Negotiating Responsibility

LAW AND SOCIETY

Law and Society Series
W. Wesley Pue, General Editor

The Law and Society Series explores law as a socially embedded phenomenon. It is premised on the understanding that the conventional division of law from society creates false dichotomies in thinking, scholarship, educational practice, and social life. Books in the series treat law and society as mutually constitutive and seek to bridge scholarship emerging from interdisciplinary engagement of law with disciplines such as politics, social theory, history, political economy, and gender studies.

A list of the titles in this series appears at the end of this book.

Kimberley White

Negotiating Responsibility: Law, Murder, and States of Mind

UBCPress · Vancouver · Toronto

16 15 14 13 12 11 10 09 08   5 4 3 2 1

Printed in Canada on ancient-forest-free paper (100% post-consumer recycled) that is processed chlorine- and acid-free, with vegetable-based inks.

Library and Archives Canada Cataloguing in Publication

White, Kimberly (Kimberly-Jo), 1966-
Negotiating responsibility : law, murder, and states of mind / Kimberly White.

(Law and society)
Includes bibliographical references and index.
ISBN 978-0-7748-1276-4

1. Insanity (Law) – Canada. 2. Competency to stand trial – Canada. 3. Mentally ill offenders – Canada. 4. Murder – Canada. I. Title. II. Series: Law and society series (Vancouver, B.C.)

KE8841.W45 2007   345.71'04   C2007-905475-7   KF9242.W45 2007

Canada

UBC Press gratefully acknowledges the financial support for our publishing program of the Government of Canada through the Book Publishing Industry Development Program (BPIDP), and of the Canada Council for the Arts, and the British Columbia Arts Council.

Printed and bound in Canada by Friesens
Set in Stone by Artegraphica Design Co. Ltd.
Copy editor: Deborah Kerr
Proofreader: Dallas Harrison
Indexer: David Luljak

UBC Press
The University of British Columbia
2029 West Mall
Vancouver, BC V6T 1Z2
604-822-5959 / Fax: 604-822-6083
www.ubcpress.ca

For my grandmothers, Joyce White and Helen Bailey

Contents

Preface

The epistemological questions I address in *Negotiating Responsibility,* regarding the way in which knowledge about criminal responsibility was socially and institutionally produced during the early twentieth century, grew from my attempt to make sense of the rich archival materials collected in the case files of individuals convicted for murder in Canada between 1920 and 1950. It was not my original plan to study responsibility knowledge. At the start, I was primarily interested in documenting the nature of psychiatric expert opinion evidence and evaluating any influence experts may have had on legal decisions – decisions about guilt and decisions about mercy. Only over time did I come to realize that the stories imbedded in the case file texts (trial transcripts, newspaper clippings, psychiatric reports, letters, and petitions) were profoundly about negotiating the boundaries between moral and legal responsibility, and that the roles played by psychiatric experts in the decision-making process were often minor. As this inquiry unfolded, it became clear that socio-legal narratives around the "expert" and "expertise," as they are represented in Canadian murder cases, did not easily fit with contemporary critical social-history literature, or with historiographies of forensic psychiatry in particular.

For instance, my findings could not adequately be explained by the now widely accepted medicalization (or psychiatrization) model, which proposes that psychiatric experts and discourses of scientific expertise became increasingly influential in social, political, and legal spheres during the early twentieth century. Evidence provided in *Negotiating Responsibility* confirms a deep paradigmatic shift between the late nineteenth and early twentieth centuries in the conceptualization of criminality with the rise of scientific knowledge about human determinism. However, the general argument made by theorists and historians (most notably, Michel Foucault, Andrew Scull, Catherine Crawford, Michael Clark, J.E. Goldstein, and Robert Menzies) that psychiatric experts wielded considerable power through the professional mobilization of scientific "truths" is not apparent in the adjudication of

Canadian capital murder cases, at least not in a straightforward way. This is not to suggest that we should discount scholarly evidence that points toward the obvious ways in which psychiatric theories about crime and social digression came to include an increasing number of behaviours and conditions under the rubric of "illness" or "disorder." Quite the opposite. I simply mean to point out that evidence of medicalization processes established in non-capital and civil commitment cases, and in cases where the legal outcome was a finding of not guilty by reason of insanity, must be considered alongside the many inconsistencies in form, substance, and use of expert knowledge that can be seen in the adjudication of capital cases, including cases where insanity was not the formal defence.

Conflicting historical evidence regarding professional and ideological formations between law and psychiatry suggests we cannot generalize across different social/cultural contexts. Several scholars, including Michael Clark and Catherine Crawford, address the importance of historical setting to the development of medical-legal knowledge and practices.[1] However, even within a particular historical context, or site of investigation, researchers rely on various forms of evidence that can inspire competing arguments/interpretations. For instance, Joel Eigen and Ruth Harris describe examples of co-operation between psychiatric experts and legal authorities in England and France, whereas others compare it to a bad marriage or an ambitious battle over professional and social power. Alternatively, Roger Smith shows that medical men were at times faced with contempt in English criminal courts.[2] Such inconsistencies flag the inherent complexity and specificity of medical-legal knowledge and bring attention to the need for further analysis.

In what follows, I trace several important discussions regarding the professional and ideological interactions between criminal law and psychiatry, highlighting conflicting accounts about the role of the psychiatric expert in criminal cases. In doing so, I maintain that conclusive and generalized claims about such critical historical developments must be read shrewdly, and with the recognition that they are in fact partial histories to be read in conjunction with other partial histories.

Making Sense of the History

Legal historians have shown that, before the nineteenth century, law and medicine in most Western countries had little interaction outside the occasional instance in which a medical witness was called in a murder trial to testify regarding cause of death. For instance, Crawford suggests that, in eighteenth-century England, common law had little need for medical evidence and that there was no pressure to improve the "quality" of medical testimony by excluding inexperienced medical experts. For the same reasons, she argues, "the epistemological problems encountered in applying medical knowledge to legal questions were rarely a focus of attention or concern in eighteenth-century trials ... Medico-legal questions simply had no perceived relevance to the art of healing."[3]

Likewise, historians' accounts of the eighteenth century are unlike those for the nineteenth, which depict medical experts practically champing at the bit to get on the witness stand. Crawford again argues that, before the nineteenth century, French medical experts actually held "disobliging attitudes" toward the idea of having to testify in court.[4] However, for most historians, the formative period of forensic psychiatry – whether it was the early eighteen hundreds in France and England or later in the century in the US and Canada – represented a time of conflict between law and psychiatry when it came to making legal decisions about insanity and criminal responsibility. Although the specific dynamics of professionalization during the formative years of Western forensic psychiatry certainly varied from place to place, it seems that some measure of disagreement predictably developed over the way in which legal responsibility was, or ought to have been, established.[5]

However, depending on how they read and interpret the relationship between law and psychiatry, and between psychiatric knowledge and legal decision making, historians draw differing conclusions regarding the influence each profession had on the way in which the other was practised. In *Madness and Reason,* Jennifer Radden argues that, as regards the issue of insanity, medical discourse came to have an increasingly powerful influence at both a theoretical and a procedural level of Western law.[6] Her investigation into the philosophy of insanity discourse generalizes across the US and Britain and suggests a "passing of responsibility" from the authority of legal decisions to a heavy reliance on expert opinions. Radden's evidence is not empirically driven: instead, she focuses primarily on the philosophical shifts in the notion of madness and the continuous desire of populations to "excuse" the insane. Her analysis defines "madness" strictly within the conceptual – rather than social, medical, and/or legal – notion of "unreason." Radden's claim regarding the desire to "excuse" the insane is not borne out by the findings of Walter Bromberg. In his *Psychiatry between the Wars,* he argues that American psychiatrists participated in "celebrated" trials only because most offenders were not afforded, or could not afford, the luxury of a "mental study."[7] He also proposes that the American public was not generally receptive to the inclusion of psychiatric testimony in criminal trials and actually resisted the idea of "excusing" criminals on the basis of mental incapacity.

In contrast to historians who suggest a well-respected professional hierarchy, or at least a co-operative working relationship, Janet Tighe compares the relationship between American law and psychiatry in the late nineteenth century to a "marriage on the rocks," a relationship between two "volatile partners" who managed to co-exist in order to maintain their professional interests.[8] She argues that each provided the other with an appearance of legitimacy through organized and public attempts to reconcile theoretical differences. However, the sort of equal playing field that Tighe describes – suggesting that each profession gave the other a leg up – is quite different from what Goldstein observes in the French context, and what Smith observes in the English context. Although Goldstein recognizes the judicial "need" for medical witnesses, she concludes that legal discourses on responsibility and mind-state had far more impact on the production of medical knowledge than did medical discourses on criminal law proceedings.[9]

Although the full degree of "impact" that one form of knowledge may have had on another is in many ways immeasurable, it is possible in the works of Goldstein and Tighe to discern how some medical men were able to acquire social status and professional legitimacy through their associations with the law, and through the application of medical knowledge to social problems. My analysis of Canadian archives produced during the adjudication of capital murder cases supports, to some extent, Goldstein's argument. Although Canadian criminal law was not affected on a doctrinal level – the laws of insanity have been the same for over 150 years – expert knowledge, infused with common-sense knowledge, nevertheless had a significant effect on the ways in which criminality and responsibility came to be interpreted in each case.

In *Trial by Medicine,* Roger Smith explores the issues of insanity and responsibility in Victorian trials and argues that the apparent surge in the number of citizens labelled insane and irresponsible – which included the poor, the old, and petty criminal types – moved the psychiatric expert to the political foreground in efforts to come to terms with the social problems of criminality and insanity.[10] However, Smith does not suggest that experts gained social/legal authority in the process, or that they vaulted to the top of the medical profession: rather, it appears from the evidence that medical men who chose to deal with the insane and criminal often faced derision from the press and the legal profession, as well as from traditional medical practitioners.[11] Although psychiatrists were stigmatized by association for defending "insane paupers," Smith argues that insanity and the insanity defence nevertheless "became" an important mobilizing problem for some of them, both signalling and aiding their struggle for professional legitimacy.

Smith breaks away from a straightforward medical-legal analysis of the expert witness to consider the symbolic meanings of legal decision on insanity. He suggests that symbolic representations were the result of social relations; therefore, as social relations changed, so did the meaning and expression of symbolic elements. He also imagines that the knowledge that came to constitute medical expertise was a reflection of social values, where the criminal trial became a critical display of "public choices."[12]

The bringing together of works on the history of law and psychiatry reveals a number of important parallels across historical accounts; but more interestingly, the literature reveals some significant contradictions. I do not consider contradictions to be a problem but do think we ought to explore this uneven terrain further. One way to better understand the historical significance of the forensic psychiatric expert in Western law, medicine, and society is to follow Smith's lead by considering the specific location in which the specialized discipline was largely constituted – the criminal trial.

The legal role of the expert witness and use of expert opinion evidence in Canadian criminal law were clearly laid out in the laws of evidence and in the *Criminal Code*. However, if we look closely, and on a case-by-case basis, at the judicial processes that unfolded during the trial and commutation stages, we can identify some of the more nuanced practices around evidence that are missed in broad-scoped or doctrinal studies. For instance, in capital cases, judges and juries were generally reluctant to accept the testimonial evidence of individual expert witnesses at face value. Even when a medical witness was granted expert status by the trial judge, his opinion was not privileged over those of lay witnesses simply because he was an "expert."

The relative lack of authority attributed to experts in some Canadian courts does not necessarily mean that what experts were saying did not influence the decision-making process, or that the medicalization/professionalization model documented by Scull and others is in all circumstances inappropriate for understanding the Canadian experience. However, as a general framework for critical analysis, it may gloss over the intricate and often highly contested nature of early medical-legal relations in the courtroom. In addition, this narrow reading does not account for the overwhelming appeal to common-sense knowledges within representations of expert knowledge. There is an important distinction to be made between "experts" and "expert knowledge" in the adjudication of Canadian murder cases. Experts were often kept at arm's length, but expert knowledge was taken up by decision makers through a variety of means.

Several social historians over the past twenty years, who have written about early medical-legal relations in the West, suggest that psychiatrists were eager to get into the courtroom because they recognized the potential career benefits of legal affiliation. Regardless of the particular place or period, questions about the professional status of experts and the legitimacy of psychiatric expertise repeatedly come up in medical-legal historiographies. For instance, some historians consider social and professional status to be the ultimate motive for psychiatrists who got involved in the "science" and regulation of criminal behaviour. Similarly, the argument that a psychiatrist's expertise and professional worth were constituted and legitimized through law has been the focus of works by Carol Jones, J.E. Goldstein, Robert Nye, and Andrew Scull, who, with varying degrees of theoretical sophistication, construct the expert as a careerist and power-monger.[13] The idea that this intense drive for power occurred within the psychiatric profession is certainly provocative, but there really isn't much evidence in the literature to show how it transpired.

In *Witnessing Insanity*, Joel Eigen examines the participation of the expert medical witness in the courtroom drama of English insanity trials, as well as the social-cultural context of England during the Victorian era. He shows how the terms "madness" and "insanity" were deployed in popular and medical discourses to represent the same image whereby the mad became "objects of derangement." Eigen reports that the development of a specialization in "forensic witnessing" in England was mostly "consumer-driven, fragmentary, and perhaps even more court-inspired than professionally generated."[14] Eigen's rejection of the reductionist argument that the rise of psychiatric expertise was a product of the social construction and regulation of insanity is important here. But again, I think it is necessary to distinguish between the proliferation and integration of psychiatric *expertise* and the professional positioning of the psychiatric *expert* in law.

To get at some of the more complex dynamics of professionalism, expertise, and the rise of the expert, it is necessary to consider the specific cultural context – the role of institutional, economic, and political forces – that may have inspired medical knowledge about criminal responsibility. At the same time, it is important to pay attention to the ways in which the form and content of medical expertise have been interpreted, or limited, by legal procedure and legal decision makers. As Eigen points out, individual legal actors were both a part and a product of their culture, "and the images and metaphors employed by *all* parties to make sense of severe mental torment needs to be placed in the context of contemporary concerns and anxieties."[15] In this book, it is precisely the knowledge processes involved in "making sense" of crime and criminals that I am interested in.

Eigen also shows how the language of expert testimony was "freighted with the imagery of a specific scientific tradition" and that it did not reflect the traditional assumption that the sole aim of the expert was to achieve the "professional colonization of the witness box."[16] This interpretation of the role or ambition of the expert differs somewhat from that offered by Nigel Walker in *Crime and Insanity in England*. The psychiatric expert in Walker's survey of the insanity defence is presented in part as an underdog, a "wrestler who is compelled to box" in a "contest ... for which he is not trained." In the legal "game" of language, intellect, and rivalry, Walker argues, the psychiatrist was forced into "obscuration and jargon" in order to "ensure that he arrive[d] at ... the right destination." At the same time, Walker is suspicious of evidence that shows the way in which psychiatrists actively criticized the laws of insanity for being too rigid and narrow in scope. He does not view the evidence of resistance to legal authority on the part of experts as terribly significant. He cautions, for instance, that in order to properly evaluate the "strength of attacks of this sort ... one must distinguish between those [psychiatrists] who accept the law's fundamental justification for its concern with 'responsibility' and those which do not."[17]

Walker further speculates that psychiatrists' opinions were based on "compassion rather than logic" because they generally subscribed to the notion that "the madman is punished enough by his madness." Although Walker appears to admire the social sentiment of some early psychiatrists, his representation of the expert witness in early modern England is limited to a legal perspective. In their efforts to have their voices and ideas recognized in the courtroom, experts are cast in this analysis as single-minded marketers in the "business" of manufacturing labels – "like slogans of over-enthusiastic advertisements." Walker further speculates that, although the "typical" judge or lawyer was "at least as intelligent as the typical psychiatrist" and could therefore understand medical jargon, it was necessary to send a simple but powerful message if a defence of insanity were to be sold to the jury.[18]

In contrast to Walker's image of the expert as a self-interested professional marketer, Eigen's analysis suggests that assertions about the status and value of a particular witness' expertise were (rightly) put forward by lawyers in order to secure an acquittal. This was, after all, the nature of the adversarial process. Claims of skill, according to Eigen, usually appeared during cross-examination and were "rarely used to legitimize testimony at the onset."[19] This observation is somewhat different from what I have found in Canadian trials, which indicate that there usually was some form of preparatory legitimation work done at the start of a witness' testimony to establish his medical and legal qualifications as an "expert."

However, the legal qualification of a particular medical witness as a psychiatric expert was not necessarily determined by his medical qualifications or specialized experience working with the insane. Many general practitioners, prison doctors, coroners, and occasionally even non-medical witnesses were able to fill the legal requirements of "expert witness." An expert witness during this period was simply defined as a "specially skilled" witness with knowledge of questions of science beyond the understanding of the common man.[20] Also, as I demonstrate throughout this book, the preliminary set-up of certain doctors as expert witnesses did not follow with an automatic privileging of their expert opinions on the issues of mind-state and responsibility. The contentious nature of the routine practice of legally qualifying witnesses as "experts" stemmed from several ongoing debates about the "science" of psychiatry and the question of who was best suited to detect true evidence of insanity for the purposes of law; was it the expert, or was it the ordinary men of the jury? In several cases that I analyzed for this study, judges were not convinced that experts were necessary (even when the defence was insanity) to determine a defendant's state of mind at the time of the crime, particularly given that insanity as a defence to crime was an issue for law, not medicine.

Both Joel Eigen and Roger Smith argue that our interpretation of medical-legal relations need not be an either/or proposition – that is, psychiatric expertise was either socially constructed or, as more positivist historians such as Edward Shorter and Erwin Ackerknecht suggest, it emerged from objective scientific work.[21] Indeed, early professional literature shows that some psychiatrists campaigned for a prominent role in deciding criminal responsibility based on significant advancements in neurology and psychiatric medicine. However, at the same time, Smith points out that both legal and medical institutions reflected popular concerns more than they influenced them. He also cautions against the temptation to make generalizations regarding cause and effect when it comes to understanding trial outcomes and their broader social meaning. As Smith explains: "To understand why any particular verdict was reached requires an examination of the special circumstances of that trial. Trials were occasions for expressing theories of human nature and associated value systems ... but it would be wrong to suppose that these theories produce particular verdicts. It is necessary to separate reasons for a specific verdict from reasons for controversy over verdicts in general."[22]

Finally, I must draw attention to Ruth Harris' excellent work in *Murders and Madness*. Harris does not explicitly focus on the expert witness, however, she does a very good job of exposing the complexity of the legal processes involved in the construction of early medical-legal discourse, which included expressions of power, compliance, and resistance. The important courtroom details drawn out by Harris have particular historical and analytical relevance here because she situates her investigation within the specific context of the French murder trial. Her scope of analysis, which takes in the landscape of French culture as well as the details of courtroom procedure, provides a new depth to our historical read of the "expert" and "expertise." Her conclusions are not especially grand, in that she does not claim to offer the definitive social history of crime and madness; nor does she claim to provide the ultimate story of legal medicine. What Harris does, and what I aim to do in suit, is trace the important links between social discourse, medical theory, legal practice, and human agency at a particular place and time.

Case file evidence dating from 1920 to 1950 indicates that the legitimacy of psychiatric "expertise" in Canadian murder cases was (re)evaluated and (re)negotiated according to the particular circumstances of each trial in ways that sometimes eroded the status of experts but at the same time did not necessarily disregard expert knowledge about mental capacity and legal responsibility. This book shows that when mind-state was raised and a medical witness called, the professional status of the expert did not seem as important as what he said in court or wrote in his report. Expert opinion was more likely to be taken as legal fact if it met the substantive requirements and language of insanity law, and if it did not challenge the sensibilities of the common man on the jury.

During this time, the perceived authority of psychiatric expert knowledge was very much contingent on the changing dynamics of the criminal trial, as well as on the larger socio-political concerns.[23] However, I make the point once more that though the law of evidence specified that professional experience was important in order to qualify a witness as an expert, some Canadian judges did not uphold a ruling standard of experience or specialized skill in deciding to hear opinion evidence. Decisions regarding the value of a particular expert's testimony seemed to be heavily influenced by the circumstances of the case and by the substance or nature of the evidence itself.

My attempt to make sense of divergent social and institutional histories of forensic psychiatry, and to locate the Canadian experience in the broader context of Western medical-legal historiographies, has led me to an unexpected line of inquiry. The degrees of variation that exist across accounts of the status and role of the psychiatric expert are historically significant and intellectually provocative. Discrepancies in research findings reflect not only the ways in which scholars locate and read historical evidence but also the range of possible interpretations of expertise and the nature of expert authority on legal issues of mind-state. *Negotiating Responsibility,* therefore, begins the process of mapping a very small yet relatively unexamined corner of this rich historical landscape. In documenting the specificity of responsibility knowledge in Canadian law and society, I intend to emphasize, rather than smooth over, the rough edges of medical-legal history.

Acknowledgments

I would like to thank Carolyn Strange for her years of guidance, patience, and wisdom. I would also like to thank Mariana Valverde, the late Dianne Martin, Richard Weisman, Randy Schmidt, and especially Robert Menzies for reading and commenting on earlier sections and drafts of this manuscript and who have all expressed enthusiasm and encouragement at times when I needed it most. I also thank the external reviewers and press editors, in particular Ann Macklem, for their comments, suggestions, and editorial expertise.

I am deeply indebted to the remarkable staff and hard working archivists at the Library and Archives Canada. They helped make the daunting task of locating and working through historical documents a most rewarding experience. I appreciate in particular the attentiveness of Tony Bonacci, who went to great lengths to accommodate my ambitious research schedule by moving materials through access procedures as quickly as possible. I would also like to thank the York University Faculty of Arts Research Grant programme, and the Office of the Dean of Arts, which helped fund the final stages of this project.

This also seems an appropriate opportunity to express my ongoing appreciation for my friends, both in and out of academia, who have given me far more than I could possibly return. Kirsten Kramar, Carole Roberts, Linda Peake, Lisa Drummond, Anna Pratt, David Sealy, and Annie Bunting stand out among them. I also want to acknowledge my students in the Law and Society program at York University who, perhaps without knowing, serve as a critical and forgiving audience to much of my work in progress.

My family – in particular my grandparents – have also been a source of quiet and constant encouragement in every aspect of my life. I have always marveled and appreciated their overestimation of my abilities.

Finally, I thank my partner, Paul, and my daughter, Sadie, for everything.

Negotiating Responsibility

1
Introduction

On 17 December 1935, Elizabeth Tilford became the first woman to be hanged in Ontario in sixty-two years. Her trial, conviction, and death sentence for the poisoning of her husband, Tyrell Tilford, caught the attention of many in Canada and beyond, and brought to the fore conflicting ideas about human nature, capital punishment, and criminal responsibility. Following the murder, Inspector Hammond, the police officer in charge of the investigation, reported that the Tilfords were poor and that they lived "loosely" and in "sordid conditions."[1] This single suggestion of the "conditions" of the married couple's life was intended to help explain a terrible domestic murder that had taken place in the small community of Woodstock. It was also indicative of the kind of knowledge that went into making sense of a wife who was accused of killing her husband. Throughout the inspector's report, [illegible] Elizabeth Tilford's [illegible] her mothering and [illegible]. [illegible], the condemned woman [illegible] as a self-interested bigamist and husband-killer. There was no question of her guilt; rather, it was the apparent reason for her behaviour that was the primary subject of the police report, and what seemed most disconcerting to the inspector. He began his account of the event with the following statement: "I do not think there is any question, or the least doubt of her Guilt, for, from my personal investigation of this case, it would be hard to find a more cunningly conceived way of putting aside those who had become useless in her view."[2]

According to this version of the story, Elizabeth Tilford married for the first time in England at age sixteen. When her husband left her for another woman after only six months, she moved on to marry her cousin, William Walker, and had several children with him. According to the inspector, she admitted quite freely that her marriage to Walker was bigamous, although some question was raised about whether her first husband was actually still alive at the time. During her marriage to Walker, she worked as a nurse and midwife, and he worked as a [illegible]. They were brought to Canada in

1
Introduction

On 17 December 1935, Elizabeth Tilford became the first woman to be hanged in Ontario in sixty-two years. Her trial, conviction, and death sentence for the poisoning of her husband, Tyrell Tilford, captured the attention of many in Canada and beyond, and brought to the fore conflicting ideas about human nature, capital punishment, and criminal responsibility. Following the murder, Inspector Hammond, the police officer in charge of the investigation, reported that the Tilfords were poor and that they lived "loosely" and in "sordid conditions."[1] This single summation of the "conditions" of the married couple's life was intended to help explain a terrible domestic murder that had taken place in the small community of Woodstock. It was also indicative of the kind of knowledge that went into making sense of a wife who was accused of killing her husband. Throughout the inspector's reconstruction of Elizabeth Tilford's nefarious life prior to her marrying, and murdering, Tyrell Tilford, the condemned woman is characterized as a self-interested bigamist and husband-killer. There was no question of her guilt here: rather, it was the apparent reason for her behaviour that was the primary subject of the police report, and what seemed most disconcerting to the inspector. He began his record of the event with the following statement: "I do not think there is any question, or the least doubt of her Guilt, for, from my personal investigation of this case, it would be hard to find a more cunningly conceived way of putting aside those who had become useless in her view."[2]

According to this version of the story, Elizabeth Tilford married for the first time in England at age sixteen. When her husband left her for another woman after only six months, she moved on to marry her cousin, William Walker, and had several children with him.[3] According to the inspector, she admitted quite freely that her marriage to Walker was bigamous, although some question was raised about whether her first husband was actually still alive at the time. During her marriage to Walker, she worked as a nurse and midwife, and he worked as a coalminer. They were brought to Canada in

1928 by the Salvation Army, which recorded that William Walker held a position as an officer of some sort and Elizabeth helped look after "insurance details."[4]

In 1929, shortly after the couple's arrival in Canada, where they lived in "apparent poverty," William Walker went blind, was unable to work, and died of unknown causes. After Walker's death, rumours surfaced that he had suspected his wife was poisoning him, so his body was exhumed and examined. But according to the police report, "too long a time had lapsed for to [sic] recover anything of a suspicious nature in this respect."[5] Elizabeth, who had managed to arrange for some disability insurance on Mr. Walker before he died, collected the full amount. She also began collecting the widowed mothers' pension allowance, and was, according to Inspector Hammond, "getting along fairly well." The inspector also noted that when Walker passed away, his widow gave him a send-off that "was more like a wedding feast, than a funeral assembly."[6]

In 1930, approximately one year following the death of William Walker, Elizabeth met and married Tyrell Tilford. Hammond reported that, after the death of Walker and before she met Tilford, the widow had a difficult time fitting in and settling down. The Salvation Army rejected her on moral grounds (apparently for living with "other men"), and her attempts to enter the folds of other churches elicited less than welcoming responses. Inspector Hammond described a woman who was desperate, turning to "spiritualism" and even "fortune telling" while travelling around with "some man under the name of Professor Blake."[7] Perhaps it was because she desired a more stable and respectable domestic life that she quickly married Tilford, a man twenty years her junior and known to come from a "very honourable family."[8] Or, it may have been, as the police report implies, that she saw the young gentleman Tilford as an easy target.

Although the inspector suggested that the Tilford family in general was well regarded, he nevertheless described Tyrell Tilford as an "ignorant type of fellow" and a "man of little ambition."[9] His family, so the story goes, was not happy about the marriage to Elizabeth but did their best to welcome the newlyweds in, even allowing them to build a small house on the family's property in Woodstock. Tyrell Tilford worked as a garbage collector, and the new Mrs. Tilford reportedly kept busy reading teacups and telling fortunes. This marriage, like her previous two, was characterized by the inspector as being quite miserable. Mrs. Tilford's children from her marriage to Walker apparently hated Tyrell Tilford. Her two eldest sons, known to be "rough characters" (one was nicknamed "Bulldog"), would frequently beat up Tilford. And Tilford retaliated by ill-treating his wife's sixteen-year-old daughter – forcing her to unload days' worth of rancid garbage. However, things seemed to turn even further downward for the Tilfords' marriage when "Professor Blake" re-entered the picture. According to the police report, Blake, who owned two farm properties, began making frequent visits to the Tilfords' house, and Mr. Tilford became very unhappy about the straying "attentions" of his wife.

After about five years of marriage, and approximately six weeks before Tyrell Tilford's death, Elizabeth Tilford enquired about the amount of insurance that could be collected in the event of her husband's death. At the time, he was reported to have been in good health. Considering all the "relevant" circumstances leading up to the murder of Tyrell Tilford, the conditions of the couple's domestic life, and the questionable character of Elizabeth Tilford herself, Inspector Hammond summed up the case:

> At the time she made these [insurance] enquiries Tilford was in very good health, with no signs of sickness. But to her, Tilford was a useless tool, just the same as Walker became prior to his death, and she wanted freedom and the widows pension, which she got before she married Tilford, and it was discussed by her and her sons and another party just before Tilford became sick, and Mrs. Tilford denied that she ever knew there was any insurance left ... whereas she knew quite well just the exact amount that would be available at death.
>
> They were still living in poverty, and in sordid conditions, very loose generally. Before her marriage to Tilford she was getting the widow mothers pension allowance, and was getting along fairly well, but of late she claimed that Tilford never paid her one cent either for her keep or that of her family. She went out to work occasionally, and one son was working part time. She claims that Tilford was always in debt, and that she had to give him money to keep him going, and she wanted him out of the way to get mothers pension again, and living in the house put up by Tilford with the assistance of the Tilford family, with nothing to pay, she would then be on easy street again.
>
> In so far as the motive for the crime goes, it has been our opinion that her husbands have proven to be quite useless for her who we imagine has been a person overly sexed, and she wanted free rein, with perhaps an eye on the farm properties of the man Blake. No other motive appears on the surface.[10]

Very little detail is given in the three-page police report about the physical evidence that linked Mrs. Tilford to the death of her husband – evidence that she had allegedly been feeding him homemade tablets containing arsenic. In concluding, the inspector simply restated that "it is quite apparent, what occurred, and I think I have outlined clearly the reasons for doing it."[11] In mapping out the "reasons" for the murder, he also constructed a clear representation of Elizabeth Tilford as a particular type of woman/

wife – the "cunning" type who would kill for money and use sex to get what she wanted.

Elizabeth Tilford pleaded not guilty to the charge of murder and maintained throughout the investigation and trial that she did not kill her husband and that she had been framed by Tyrell's family. Following the guilty verdict, and the judge's reading of the sentence that she was to be "hanged by the neck" until dead, the prisoner shouted, "Your lordship, it is not right. Oh, if I only had a chance – a chance to give my evidence. Oh, dear, dear! Framed! Absolutely framed! May God have mercy on the Tilfords' souls."[12] Despite Elizabeth's cries of innocence, there seemed – from official reports, newspaper clippings, and letters from the public – to be wide agreement on the fact that she was legally guilty of the crime of murder. A *Toronto Mail and Empire* article reported that a petition circulated by her children received only a "few hundred signatures." This showing of support was, in comparison to that garnered by other clemency campaigns, "disappointingly small."[13] Yet, in the midst of this generally cool public reception, multiple interpretations of her motivation emerged, and some observers even voiced hesitation regarding the extent to which she should be held *responsible* for her behaviour.

Evidence from case file records suggests that though Mrs. Tilford was not able to rally much support for mercy on claims of her innocence, many members of the public did write on her behalf asking the minister of justice to commute her death sentence to life in prison – a symbolic move that would not dismiss her guilt but would acknowledge the existence of "conditions" beyond her control. One such condition that could influence interpretations of criminal responsibility in murder cases was insanity, and several letters written to the minister following Tilford's guilty verdict expressed concerns about her state of mind. Some insisted that the sheer nature of her crime(s) indicated some form of "sickness" or mental abnormality. However, the specific cause of her purported sickness varied from writer to writer and included a range of social, biological, and psychological conditions, including menopause, poverty, feminine nature, and domestic disharmony.[14]

Others who wrote in support of mercy for Tilford expressed concern about the moral health of the nation, the conditions of an economic depression, and the undesirable message that would be delivered were a woman to be executed at that time. But here, too, we find variations from writer to writer on precisely what, in the deliberation of this case, was threatening the health of the nation. For instance, several local women wrote letters arguing that the execution of a "Christian" woman and "mother" would bring a particular brand of "dishonour" to Canada.[15] Others, in pointing to the weakened social and economic circumstances of the country at that time, were more specifically concerned about the potential social damage that might be caused by executing a woman in the midst of a depression. Some went so far as to question or denounce the very idea of capital punishment as a legitimate practice.

For example, with a clear sense of what the role of law ought to be in the enlightened 1930s, Mr. and Mrs. Keill wrote, "at previous hangings of women in Canada there has been no small amount of disapproval among many very intelligent people. And after the last execution of a woman, there was a greatly increased abhorrence of the act ... In these sad days of depression such executions tend to further sadden and embitter the people. While, on the other hand, a show of mercy raises the spirits of those enduring great trials. Nothing can be gained by this woman's death. Considerable can be gained by clemency at this time."[16] Despite evidence of growing public disapproval for hangings during this period, historians have documented the 1930s, with an execution rate of 61 percent, as the harshest decade in Canada's history of the administration of capital punishment. Prior to the 1930s, execution rates hovered at, or just below, 50 percent.[17] And though justice ministers consistently maintained that capital case dispositions were guided by strict principles of judicial fairness,[18] the public seemed to be quite aware that the machinery of law was vulnerable to political tampering and, in some cases, capable of misfiring.

Commentary on capital punishment was certainly not one-sided. Some thought it was a fine, and necessary, tool of law. Others did not necessarily protest the practice of executions but opposed hanging as a method. As lawyer R.H. Greer stated in a *Toronto Daily Star* article, "I am opposed to hanging as the method of capital punishment; it is a dog's death ... It should be possible, through a commission to determine some much more humane form of executing criminals. I am not opposed to capital punishment in certain types of cases but I am opposed to hanging."[19] However, for many who demonstrated outright disdain for capital punishment, their sentiments were very much tied up with a growing public interest and confidence in the possibilities of "science" as a legitimate and more sophisticated form of knowledge through which to understand crime, and hence to (re)constitute criminals as subjects of science. As Margaret Sim, writing on behalf of a group of women from Hamilton, stated, "let us do honor to our enlightenment, our scientific attainments, our sure instinct to pity, and let us encourage a boundless charity so that the whole nation will be enriched. We do not believe, we again re-iterate, that we will be honored, or uplifted, nor will the life of the nation be enriched by the hanging of a poor, sick woman."[20] Similarly, in a newspaper editorial titled "Mrs. Tilford Should Not Be Hanged," an unnamed author argued that the practice of capital punishment was "perhaps a shameful necessity until our whole treatment of crime is made Christian and scientific." From this author's perspective, it was argued that

> Instead of the short and simple but sometimes hideously unsatisfactory method of getting troublesome people off our hands justice demands that the highest psychiatric skill and experience should be utilized to determine what treatment society should mete out to so extraordinary an individual in the interest of social protection and her own possible redemption. It seems a most deplorable thing that the more unnatural and shocking a crime is the stronger is the demand for swift and passionate vengeance, when the very nature of the crime should moderate the instinctive wrath by suggesting the more powerfully that the wrong-doer is less of a devil and more of a victim of an abnormal temperament.[21]

It is interesting, however, that though popular as well as legal theories about Tilford's "abnormal" mentality were freely floated, and clearly informed by "new" scientific and psychiatric discourses about the causes of criminal behaviour, no psychiatric *experts* were invited to participate in her case. In fact, most of the substantive discussions around Tilford's state of mind took place outside the courtroom and/or tended to be directed toward establishing the nature of her temperament, or *character*. Representations of character, as we shall see throughout this book, were very often framed by narratives of mind-state, and produced in part through the selective appropriation of psychiatric knowledge.

In an attempt to counter the barrage of character witnesses presented by the Crown at Tilford's trial, her defence counsel submitted the feeble argument, without medical evidence, that the defendant's state of mind had been affected by town gossip over her "unduly friendly" behaviours with another man – the elusive Professor Blake. However, in the end, the judge was won over by the Crown's more convincing argument that Tilford was exactly the "type" of woman who would maliciously kill her husband for his life insurance money. The judge stressed in his final charge to the jury of twelve men that it was important for them to decide which interpretation of the events and which characterization of the accused they would use to render their verdict. The judge reminded the jury that "she was the wife of this man" and that they must decide whether she was in fact a "wronged woman" or "a diabolical creature" who only pretended to have affections for her husband. In concluding, he drove home the urgency of a clear decision regarding Mrs. Tilford's character:

> There is no half-way house, gentlemen – no half-way place you can rest. You have to make up your minds which type that woman was on all the evidence. Was she, as counsel for the defence says, a very much wronged woman, injured by the scandal, gossip and talk of the town; or was she the type of woman who would stop at nothing to gain her own ends, and the life of her husband be of no matter so far as she was concerned if it served

> her purpose to get rid of him? You have to take your choice. She is either one or the other. If she is a Doctor Jekyll and Mr. Hyde, there is no half-way house that I can see. Which category does the accused stand in?[22]

The jury found Tilford guilty and did not recommend mercy – meaning that they did not feel the accused was worthy of commutation. The judge concurred, and after polling the jury, made the following statement:

> Gentlemen of the jury, I am sure the responsibility of this important case weighed very heavily on you. Let me say that I am proud of this jury, that I know under what stress, and what it cost the jury to bring in a verdict of this kind, and I think the County of Oxford is to be congratulated in having men who will sit on a jury and do their duty, and having the courage of their convictions. I think I can say that I concur with the verdict that you have found in this case.[23]

Defence counsel made an attempt at an appeal, but it failed, and Elizabeth Tilford was hanged.

The courtroom version of Tilford's life, character, and presumed reasons for killing her third husband matched quite closely the pre-trial account of police inspector Hammond. However, legal representations of the crime, and the formal condemnation of Tilford as a particularly dangerous type of woman/wife, did not resonate uniformly with the public; nor did they overshadow intense expressions of sadness and discomfort following her execution. The 17 December 1935 *Ottawa A.M. Journal* described the sombre tone of her execution day: "A small crowd of curious citizens gathered outside the high walls of the courtyard shortly before the lights went on inside. It was broken up by several policemen who kept citizens on the move. An hour before the execution, the 56-year-old woman, thrice widowed and mother of nine children, four of whom are living, was in a state of collapse in her cell. She was able, however, to walk to the scaffold. Snow was falling as she slowly entered the courtyard."[24]

In tracing just a few of the interwoven narratives that helped shape and give meaning to sometimes divergent representations of crime, criminality, and criminal responsibility in the case file of Elizabeth Tilford, we begin to see how little a guilty verdict actually tells us about the history and practice of criminal law in Canada. It is certainly true that the opinions expressed in a selection of newspaper articles and other selected documents that made their way into Tilford's file exemplify a mere sampling of the range of positions that may have been held by the public and legal officials on her case. Nevertheless, they provide a strong indication of the routine interplay between law and society, and between legal and social actors, when it came to interpreting the boundaries and consequences of criminal responsibility.

The contents of Elizabeth Tilford's case file, and the case files of other individuals sentenced to death for murder, also serve as valuable textual representations of the institutional structures that framed each case. In particular, we can observe the impressions of the author of the case file (the chief remissions officer) and the messages he *intended* to convey to the minister of justice in (re)constructing the summary of the evidence and trial hearings. However, much of the institutional structure surrounding capital case decision making was hidden from public view. Only in the past twenty years or so have critical social historians started to uncover some aspects of this important piece of Canada's legal history. For instance, good evidence now shows that the chief remissions officer, whose role was intended to be purely administrative, was in fact a key player in the disposition of capital cases, and may even have influenced decisions regarding the use of the royal prerogative of mercy.[25] It is possible to observe hints of this influence in the case files. I again take Tilford's case as an example.

In summarizing the case facts in his report, the chief remissions officer restated some of the trial judge's concluding remarks on the question of motive, sharpening the characterization of Elizabeth Tilford as a conniving gold digger:

> Motives were advanced by the Crown, suggesting why the accused might have administered the poison. In March last, Tyrell Tilford and the accused were in very straightened [sic] circumstances. The accused made enquiries about insurance moneys before the death of her husband. Furthermore, on the Thursday night before his death, she had his will drawn, leaving everything to her, and, finally, evidence was offered that she was very friendly with one Blake, a widower, who was possessed of property. Her own conduct both before the death of the deceased man, and after his death, was inconsistent with that of an innocent woman.[26]

The final statement of the chief officer's report was his personal vote in support of the verdict. He concluded that, "upon consideration of the facts and circumstances of this case, the undersigned is of the opinion that the law may well be allowed to take its course."[27] The decision to convict and execute Tilford for the murder of her husband seems to clearly reflect a series of judgments made within the doctrines of Canadian criminal law and through the application of legal rules. However, institutional assessments of her character, nature, and circumstances also produced distinctly political representations of her as a calculating murderess.[28]

These multiple ways of "knowing," or claiming to know, a single legal subject such as Elizabeth Tilford disclose something important about the cultural and institutional dimensions of law and legal decision making. In particular, the documents compiled in the case files of those sentenced to death for murder allow for an exploration of the textured and contingent nature of responsibility knowledge as it was (re)produced in order to make sense of murderers and of murderous acts. These more qualitative readings of the files, which necessarily require looking beyond the official verdict in each case, suggest that the law was anything but fixed on the subject of responsibility and that legal outcomes were not simply the result of a measured application of legal rules.

Although evidence of unevenness between the way in which the law defined the official threshold of criminal guilt and more multifarious socio-legal and scientific knowledges evoked in representations of responsibility is, I think, an important element, it is not novel. The perceptible divide between the law on the books and the law in action has long been a key site of analysis among legal realist and critical socio-legal scholars. However, this divide between doctrine and practice seems always to have existed and perhaps should not necessarily be viewed as dysfunctional. Rather than "explaining away" the many contradictions in legal practice, Patricia Ewick and Susan Silbey argue that "the apparent oppositions and contradictions – the so-called gap – might actually operate ideologically to define and sustain legality as a durable and powerful social institution."[29] Their use of the term "ideology" here does not simply connote a "single giant schema that determines how people think": rather, the authors borrow Michelle Barrett's words to describe ideology as a "complex process by which meaning is produced, challenged, reproduced."[30] Ideology, then, is not an abstract concept but a form of "sense making" that is "inextricably tied to practical consciousness" and consequences.[31]

I find this to be a useful way of framing and thinking about the subject of this book – as a way of connecting the theoretical to the empirical, the abstract to the concrete, the ideals of law to the effects of law. The form and content of capital case files provide a rare opportunity to trace some of the ideological processes of judicial sense making, and to observe how, through the ideological processes of sense making, we continually (re)produce the "specific structures and contests for power" within which we live and experience law. According to Ewick and Silbey, "the internal contradictions, oppositions, and gaps are not weaknesses in the ideological cloth. On the contrary, an ideology is sustainable only through such internal contradictions insofar as they become the basis for invocations, reworkings, applications, and transpositions through which ideologies are enacted in everyday life."[32] Along these lines, I am therefore not so much concerned with the inevitable and perhaps even desirable gap between what the law said and what the law did as I am with how knowledge about responsibility was produced, ordered, and contested in each case, and how convergent knowledge forms helped sustain, strengthen, and legitimize law's "ideological cloth" by providing meaning to trial and commutation outcomes. In other words, I am concerned here with the *effects* of responsibility knowledge on the adjudication of capital cases, where the decided outcome literally meant life or death for the accused.

Themes of the Book

Given the sorts of questions in which I am interested, I have organized the book thematically through overlapping discussions of context, expertise, common sense, identity politics (including race, citizenship, and social status), character, and domesticity. In drawing attention to some of the subtler dynamics of legal decision making, several socio-legal and medical history scholars have traced the complex ways in which scientific knowledge, particularly psychiatric knowledge, has provided the language to articulate legal decisions about guilt, responsibility, and mental capacity in criminal and civil cases.[33] Although the impact of psychiatric knowledge on Canadian law and society over the past century is pretty much undeniable (even if the nature of that impact has been debated), my interest in the subject of psychiatric expertise is a bit different, and best described as two-fold. First, I am interested in understanding the role and authority that may or may not have been afforded certain psychiatric expert witnesses in defining the boundaries of criminal responsibility in particular cases. Second, and more significantly, I am interested in understanding the ways in which "common-sense" knowledges about criminality and responsibility in fact helped constitute the boundaries and legitimacy of certain forms of psychiatric "expertise" during this period.

Other critical social historians (such as Roger Smith, Andrew Scull, Joel Eigen, Carolyn Strange, Ruth Harris, and Martha Umphrey) have demonstrated that the murder trial provides a particularly good discursive site for evaluating the interplay between social-cultural attitudes and processes of legal decision making. As the many documented public reactions to Elizabeth Tilford's case indicate, Canadian murder trials during the early twentieth century were very much public affairs.[34] Before the dawn of television and other technological forms of mass communication, newspapers frequently reported in great detail the spectacle of overflowing courtrooms and the sharp interest of community members in trial deliberations. We can also trace in capital murder case files the ways in which legal officials gauged the public's view toward mercy in each case in order to determine what message a decision to execute or commute would/should send.

Individuals and groups from across Canada made their views on a particular case known by writing to newspaper editors and government officials in the form of organized petitions, eloquent letters drafted on business letterhead and personalized stationery, near-illiterate scribbles on scraps of paper, or through the pen of a third party who would write for those who could not. Although the case file documents reveal the public's active interest in how certain cases were decided, it is important to distinguish which members of the public were in fact interested and/or able to have their views weighed in. Of course, many voices were also silenced during the judicial process and are not represented in the case file records. Most notably absent in these accounts are the voices of those who were on trial. Still, the murder trial, being an intensely cultural process, brought together a cross-section of ideas, institutions, and individuals with the common goal of trying to make sense of, and determine just responses to, acts of murder.

However, there were definite limits to what counted in law as a legitimate explanation for a murder, or murderer, in each case. Evidence here suggests that if public opinion did matter, it was only to the extent that it did not upset the basic moral tenets of the criminal law. And in the context of Canada's social, political, and economic climate, dominant rationales of justice and responsibility in the first half of the twentieth century seemed to be bound by a deep sense of citizenship, national identity, and a pragmatic understanding of the social role of the rule of law – common sense if you will. The ideals of British justice and citizenship, and the moral sentiments of the celebrated "common sense" of British-Canadian men in particular, ran through every aspect of the adjudication process. "British" and "Britishness" were used with specific racialized connotations – and employed by judges to evoke a particular sensibility.

As is the case for popular opinion, much has been written about the notion of "common sense" and the defining characteristics of "common-sense knowledge."[35] Again, I will not attempt to provide a grand theory about what common sense *is:* rather, I am interested in how common sense was understood and articulated by legal actors (judges, juries, lawyers, experts, and witnesses) as well as non-legal actors regarding questions about mind-state and responsibility. In particular, I am interested in the way in which common sense was constituted in medical-legal discourse as distinct from expert knowledge. As I show later on, there were very definite ideas about the strengths, weaknesses, nature, and role of common-sense knowledge in legal decision making. I challenge this theoretical distinction between common sense and expert knowledge throughout the book.

As well as detailing the ways in which systems of language and knowledge were organized by and through social institutions and interactions to produce contextually specific accounts in each case, this book chronicles a partial history of interfacing and overlapping ideas – ideas about criminality, about law, about expertise, and about responsibility. For instance, I consider how medical-legal standards for defining responsibility were formed and negotiated according to essentialist theories about individual difference, mental capacity, and scientific certainty. In tracing the history of ideas, we can begin to make out the ways in which the boundaries of criminality and responsibility were constituted over time and from case to case. As well, we can begin to make sense of the ways in which the socio-political significance of those ideas was simultaneously, or subsequently, transformed.

For example, the emergence of an anthropological/scientific language about "race" origin and difference in the eighteenth and nineteenth centuries provided early twentieth-century Anglo-Canadians – concerned with the identity, quality, and security of the Anglo-Saxon race in Canada – with a system of knowledges or logics within which to interpret, order, articulate, and respond to criminality.[36] Over time, categorizations of race based on speculations about natural race order became part of the ideological and scientific formation of criminal *classes, types,* and *kinds*.[37] Of course, the historical movement of ideas and knowledges was not as linear as this, but it does help to understand the cultural significance of the language used in the formation of responsibility knowledge. I also want to point out just how transparent were the operating assumptions about human *types* during this period, and how obviously they structured the policies and practices of Canadian criminal law and forensic psychiatry. One need not dig deeply to see that certain types of women were generally considered incapable of appreciating the consequences of their actions, and that "race" was central to essentialist theories about human nature, class, and individual character.

For instance, when the defence lawyer for Louis Jones, a black man convicted for the murder of his wife (also black) in 1927, implored the minister of justice to consider the "expected" level of violence and vulgarity among people of his client's "class,"[38] or when the constable who arrested George Dvernichuk, a Ukrainian immigrant, for the murder of his neighbours in 1930, described his behaviour as "typically foreign,"[39] a set of ideas about foreign types and the criminal classes was already in place. Criminological knowledge about types and kinds further acquired particular meaning through the processes of fact-finding and legal advocacy, which often revolved around the presumed character of the defendant and victim(s).

Similarly, the presence of strong social ideals and legal sanctions around conjugality and marriage during this period helped charge the moral undercurrents of legal decisions in domestic murder cases. James Snell observed that, at the beginning of the twentieth century, the "ideal of the conjugal family" dominated Canadian consciousness and was reinforced by rigid patriarchal divorce laws. According to Snell, sentiments about the virtues of conjugality were profound and "incorporated virtually all the principles and ideals valued by Canadian society." He argues that the moral sanctity of the family was "shared by Canadians of almost all ethnic and religious origins and engaged in almost any sort of occupation" and that marriage became the foundation of a "civilized Canadian society."[40] However, as Mona Gleason argues with good evidence, the construct of "the family" was also quite exclusionary. She shows, for instance, that "immigrant, working-class and Native families were not part of the ideal."[41]

Although Snell's portrayal of "Canadian society" may be criticized for being far too homogeneous, and his analysis of divorce law as decidedly functionalist, his general research findings point to some of the ways in which the language of domesticity and ideas about conjugality may have provided a conceptual and illustrative framework for members of the public, psychiatric experts, and legal decision makers to make sense of murder committed between "wives" and "husbands." However, where Snell holds that the "ideal of the conjugal family" was uniformly shared among Canadians, I would argue, more in line with Gleason, that the significance of conjugality (like race, gender, or citizenship) and the consequences of ascribing to the "conjugal ideal" in decisions about moral and criminal responsibility were not consistent. In accordance with the general principles of law, the significance of the domestic space and the moral boundaries of conjugality were constituted on a case-by-case basis and in relation to various other socio-political and individual circumstances. Therefore, in order to decipher the legal standards that were used to interpret facts and render formal decisions, and in order to better appreciate the general and particular effects of these processes, it is necessary to consider the specificity of circumstances that were at play during each trial.

The inimitable archival materials that make up the case files of capitally convicted women and men reveal quite vividly the social tensions and institutional frameworks that defined the parameters of criminal responsibility, and highlight the systemic leanings of legal decisions and medical diagnoses. In drawing closer attention to the role of common sense in responsibility knowledge, this book brings to the fore the more subtle dynamics in decision making that are not represented in the doctrines of law and medicine, such as the legal qualification of certain doctors and lay witnesses as "experts," the legitimation of certain kinds of knowledge as "expertise," and the remarkable instability of responsibility knowledge during that time. In these case files we can see, in a very tangible way, the contingent relations between law and society, what James Walker describes as "the operation of common sense on the perception of problems and consequences, and on the choice of solution."[42]

Chapter Overview

This book generally draws on a sustained and collective analysis of sixty-six capital murder case files, using a smaller set of case files for close readings. In Chapter 2, I discuss their contents and the institutional context in which they were produced. Here I look critically at the institutional practices around the disposition of capital murder cases, the remissions branch, and the role of the chief remissions officer as principal author of the files.

In Chapter 3, I show how dominant themes of criminological knowledge came to influence the adjudication of murder cases by shaping the content and meaning of certain case file texts. Here I am concerned with expert theories of crime and criminality and with popular sentiments on these subjects. As Canadian historians have established, this period was marked by a number of events that informed the ways in which Canadians came to understand and respond to criminality. For instance, a substantive shift in criminological thinking occurred with the emergence of "germ theory" and the science of "degeneration" toward the end of the nineteenth century.[43] In subsequent decades, medical, legal, and popular knowledge about degeneration and criminality adapted to accommodate the experiences of, and ideas about, the effects of particular social conditions, such as war and economic hardship, on both individual citizens and the Canadian citizenry. In the context of this cultural climate, I trace the professional and ideological relationships of law and psychiatry as regards insanity and criminal responsibility as well as the dialectical relationship between expertise and common sense.

I argue in Chapter 3 that expert and common knowledges were not distinct; rather, they were bound up in and with each other in the production of a knowledge about the reasonable and responsible person. Critical medical-legal historians have recently provided a wealth of evidence to show the overt and covert discriminatory practices of those with economic, professional, racial, and sexual power. Few, however, have recognized the considerable influence of common-sense knowledge in defining the cultural boundaries of criminal responsibility and the legal use of psychiatric expertise. This analysis of the relationship between expertise and common sense illustrates how certain medical witnesses were legally qualified as *experts,* and the selective ways in which certain aspects of expert evidence were taken up as legal fact while others were rejected.[44] The case of Frances Harrop demonstrates the implications of these processes and shows that though professional status was sometimes important in getting a doctor's opinion legally qualified as expert opinion, it did not guarantee that his testimony would be privileged in decisions about legal responsibility.[45]

Chapter 4 highlights some of the socio-political and legal dynamics that brought together various knowledges about criminality and human nature in order to resolve the legal question of guilt, establish moral responsibility, and, in the end, determine an appropriate sentence. Here I examine some of the ways in which responsibility has been, in part, negotiated through particular narratives of mind-state. Drawing on Michael MacDonald's description of the various discursive "marketplaces" in which mind-state, and "insanity" in particular, has historically been bartered, I begin by outlining the points in the judicial process where negotiations of responsibility and mind-state typically took place.[46] I also briefly examine the laws of insanity as a defence in criminal cases but then look more closely at alternative legal spaces beyond the insanity defence, where mental capacity was also negotiated.

Chapter 4 establishes the importance of looking beyond the insanity defence and the laws on insanity to get at the broader cultural meaning and ideological boundaries of "insanity" during this time. For instance, I look at the post-trial commutation stage and the defence of provocation, two other procedural/doctrinal marketplaces within which standards of criminal responsibility were routinely contested, negotiated, and classified through assessments of the accused's mental capacity.

I also consider the power of narrative in legal decision making, with the understanding that certain criminological narratives provided important discursive marketplaces within law. Here I expand the analysis of degeneration theory by considering how this particular way of thinking about criminality affected judicial decision making. In doing so, I examine the effects of appropriating scientific/expert knowledge and the implications of certain sociopolitical events on interpretations of criminality. For instance, I look at how war and poverty were seen to produce mental deficiency in certain vulnerable individuals, and how the perceived mental effects of war and poverty worked their way into evaluations of criminal responsibility. I end the chapter with an examination of the ways in which popular, legal, and medical assessments of mental capacity relied upon the ideals of British character and citizenship.

Chapters 5 and 6 focus on the relevance and implications of certain character designations and the ways in which assumptions about race difference and the conjugal ideal informed specific narratives and representations of criminal responsibility. Chapter 5 addresses the ways in which psychiatric and common-sense knowledges about mental capacity linked essentialist theories about racial inferiority to a range of behavioural tendencies and predispositions. For instance, "Indians" and "half-breeds" were characterized as naturally violent and lacking in moral discretion; it was common knowledge that the "coloured" had a loose character and an affinity for vile language; southern European immigrants were known for their "communistic" ways and drinking habits; and non-Anglo women (as well as Anglo women who kept bad company) were often seen as sexually perverse and immoral. We see in this chapter that against a backdrop of scientific certainty and deep confidence in truth-seeking techniques, legal measures of mind-state and criminal responsibility hinged on very flexible ideas about racial identity that were grounded in common-sense understandings about British authority, white supremacy, and the role of the rule of law. That said, these dynamic institutional processes played out quite differently in each case and, I would argue, cannot simply be explained through a functionalist account of racial domination and oppression.

Chapter 6 investigates the significance of the domestic space in the adjudication of capital cases involving spousal murder. The case studies I included here help us to understand the legal implications of certain representations of mind-state and responsibility as defined through narratives of gender, domesticity, and conjugality. The cases of Paul Abraham, Mary Smith, Dina Dranchuk, and James McGrath each reveal the textured and contingent nature of criminological thinking during this period. They show, for instance, the ways in which common sense defined the form and substance of expertise, the importance of character in interpretations of criminal events and criminal behaviour, the recognition of social-structural and political conditions in understanding the meaning of murder, and how race, class, and gender divisions were legitimized through simultaneously operating theories about criminality and responsibility.

This study ends, appropriately, at a point just before the launch of the 1953 *Royal Commission on the Laws of Insanity as a Defence in Criminal Cases,* and taps into several important issues related to crime and criminality that developed during the first half of the twentieth century and were subsequently taken up by the royal commission. Most notably, the commission addressed a growing concern about the role and authority of the psychiatric expert in Canadian criminal law and the qualitative boundaries between criminal responsibility, diminished responsibility, and not guilty by reason of insanity. At the onset of the commission, the minister of justice determined that the *Criminal Code* provisions on the defence of insanity were so complex that a public inquiry should be held to determine whether the law should be amended in any respect. The initiation of the *Royal Commission on the Laws of Insanity* therefore marked an important point in Canadian legal history and helps define the significance of the time period covered in this book.[47]

If criminal responsibility has generally not been the subject of intensive social-historical inquiry, a historical understanding of the discursive nature and consequences of these social and institutional processes in Canada – as distinct from the British or American experience – has been virtually nonexistent. This book fills a substantial void in Canadian socio-legal historiography and provides a critical point of reference to evaluate current legal practices and initiatives in criminal law reform that continue to (re)define responsibility through politicized (re)interpretations of criminality and mind-state.

2
The Making and Mapping of Capital Murder Case Files

This chapter sets out the analytical parameters of the book, as well as detailing the empirical aspects of this study, such as the contents, production, and selection of capital case files. Each person identified in this book was found guilty of capital murder and sentenced to death. Yet, despite the fact that the same legal conditions may have applied in each case, wild variations appear in the conditions of responsibility knowledge, which in turn produced varying representations of individual responsibility within and across cases. By reading each case file as a unique cultural text, we soon learn that a formal verdict of *guilty* actually tells us little about the nexus of social, political, and institutional knowledges that came together to help define the structural and/or ideological boundaries of *responsibility*.[1] For instance, the absence of an insanity defence did not mean that the issue of mind-state was not central to medical, legal, and popular narratives of criminal responsibility.

To make this point, let us return to the case of Elizabeth Tilford. There we observed a contrast between the appearance of a clearly drawn formal verdict of guilty delivered by the judge (and reinforced by the remissions officer) and the more textured and overtly politicized narratives about mental health and (ir)responsibility from certain members of the public. We might also notice in Tilford's case the apparent gaps between the ideals of law – as a fact-finding, truth-seeking machine of justice – and the human performance of those ideals in the form of legal decision making. It is important, however, to move beyond explaining and (re)constructing these processes in simplistic oppositional terms – the law versus the public, formal versus informal, guilty versus innocent, the ideal versus the practical. Although it is helpful at times to deconstruct the components of a particular form of knowledge, or combination of knowledges, in order to point out its many parts, contradictions, and gaps, it is also necessary to appreciate the inextricability, instability, and necessity of these internal tensions to the complex cultural practices of sense making. To understand the nature and meaning of responsibility knowledge, we must see a guilty verdict as only one thread in law's "ideological cloth,"[2] and see law's ideological cloth as a loosely woven and permeable patch of cultural fabric.

The Case Files

The empirical evidence to support this study is based on the case file records for 66 of the 579 individuals convicted for murder between 1920 and 1950 inclusive.[3] According to the records in *Criminal Statistics,* approximately 1,443 people were charged for murder during this period.[4] Of those charged, 12 percent were reported as detained for "lunacy" and did not go to trial. Another 48 percent were "acquitted" of murder charges and released or charged with a lesser offence. The remaining 40 percent of those charged with murder were convicted; 55 percent (319) of these were eventually executed. I am interested in this last group of murder cases, in which each of the accused was found fit to stand trial, convicted for murder, and sentenced to death.

Because there were relatively few cases of women sentenced to death for murder during this period (4 percent), I hoped to include all of them in my sample. Unfortunately, three of the twenty-six files of women convicted for murder were unavailable for viewing at the time of this research. I selected the case files of men from *Persons Sentenced to Death in Canada, 1867-1976,* an inventory of capital case files organized by the Government Archives Division of Library and Archives Canada. Each case in the series is assigned a catalogue number and classified by year. From the catalogue numbers, I randomly selected two cases per year for the years 1920-50, for a total of sixty cases.[5] Eight of these were already included in my sample of women. Of the remaining fifty-two cases of men, nine were subsequently dropped, six because they were incomplete or poorly documented, and three because they were unavailable.[6] Therefore, my final sample includes the complete, or nearly complete, case files of twenty-three women and forty-three men who were sentenced to death for murder. None of the original sixty-six cases was chosen according to previous knowledge of the file contents, and each of the thirty years covered in this study is represented by at least one case. The case studies discussed in each chapter are not exceptional in nature and were primarily chosen due to the richness of the file contents.

When I first surveyed each file, I was interested only in establishing a profile of the contents and gathering enough information to ascertain the key issues and characteristics of each case. I documented the essential demographic factors, including gender, age, racial/ethnic identification, occupation, and year and location of the trial, as well as any information that seemed to shed light on the adjudication process and, in particular, on the role of the psychiatric expert in this process. For instance, in each case I identified factors that were noted in one way or another as significant to the outcome of the case, such as the victim-offender relationship, the method used by the defendant to kill, the alleged motive, the official legal defence, whether the defendant's state of mind was raised as an issue at trial or during the commutation stage, whether expert opinion evidence was admitted, and whether mercy was recommended. Appendix A-1 provides the details of this initial survey and a synopsis of the basic information gathered from each file. Appendix A-2 presents the same information on a case-by-case basis.

I do not present the cursory information in the appendices as statistically meaningful in any way; nor do I wish to suggest a correlative relationship between factors based on these summary statistics. In fact, I have intentionally not taken the statistical analysis of these cases any further. I provide this information only to establish the general representativeness of the case files. As I have already made clear, a more qualitative and interdisciplinary approach to reading the case file documents is necessary in order to understand the specific dynamics of each case, and to understand the meaning and significance of any interplay between legal and extra-legal factors such as outcome and race, or defence and gender.

In terms of gender frequencies, this collection of files is significantly, and necessarily, skewed by the intentional overrepresentation of women convicted of murder during this period. However, it is still safe to say that the cases of women, taken on their own, are representative of all cases of women convicted for murder during this period, and likewise that the cases of men are representative of cases of men convicted for murder at this time. The general demographic features of these sixty-six cases, and the nature of the documents contained in the files, appear to be a fair representation of all capital case files compiled during this period. They are also consistent with statistical information gathered by Kenneth Avio in terms of the frequency of commutations and recommendations to mercy – even after accounting for the overrepresentation of women.[7] The individuals represented in this collection, both women and men, were typically lower working class, lived mostly in the central and western provinces, and were predominantly non-Anglo – with 35 percent identified by court records as originating from south-central and eastern European countries. They were most likely to be between the ages of twenty and thirty-nine and most often killed a member of their family or someone they knew. Again, I must say that though it is useful for descriptive purposes to make general observations about capital cases in Canada, a qualitative reading of the case file texts reveals far more inconsistencies than similarities.

Authoring and Authorizing: The Institutional Production of Capital Murder Case Files

In early-twentieth-century Canada, the governor general, acting as the Crown's representative, was the official authority over whether the royal prerogative of mercy would be exercised. However, by this time the governor general's signature on commutation and execution documents was literally rubber-stamped and did not necessarily indicate his actual authorship of the final decision.[8] Instead, decisions about executions and whether to exercise mercy were the result of a series of institutional procedures and structures beyond public view. As Carolyn Strange describes it, clemency decisions took place "in judges' chambers, in bureaucrats' offices and in the plush quarters of the federal Cabinet."[9] Formally, it was the job of the justice minister to review all capital case files and report his decision regarding clemency to the governor-general-in-council for the final word, but because Cabinet minutes were not recorded, very little has been known about how final decisions were made. Only recently have historians, relying on evidence in capital case files, ministerial records, and chance archival findings, begun the important work of mapping the executive decision-making process. One such chance finding was a 1941 booklet entitled *Capital Cases Procedure under Section 1063 C.C.,* published by the Department of Secretary of State.[10]

The 1941 booklet expanded on the guidelines for capital case procedures previously set out in section 1063 of the *Criminal Code of Canada* by providing more detailed instructions for capital case file dispositions as well as administrative instructions for executions. As noted by Bruce MacFarlane, QC, the lawyer who uncovered the booklet, "the instructions provide an invaluable insight into the thinking of the government during the period when it was most active in the execution of Canadians."[11] The publication also reflects, as Strange observed, "the federal government's desire to appear systematic, rule-bound, and utterly impartial, in spite of mounting evidence that capital justice was haphazard, unregulated, and idiosyncratic."[12]

An important aspect in the disposition, or ordering, of capital cases that can be gleaned from the 1941 manual is the requisite documentation that was to be arranged following every death sentence and forwarded to the minister of justice for review.[13] The following is an excerpt from the *Capital Cases Procedure* manual under the heading "Résumé of Instructions":

> During the Two Weeks Following the Trial:
>
> (a) The trial judge should send directly to the Secretary of State [via the remissions branch] his report containing a substantial summary of the salient facts of the case, together with any remarks or recommendations from his personal notes taken during the trial with reference to the exercise of executive clemency.
>
> The report is then referred to the Minister of Justice, who, after perusing the evidence, gives to each capital case the most anxious consideration. When reaching a decision before making his report to Council, he finds it

> very helpful to have the views of the trial judge regarding any feature of the case which has a bearing upon the exercise of executive clemency.
>
> (b) It is also imperative that the trial judge should give instructions to the stenographer to complete and forward to the Secretary of State the transcript of evidence at the earliest possible date, together with his address to the jury.

The instructions further "invite" the judge, when making his report, to "give his personal detailed observations regarding medical testimony on any insanity issue and concerning the prisoner himself."[14] Judges' reports, though produced in an official capacity, were highly discretionary and value-laden texts. As we shall see in later chapters, judges' evaluations of the cases and individuals tried in their courts did indeed extend beyond strict discussions of law to include personal reflections on the event, the trial, and the convicted murderer.

The manual also stated that the minister was to be sent any sketches or photographs that were "filed as exhibits" at trial, a copy of the evidence, including an index of witnesses and exhibits, and a copy of trial transcripts, including all proceedings subsequent to the judge's charge (reading of the verdict, accused's response, remarks of the jury and judge, and reading of the sentence). In the remissions branch, the chief remissions officer was responsible for receiving and arranging capital case file documentation. From 1924 to 1953, this bureaucratic position was held by one man, Michael Gallagher.[15] In preparing each file, he wrote a summary report, highlighting the nature of the offence, the facts of the case, and notable evidence taken from the trial transcripts; he also included supplementary documents such as medical/psychiatric assessments – assessments that he had often ordered himself. How, and by whom, the case files were produced are important because it seems that the summary report from the remissions officer and the judge's report filed after the trial were perhaps the most influential documents in clemency decisions.

Most of the official documentation contained in the case files allowed the author a considerable amount of discretion. For example, the summary report of the chief remissions officer was a sharply edited version of the full trial transcripts. The process through which this edited text was produced is easily traced by observing which transcript passages he marked with coloured pencil to be included in his summary. Therefore, it is possible to determine which circumstances of the crime or which aspects of expert evidence, for example, he considered to be most noteworthy. Given that trial transcripts could run into thousands of pages, and the condensed remissions report was typically a document of fewer than fifteen pages, much of the evidence presented at trial was intentionally omitted.

In addition to providing an abbreviated version of the trial proceedings, each remissions report concluded with the chief officer's recommendation on how the case should proceed. The executive almost always followed his recommendation; in a few cases, it prevailed over differing recommendations from the trial judge or jury. Gallagher, given his long reign as chief officer, had considerable influence over the routine administration and interpretation of capital cases during the twenties, thirties, and forties.[16] And during this time, he was known as a bit of a hard-liner. For instance, following the Second World War, he was reported to have despised social workers and other "do-gooders" whose proposed approach to corrections was more individualized and rehabilitative than his.[17] Despite his important role in the production of capital case files, there is little record of the chief officer's official duties. Perhaps the most telling bit of evidence here comes from a memo that was drafted by Gallagher himself and found in his personnel records as part of an application for a pay raise.

Carolyn Strange provides a synopsis of the memo and paints a clear picture of Gallagher's own sense of authorship and authority over capital case file dispositions. Gallagher considered that his "most important" duties relating to "Capital Case Work" included summarizing and reporting the facts and legal points of each case as well as "investigating alleged impaired mentality; appointing alienists [psychiatrists] to report, instructing them and considering their findings; collecting data bearing upon character, embracing elements of general reputation, individual disposition and personal temperament and considering all material obtained or submitted bearing upon the innocence of the accused, improbability of guilt, community sentiment, mitigating circumstances of case or redeeming features deemed proper ground for commuting death sentence."[18] This account of his professional duties suggests that Gallagher did not see his work on capital case files as simply administrative but as investigative and directive. In collecting and "considering" evidence toward establishing the condemned person's "mentality," "character," "reputation," "disposition," and "temperament," Gallagher obviously saw it as his duty to provide the minister of justice with additional evidence regarding *who* the condemned person was, including "redeeming features deemed proper ground for commuting death sentence." His remarks also clearly indicate that evidence bearing upon "community sentiment" was actively sought and considered, at least by Gallagher, to be relevant to executive decision making.

Strange provides further evidence to show that the underlined bits in a file, as well as the remissions officer's concluding recommendations regarding mercy, did in fact shape clemency decisions. In 1941, while defending the work of the remissions branch in the House of Commons, Justice Minister Guy Favreau spoke of the care and efficiency of the branch officers and of his reliance on their interpretations and recommendations in rendering his own decisions about clemency:

> In cases where it is the recommendation of the officers of the branch that the law should take its course, of course it is the duty of the minister himself to read the evidence and to convince himself that that is the report which should be made to council. When the recommendation is for clemency, I always read the parts of the evidence which are specially brought to my attention, but I do not feel under the same sort of imperative duty to read every word, to look at every comma of the evidence, because the recommendation is that the law should not take its course.[19]

Government records strongly suggest, therefore, that once a death sentence was handed down and the trial information reached the remissions branch of the Department of Justice, the chief remissions officer became the principal author of the capital case file. We also now know that he was most certainly a key player in the decision-making process, and that Gallagher, at least, had a clear sense of his importance and influence in capital case procedures. And there is evidence to suggest that the authoritative persuasion of the remissions officer's recommendations may have been well established even before Gallagher's time.

For example, in the case of Florence Lassandro (1922), a woman charged and convicted for her connection to the murder of a police officer, the trial judge wrote in his report to the minister of justice that she should escape execution and be held less responsible than her male co-conspirator only because she was a woman, and for "no other reason."[20] However, this chivalrous gesture from the judge in recommending mercy for Lassandro was later levelled by the chief officer. In the remissions report, the officer dismissed "sex" as a mitigating factor and instead drew the minister's attention to the fact that Lassandro's male co-accused made an "immense fortune in bootlegging" and was able to delay the process by securing reprieves "granted as of course," therefore forcing the case to reach the highest court. He urged that these matters of due process "can hardly be considered as entitling the appellants to escape the death penalty."[21]

Therefore, even before Gallagher's appointment to the position in 1924, weighing in on capital cases was probably already considered to be within the chief remissions officer's duties. And given that both Lassandro and her co-accused were executed, this case also suggests that perhaps his recommendation carried some clout. The recommendation by the remissions officer that mercy not be granted in Lassandro's case, going against the judge, also points to some of the subtler ways in which assessments of criminal responsibility, and the nature of mitigation bias, varied among legal/government actors.

Reading the Case Files as Cultural Texts

According to the 1941 instruction manual, the standard information required for each case file was limited to trial documents and official representations of the case, but most files contained plenty more. Each file served as a repository for documents produced on the case from the arrest date of the accused until his or her execution, natural death, or release from prison was reported. Official documents – such as verbatim trial transcripts, judges' reports, summary reports, police reports, medical assessments, jail records, coroners' reports, military records, and death certificates – were produced as a requirement of the official position of the author and with varying degrees of discretion.

Texts produced through a standardized format and procedure, such as trial transcripts, jail records, arrest sheets, and death certificates, allowed for seemingly little discretion in the way the documents were constructed. This is not to say, however, that these records are void of individual and institutional biases. Even a verbatim trial transcript, intended to record exactly what was said at trial, is shaped by the highly selective way in which legal discourse represents "reality." The constitutive quality of trial transcripts is discernible in the revised and editorialized versions of events and evidence presented in court by judges, lawyers, experts, lay witnesses, and the accused through the mechanics of legal procedures. Transcripts are, by their very nature, a by-product of a series of tightly scripted institutional narratives and must be read foremost as fictional texts. However, they are an important record of what happened in court, and they provide some of the most telling evidence of how narratives about criminal responsibility and mind-state were constituted through legal language and institutional structures.

The case files also contain an array of unofficial, or supplementary, documents, including correspondence between official personnel, letters from the public, telegrams, memos, petitions, and newspaper clippings. It is likely that these texts were compiled by the remissions officer as a means to establish character evidence and to measure public opinion, or "community sentiment." Again, although providing assessments of character and community sentiment was considered an important aspect of the chief remissions officer's duties, it is difficult to determine the extent to which this evidence was influential, since commutation decisions were not made public record. We do know, however, that public opinion was considered important by legal decision makers and has historically influenced trial outcomes in a variety of ways. We also know that measures of "community standards" continue to influence sentencing decisions in Canada to this day.[22] In some case files, we can see that selected passages from letters written by members of the public to the minister of justice were cited in the remissions report to make a point about how the public perceived a certain case or individual. The remissions officer would also include newspaper stories, editorials, and letters to the editor, highlighting certain parts to indicate the will of the public.

The concept of "public opinion" is certainly over-inclusive in that it suggests some degree of uniform thinking. The phenomenon has been defined in a number of ways, and I will not attempt to provide a thorough analysis of it. But for the purposes of this discussion, I do like this early definition: "The term public opinion is given meaning with reference to a multi-individual situation in which individuals express themselves or can be called upon to express themselves, as favouring or supporting or else disfavouring or opposing some definite condition, person or proposal of widespread importance in such a proportion of number, intensity and consistency as to give rise to the probability of affecting action directly or indirectly towards the object concerned."[23] It would be an exhaustive and perhaps impossible undertaking to document anything resembling a complete representation of "public opinion" on capital cases during this period. However, we can tap into some of the ways in which legal officials calculated and reported measures of public opinion in relation to each case; in some instances, we can make fair estimates of the influence that public opinion may have had on legal outcomes. The point again is that public opinion *mattered* in these highly politicized cases – sometimes a lot – and evidence shows that attempts were regularly made by legal officials to gauge dominant trends in public attitudes, even if "the public" was not fully represented.

The documents in capital case files were produced by a variety of authors, each with different material interests in the case. Because the issue of self-interest is always at hand – meaning that there was inevitably some practical or conjectural advantage gained by the author – caution must be taken in assessing the representations made in the document itself. For instance, the way in which a psychiatrist determined a diagnosis and structured the language of his report may have been influenced by the predetermined language of the laws on insanity and his desire to have his "expert opinion" heard as evidence. Likewise, newspaper editorials and letters written by members of the public quite often reveal the social position and moral perspectives of each author. Reading the case file documents, therefore, requires a mindful approach in recognizing both the positions authors take and the representations that are conveyed through the texts. However, it is precisely these dynamic idiosyncrasies that make this collection of texts, intended to reflect public and professional sentiment, so valuable.

Each murder, and murder trial, took place under different circumstances, with its own participants, audiences, and decision makers. Thus, from frequency estimates we cannot infer answers to all of those very important *how* questions – such as *how* evidence on mind-state was taken up in each case, or *how* these processes may have differed from case to case, or *how* this information may or may not have influenced trial and commutation outcomes. A number of the social and institutional processes involved in the adjudication and disposition of capital murder cases are not easily quantified, including the role and significance of expert and common-sense knowledges on judicial decisions, and the influence of the remissions branch on the exercise of the royal prerogative of mercy. Statistical evidence can help shape particular research questions or suggest how we might go about further evaluating these processes, but to understand the *effects* and *meanings* of judicial decision making and the socio-political significance of particular trial outcomes, a range of analytical tools is required. In this book, I draw heavily from the tools of constructionism and text analysis, including semiotics, ethnomethodology, and narrative and discourse analysis.[24]

One of the challenges of text analysis is to establish the scholarly integrity of qualitative findings based essentially on interpretation. The interpretation of a particular concept or idea as historically/contextually meaningful goes beyond counting the number of times it appears in texts from a particular period/context. For instance, in the early twentieth century, references to "feeblemindedness" increased in medical, legal, and popular texts. However, this frequency observation does not tell us anything about the social-cultural significance of the idea of feeblemindedness or the "feebleminded" during that period. To understand the processes at work, we need to consider *how* meanings were organized through language and systems of knowledge, and how language and knowledge are represented through text.[25]

Reading a text therefore involves the analytical process of simultaneously taking account of the interests of the text's author and its various audiences, as well as of the fact that an author's intentions and a text's meanings are shaped by the social and institutional contexts in which they were produced.[26] By recognizing the legal structuring and organization of the documents, we can learn much about the institutional processes that shaped and stabilized legal narratives of criminal responsibility. But in reading the files as cultural *texts,* we can also learn something about the historical significance of legal decisions and how criminality was, at least in these cases, understood and negotiated in the Canadian context.[27]

Taking notice of the selective points of view from which the case file documents were produced also requires recognition of my own positioning in the production of this historical account. My prejudices are certainly evident in the way I structured my research questions, selected my sources, and interpreted the meaning and significance of the material. In my view, text analysis is the most provocative approach to studying documents of this nature. They are politically charged and have political consequences. Therefore, by taking account of the institutional constraints on the formation of the documents, the socio-political and moral underpinnings of the texts, and the invested interests of certain authors writing for particular audiences, my reading of the cases is very much interpretive and tentative, rather than formalistic and resolute. My assessments about the historical significance of the cases and what they can tell us concerning the complex ways in which we have made sense of murder and murderers in the past are necessarily provisional. Much work remains to be done. My only hope is that this preliminary work will open the possibility for new questions, new research, and perhaps very different interpretations.

Conclusion

Official representations of law may at times suggest that the legal criteria for establishing criminal responsibility were sharply defined and did not accommodate subtler social-cultural shadings or other non-legal factors such as citizenship, gender, and class. However, at every stage of the murder trial we find the accused's life circumstances, ancestry, character, and disposition under moral scrutiny in order to determine whether she or he possessed the requisite guilty mind. Even when the question of legal responsibility appeared to have been settled with the guilty verdict at trial, plenty of room remained for negotiation in determining whether mercy should and would be granted. Therefore, criminal responsibility was not at all a fixed concept in Canadian law with clean-cut boundaries and predictable measures. The standards and meanings of responsibility were (re)negotiated according to many factors, including, as we would expect, the context and circumstances of each case, the decided character of those involved in the murder, and the concerns and sensibilities of legal decision makers.

In the next chapter, I look outside the institutional structures that gave rise to the production of the capital case file to consider some of the dominant themes of criminological thinking that came to influence the adjudication of murder cases, and in turn shaped the content and meaning of case file texts. In doing so, I also trace the professional and ideological relationships between law and psychiatry on the subjects of crime, insanity, and criminal responsibility as well as the dialectical relationship between expert and common-sense knowledges.

3
Criminological Thinking and Ways of "Knowing" the Criminal

This chapter chronicles some of the ways in which cultural knowledge about criminality and mind-state in early-twentieth-century Canada helped give meaning to specific courtroom dynamics, trial outcomes, community responses, and commutation decisions. During this time, dominant narratives on the causes of crime and criminality drew heavily on the ideology, language, and science of degeneracy and determinism. This was true for expert as well as lay, or common-sense, thinking. If we consider that murder trials were both a part and an expression of Canada's cultural fabric – a complex of ideas, institutions, individuals, events, and movements – then capital case file texts offer an exceptional opportunity to tease out some of the contrasting views on the subject of criminality that existed simultaneously between and within different social institutions and audiences. Through the process of unpacking the content and meaning of criminological knowledge as it came to be represented in each case, and by examining different social, individual, and institutional standpoints, we also gain insight into the historical and political climate in which each murder was understood and dealt with.

Although an exhaustive and systematic analysis of the social, institutional, and individual practices that constituted early-twentieth-century Canadian culture is ontologically impossible, I do attempt here to identify some of the ways in which predominant social and institutional conditions shaped case file texts, and to relate specific narratives of criminality and mind-state back to that broader socio-political and institutional context. For instance, several cases reveal the historical and legal effects of a deep paradigmatic shift during the late nineteenth and early twentieth centuries in the basic conceptualization of criminality. This shift in criminological thinking occurred in tandem with the rise and popularity of determinist psychiatric knowledge about certain kinds of insanity, mental degeneracy, and feeblemindedness. The increasingly stable and popular idea that deviant, immoral, and/or "insane" behaviour was *caused* by biology, physiology, and, in certain cases, environment was far-reaching in Canada; it was epitomized in a momentous eugenics movement during the 1910s, '20s, and '30s. The material of determinism, however, was extremely porous, allowing for the passing through of political concerns, social trends, and new science while at the same time maintaining its essentialist core.

One striking example of the flexibility and permeability of criminological knowledge can be seen during the inter-war period of the 1930s, when attention turned to the social, moral, and individual effects of a nationwide economic depression. As the depression set in, the language of criminological knowledge began to take in concerns about the effects of adverse environmental conditions such as poverty, war, and unemployment on the mental health of certain vulnerable individuals. As I demonstrate more fully in Chapter 4, the incorporation of external factors related to economic hardship and domestic (in)security into narratives of criminological determinism and mental capacity would also come to influence medical, legal, and popular interpretations of criminal responsibility in some capital murder cases.

Likewise, during the Second World War and the post-war period, a number of moral panics ignited over the biological "health" of the family and the quality of Canadian citizenship. Although the purity of Canadian "stock" had been a concern among Anglo-Canadian citizens during the late nineteenth century, this was compounded by the depletion of "healthy" men during the war and a growing immigrant population. Reports of increased crime rates, particularly in urban centres, prompted the production of new ways of "knowing" (identifying and explaining) what was becoming one of the nation's most dangerous classes of criminal – the "feebleminded" immigrant. Criminological knowledge during this time was, to borrow a term, very much a "hybrid knowledge," including many forms of expert, institutional, and common-sense knowledges.[1] Therefore, shifts and dynamics in popular thinking about crime and criminals cannot simply be explained as a response to new science on criminality.

After looking briefly at some of the broader legal consequences of degeneration theory and the professional tensions between law and psychiatry on the subjects of crime and insanity, I focus more specifically on the dialectical relationship between expertise and common sense. I begin my analysis of expert knowledge by examining how the finding of legal facts, the qualification of certain medical witnesses as "experts," and the adjudication of expert opinion evidence in the courtroom relied heavily on common-sense knowledge about individual responsibility and criminal behaviour. Interestingly, in some accounts of expert evidence we can observe significant slippage between what could be superficially classified as expert knowledge and what might be seen as common-sense knowledge. I argue here that the dichotomy between expertise and common sense was forged in many respects, perhaps in order to maintain professional elitism and protect claims to particular forms of knowledge. Regardless of any degree of agency that can be read into these discursive processes, evidence presented in the later part of this chapter most certainly calls into question overgeneralized theories about knowledge, power, and expertise. To stake down this point, I draw on evidence from the case file of Frances Harrop (1940). Harrop's trial transcripts illustrate quite expressly the interplay between common-sense knowledge and expert knowledge, shedding light on the processes through which medical witnesses were legally qualified as "expert witnesses" and the ways in which certain aspects of expert witness testimony were then selected and omitted as legal "fact."

The appeal and popularity of degeneracy theory, when combined with a significant economic crisis and the political effects of war, provided fertile ground for new ways of thinking about crime and "knowing" criminals. Cultural knowledge about criminality produced through and within these historical events was, quite literally, written into the case file texts of capitally convicted offenders and represented in legal narratives of mind-state and responsibility. There were, of course, many other historical events – such as the rise of the labour, social welfare, suffrage, and early feminist movements – that I do not address in this book but that were also certainly part of the backdrop against which the case files were compiled. Therefore, this chapter only begins the work of mapping criminological thinking as a way of understanding and conceptualizing responsibility knowledge in Canadian law, medicine, and society.

Degeneracy and Feeblemindedness

Ideas about degeneracy and feeblemindedness metamorphosed during the inter-war and post-war periods in Canada to include competing accounts of the perceived social and psychiatric effects of the conditions of war and economic hardship. Individuals classified as degenerate, defective, or feebleminded were subsequently identified as the primary contaminants of Canada's social, moral, and biological health.[2] The (re)constitution of external events, as embodying an inherent degenerative quality, provided particular meanings to medical, legal, and popular interpretations of criminal responsibility in this period.

Before the nineteenth century, the relationship between insanity and criminality was not highly contested among medical professionals: rather, it was generally thought, to varying degrees, that criminality was in fact a form of insanity. However, toward the mid-nineteenth century, doctors began writing on the legal and psychological issues of motivation and intent, and medical texts soon differentiated between acts committed *with* and *without* criminal intent. According to some medical experts, the former constituted a crime to be dealt with by the law, whereas the latter characterized "the antisocial act of the insane man" and came under the jurisdiction of psychiatry.[3] In British law, however, motive and intent were distinct; motive was usually understood as a *symptom* of guilt and intent as a condition of guilt.[4] To put it another way, motive, from a legal standpoint, had to do with why an individual committed a crime, whereas the question of intent was concerned with whether an individual meant to commit a crime.

Although this distinction may seem clear enough, motive and intent were often conflated in legal evaluations of mind-state, or *mens rea,* as well as in psychiatric determinations about mental capacity. However, the underlying assumption in both legal and psychiatric interpretations of intent was that those who acted freely were guilty and punishable, and those who acted without intent were not legally/morally responsible and therefore excusable.[5] Trial evidence indicates that it was within the context of the legal notion of the "excuse" – fundamentally a recognition of human weakness – that theories of degeneracy were most easily taken up. However, as scientific knowledge about human nature and feeblemindedness proliferated to include an increasing number of personal qualities thought to interfere with one's ability to act freely, legal understandings and evaluations of intent became unstable. In particular, debates seemed to focus on what to do with those individuals who were not found legally or medically insane yet were still considered – by medical, legal, and/or social standards – to be mentally weak.

Although the ideas of heredity and degeneracy were born in agricultural science, not psychiatry or criminology,[6] it was ambitiously adopted into these disciplines as a way of explaining the social repercussions of criminality and the nature of the newly identified feebleminded criminal. In an article entitled "Nature of Feeble-Mindedness," Dr. Abraham Myerson, an American specialist on the "inheritance of mental diseases," defined feeblemindedness as a "heterogeneous group of conditions which are only unified by one of many symptoms, viz., that they present an intelligence so low that it is declared pathological." Myerson divided the feebleminded into sub-classes, including cretins, "mongolians," spastic types, idiots, and microcephalics (having a small head). However, of particular social concern were those he identified as "unclassified," meaning that experts at the time had "no hint as to causation" beyond general assumptions about heredity. The doctor explained that "individuals of this group present a varied aspect. In many instances they show gross anomalies of appearance; in others no anomalies of any importance are present. They represent the group most commonly remaining in the community ... In a general way they approach more nearly the diversity and the characteristics of the normal population, and they represent the most difficult social problem."[7] This more insidious class of unspecified feeblemindedness posed a particular challenge to medicine, law, and society because it was difficult to detect and manage. According to

Myerson, the more obvious classes of feeblemindedness presented "no special difficulties." Particularly once institutionalized, they presented little social or genetic threat. However, he cautioned, "among the unclassified ... we find persons who carry on in the community and who have access, so to speak, to copulation and reproduction; who pass amongst the mass as relatively normal. This unclassified group then probably represents our greatest problem and it is concerning this group that we have the least definite knowledge."[8] The evaluation and detection of feeblemindedness in this period continued to rely on crude observations of "physical inferiority," including blindness, deafness, bad posture, shortness, tallness, bad teeth, heart defect, strabismus, and skeletal or cranial deformity, to name a few.[9] However, the real fear was generated around those feebleminded individuals who remained undetected, had unregulated "access" to reproduction, and about whom scientific knowledge was lacking.

In Canada, theories about determinism and degeneracy were widely linked to crime, insanity, immorality, social and sexual descent, and racial inferiority. The interconnectedness of these ideas can be seen in a 1920 report published in the *Canadian Journal of Mental Hygiene,* which surveyed the rising prevalence of feeblemindedness in Manitoba, a province that received a disproportionate percentage of non-Anglo immigrants during the early twentieth century.[10] According to the authors, Drs. Charles Kirk Clarke and Clarence Hincks, "the feeble-minded, insane and psychopathic ... were recruited out of all reasonable proportions from the immigrant class, and it was found that these individuals were playing a major role in such conditions as crime, juvenile delinquency, prostitution, pauperism, certain phases of industrial unrest, and primary school inefficiency."[11] Assisted by the new quantitative technologies of scientific observation, measurement, and classification, detecting and identifying feeblemindedness in its many subversive forms became a key concern among socially and politically minded Canadians, including several psychiatrists who claimed to have the needed skills and expert knowledge to sift the defective from the healthy, the evil from the ill, and the insane from the sane.

Although the law on insanity as a criminal defence was not altered in response to advances in psychiatry and new classifications of mental defectiveness in social-psychiatric theory, subsequent chapters show that the interpretation of the M'Naghten rules did expand and contract to accommodate the social-political circumstances of the time and the characteristics of each case, as well as certain aspects of psychiatric knowledge about mental deficiency. Throughout this period, a professional and ideological tension existed between law and psychiatry on the causes, nature, and evidence of mental defectiveness. However, the dominant image of the "degenerate" as the physical and conceptual representation of human weakness and social malady also pervaded popular sensibilities and inspired a range of initiatives intended to truncate the growing problems of criminality and feeblemindedness in Canada.

By the 1920s, psychiatric texts reported the basic causes of insanity to be heredity, vice, syphilis, and head trauma.[12] Disorders of perception, personality, and judgment often fell under the heading of "general psychiatry," whereas classifications of feeblemindedness, mania, alcoholism, and dementia were typically considered the domain of "special psychiatry." Most classes of organic disorders (including tumours, old age, and physical abnormalities) that were considered the fundamentals of general psychiatry during the nineteenth century were, by the early twentieth century, part of a miscellaneous group of disorders.

During the early decades of the twentieth century, the symptomatology of insanity and the classification of mental disorders underwent substantial clinical refinement. For instance, there emerged a new genre of paranoid and delusional types identified as "dementia praecox" (often considered the precursor to schizophrenia). The subject of criminality, and its clinical relation to insanity, seemed to receive comparatively little attention in early-twentieth-century psychiatry texts. However, the growing interdisciplinary study of criminology filled this intellectual space. Some psychiatrists made criminology the focus of their careers, as did psychologists, sociologists, anthropologists, social workers, legal experts, and political activists. Publications that grappled with the specific issues of criminal behaviour and criminal responsibility became increasingly popular.[13] Whereas earlier medical-social discourses typically identified criminality as a *form* of insanity, by the early twentieth century, the expression of or tendency toward criminal behaviour appeared in medical and criminology texts as a *symptom* of certain types of insanity or feeblemindedness, which were classified as manifestations of biological, moral, and/or mental *degeneracy.*

However, the real threat of degeneracy lay in what would occur should "degenerates" and other "defective" individuals happen to reproduce. An essential feature of degeneracy theory was that the undesirable and often undetected traits of defective individuals would be inherited by their children, in whom symptoms were expected to manifest in an exaggerated form. The future deterioration of the Canadian citizenry was as much a concern as the individuals who posed an immediate risk to the health of society. However, during this period, the significance and meaning of "degeneracy" and "feeblemindedness" went beyond science and law to also influence the way in which the public would come to make sense of crime and criminals.

Although certain individual psychiatrists, such as Dr. Charles Kirk Clarke, were quite visible in the foreground of social and political initiatives aimed at regulating criminal activity and the feebleminded in Canada, psychiatric experts were not great inventors of new science on crime. Rather, social movements that turned toward strengthening mental fitness, moral reform, racial purity, and social hygiene were personally and professionally endorsed by psychiatrists through claims of expertise and objectivity. Also, as I show in the next part of this chapter, the *idea* of expertise was perhaps a more powerful phenomenon than was the expert himself. The notion that expert insights and solutions to social problems were beyond the abilities of common folk is very much embodied in professional and popular writings of the day. However, a close reading of capital case files suggests that psychiatric expertise did not seriously challenge common-sense thinking. Rather, expertise often simply illuminated that which everyone already seemed to know, including the idea that certain *kinds* of people were constitutionally inferior/superior to other *kinds* of people.

Therefore, if psychiatrists did obtain some public, professional, or legal power as forensic "experts" by claiming to know the criminal, it nonetheless seems, at least in the context of these murder cases, to have been limited. It also appears that the way in which certain aspects of an expert's testimony came to be accepted as legal fact was based largely on their appeal to common sense. In addressing the court at trial, psychiatric experts called by lawyers to persuade the jury one way or another consistently invoked the language of law and the language of "common men" in order that their opinions would be heard and accepted. It was important to the adjudication process that what experts said made sense to the jury, as well as to the judge, who would often comment on the substance and viability of expert evidence in his charge to the jury.

Capital case file evidence shows that while many theories circulated throughout Canadian professional and lay communities concerning the precise nature and causes of degeneracy, feeblemindedness, and insanity, the essentialist core of degeneracy theory seemed to be understood by many and was rarely contested – at least when it came to assessing those charged with murder. Standards of criminal responsibility were therefore not strictly set according to legal criteria or psychiatric theories but on the common knowledge that people were qualitatively different, and that differences were meaningful and measurable.

Constituting the "Expert" in Canadian Criminal Law

According to Sheila Jasanoff, both law and science theoretically aspire to be "wholly rational" in their search for and judgment of truthful data. To this end, she argues, experts are tempted to give "definitive rather than qualified answers, to deemphasize the existence of other schools of thought, and to exaggerate the significance of their own inferences." Moreover, Jasanoff suggests that the legal process of truth-finding "offers no hard-and-fast rules for separating facts from scientific opinions, opinions from mere speculation, or speculation from legal conclusion." As she sees it, the borderline between "value decisions that should be the prerogative of judges and the factual matters that are properly reserved for experts is itself a construct, negotiated anew from expert to expert and from case to case."[14] Building upon Jasanoff's findings and adding to the varying accounts of the judicial role of the expert witness in medical-legal historiographies, the remainder of this chapter suggests that in early-twentieth-century Canada the expert witness and the legal concept of *expertise* were primarily social-institutional constructs that acquired limited degrees of legitimacy through the adjudication of criminal responsibility.

By the 1910s, the psychiatric expert witness was a regular feature in the Canadian murder trial. The growing presence of psychiatrists in the courtroom perhaps suggests they came to hold an important role in trial proceedings and that their opinions were increasingly valued by legal fact-finders. This notion, if accurate, would fit nicely with the medicalization thesis. Although there is some variation within the literature, social historians typically describe medicalization as the infiltration of medical or psychiatric knowledge into social, political, and legal practices, the assumption being that a centralized institution of medical knowledge wielded a certain amount of power that was exercised in an oppressive manner and further strengthened through legal affiliations. Critical works by Robert Menzies, Angus McLaren, and others certainly provide a wealth of evidence of the medicalization process in Canadian social and political spheres.[15] However, a close reading of trial evidence suggests that this analytical model does not adequately account for the often highly contested substance and status of the psychiatric expert and expert knowledge in Canadian courtrooms. It appears that in some cases, the fact that the expert was a key player during the trial did not necessarily mean he was the star player. In fact, an expert often played only bit parts, or acted as a one-person chorus.

In the following exploration of the laws of expert evidence – where expert testimony was supposedly admitted for the purpose of helping the jury to decide on the facts of a case – I am especially interested in the legal qualification of certain doctors as "experts" during the trial stage, as well as the adjudication of expert opinion evidence in the constitution of legal facts. Throughout the adjudicating process, we can identify a number of tensions between law and psychiatry, including debates on the legal test for insanity, the unstable authority of expertise in legal determinations of mind-state and criminal responsibility, and the formative and substantive relationship between expert knowledge and common-sense knowledge.

As evidence will show, these are not separate issues: rather, they are tied up with, and in, each other. For instance, the intimate connections between expertise and common sense strongly influenced the way in which expert testimony was legally taken up and, ultimately, the way in which the mind-state of a defendant was established. Likewise, the ideological/professional gap between law and psychiatry helped to establish the boundaries of expertise, shape the nature of expert opinion evidence, and contribute to the production of common-sense knowledges about criminality and criminal responsibility.

The Laws of Opinion Evidence and the Expert Witness

Historically, the rules for determining whether a witness's testimony could be legally received as expert evidence are both judicial and statutory. In establishing the test for insanity in *R. v. M'Naghten* (1843) (hereafter referred to as the M'Naghten rules), the law lords of England were asked to state their position regarding the role of the expert witness in legal decisions about insanity. They proposed that

> The medical man ... cannot in strictness be asked his opinion in the terms above stated [regarding the definition of insanity], because each of those questions involves the determination of the truth of facts deposed to, which it is for the jury to decide, and the questions are not mere questions upon a matter of science, in which case such evidence is admissible. But where the facts are admitted or not disputed, and the question becomes substantially one of science only, it may be convenient to allow the question to be put in that general form, though the same cannot be insisted on as a matter of right.[16]

This response from the judges suggests that during the mid-nineteenth century, when *M'Naghten* was decided, insanity was far from a mere question of science. However, by the early twentieth century, there seemed to be more recognition, at least in legal texts, that insanity did fall under the specialized knowledge of psychiatric experts. Yet the crafting of the law continued to protect the authority of judges to decide the parameters of expert opinion and that of juries to decide the factual relevance of opinion evidence.

According to British law, an "expert" was a "specially skilled" witness who offered his opinions and knowledge on legal questions of science.[17] In a Canadian text written to help doctors understand and prepare for interactions with the law, Kenneth Gray, a lecturer in medical jurisprudence at the University of Toronto and medical-legal adviser to the Department of Health and Hospitals in Ontario, explained,

> Any duly qualified medical practitioner (that is, any medical doctor licensed to practice) is accepted as an expert witness for all matters pertaining to the science or art of medicine. The court will permit any licensed practitioner to give an expert opinion on any relevant medical subject, whether he be a

> specialist in the subject or not ... That is not to say that the court will give the same weight to his evidence, as it may give to evidence of some other medical witness with greater experience and qualification, but for what it is worth, his opinion will be received.[18]

However, trial evidence suggests that it was not always the case that "any duly qualified medical practitioner" was accepted as an expert witness; nor were the opinions of those with "greater experience and [medical] qualification" necessarily given more weight. Gray went on to say that, in some cases, "an individual may be qualified as an expert witness in respect of some phases of medicine, even though he is not a licensed medical practitioner. It is for the judge to decide whether the study and experience of a particular person are sufficient to qualify him as an expert."[19] This process is quite evident in capital cases, although it does not seem to be a practice that was explicitly recognized by legal officials during courtroom procedures. In certain cases, lay witnesses were permitted to testify regarding evidence of a defendant's state of mind, and their testimonies were sometimes given considerable weight. However, I did not come across any cases in which a lay witness was, as Gray described, openly "qualified as an expert witness." What distinguished expert witnesses from ordinary ones was the provision that "ordinary" opinions, inferences, or beliefs were legally inadmissible, whereas the opinions of "expert" witnesses were admissible as evidence regarding the facts of a case.

To justify the admission of expert testimony, two elements were required:

> (1) The Subject matter of inquiry must be such that ordinary people are unlikely to form a correct judgment about it, if unassisted by persons with special knowledge.
> (2) The witness offering expert evidence must have gained his special knowledge by a course of study or previous habit which secures his habitual familiarity with the matter in hand.[20]

On the issue of insanity, or mind-state more generally, the question was often raised whether a medical expert was actually a better judge of human nature than the ordinary man. The law of evidence was intended to limit the role of the expert to determining if the "symptoms exhibited by A *commonly* show unsoundness of mind, and whether such unsoundness of mind *usually* renders persons incapable of knowing the nature of the acts which they do, or of knowing that what they do is either wrong or contrary to law."[21] However, attempts to (re)establish or (re)claim the boundaries between expert knowledge and common-sense knowledge were sometimes undermined in cases where judges and lawyers maintained that the facts around mental capacity could be decided by any reasonable jury and that experts were not necessary. There were indeed legal standards for the qualification of expert witnesses and for deciding when expert opinion was perhaps necessary. However, these standards, like the standards for criminal responsibility, were, as Jasanoff claims, "negotiated anew from expert to expert and from case to case."[22]

The Trial of Frances Harrop

In capital murder trials, common-sense interpretations of events and evaluations of criminal responsibility often included versions of psychiatric knowledge. I use the term "common sense" here to describe what Tony Ward refers to as the "knowledge which fact finders apply in deciding whether a narrative is plausible or not."[23] Legal determinations of criminal responsibility in the trials I examined depended on the judicial selection of certain narratives as more truthful and hence more factual than others. It could be said, therefore, that this selection process permitted Canadian courts to actively engage in the generation of the very facts they would later come to adjudicate.[24] The trials of women and men convicted of murder before 1950 suggest that the opinions of *medically* qualified psychiatric experts were not always given judicial privilege in the courtroom; instead, they suggest that, to determine facts concerning the defendant's state of mind, judges routinely solicited and legally qualified the psychiatric opinions of coroners, general practitioners, and lay witnesses who were inexperienced in dealing with clinical forms of insanity.

However, during the post-conviction stage, when the legal question moved from that of guilt to whether to commute the death sentence, experts seemed to be given more credence and authority in their assessments of defendants. Although it is difficult to know exactly how the decision-making process took place – given the closed-door policy of commutation proceedings – this analysis of the judicial construction of fact and the medical witness as *expert* reveals some of the historical, practical, and theoretical implications of legally engaging psychiatric expert knowledge, as well as the hybridity of expert and common-sense knowledges. This hybridity is quite visible in the trial documents of Frances Harrop's file.

Early one April morning in 1940, Mrs. Harrop shot her husband in the head, killing him while he slept. During the trial, her lawyer established through the testimonies of numerous friends and neighbours that she had been physically abused for many years and that her husband often made threats to kill her. Defence counsel raised three defences: provocation, self-defence, and insanity.[25] The accused made the statement to police, and again at trial, that it "was a case of his life or mine; he would kill me or I would kill him."[26] The Crown called two medically qualified psychiatric experts to help the court understand what appeared to be a sudden decision to end her husband's life, as well as her observed "calm" and "frank" demeanour following the murder.[27] However, Dr. Harry Speechly, the Crown coroner who was originally called to testify as to the cause of death and nature of the victim's wounds, was also invited in defence counsel's cross-examination to give his opinion on the mental state of the accused at the time of the crime.

The legal practice of asking general practitioners to make psychiatric assessments was common in Canadian trials. Such assessments were often followed by a courtroom discussion as to whether the witness could legally be considered an expert. Debates of this sort were, for the most part, procedural and had little to do with whether expert testimonies would eventually be incorporated into legal decisions about the facts of a case or the extent of a defendant's legal responsibility. The boundaries of expertise were therefore quite flexible, for the understanding was that a witness did not need to be a medically qualified psychiatric expert in order to have a general knowledge about insanity and human nature. Although some aspects of human behaviour, including insanity, were legally classified as beyond common knowledge, many lawyers and judges insisted that general knowledge and common sense were in fact the best tools with which to evaluate the actions of an accused. Some experts, too, seemed to understand that appealing to common-sense ideas was probably the best way to influence the jury. Therefore, witnesses without specialized knowledge were also invited to testify and offer opinion evidence about psychiatric theory, the history of insanity in a defendant's family, or the nature of a defendant's disposition and past behaviour.

For example, in cross-examination, defence counsel urged Dr. Speechly, the coroner in Harrop's case, to give his opinion of the defendant's mental and physical condition. The Crown did not object to the coroner testifying on the matter, even when Speechly made it clear that he was "not an expert." Regardless of his denial of specialized experience in psychiatry, the judge established in the following courtroom exchange that a witness did not need to be an "expert" in order to give his opinion on insanity:

> Q [judge]: I take it from the fact that you have been practicing for 50 years, and the fact of your medical knowledge gained in this period of time, that you are conversant with the state of a woman's mind?
> A: Naturally so. I am not an expert. I am a general practitioner. But a general practitioner who has practiced for 50 years must be rather a fool if he can't give an opinion on a thing.
> Q: It is something that one gets in general knowledge and one needn't be an expert?
> A: Yes, my Lord. I don't pose as an expert.[28]

In fact, the law did not require Dr. Speechly to be an expert in mental diseases to testify. However, I submit that the idea that one could "pose as an expert," and the doctor's desire not to position himself as such, suggest that some meaningful understanding existed concerning what constituted both an expert and the boundaries of expertise. Once the coroner's medical qualifications, which did not include specialized knowledge or experience in psychiatry, were legally established, defence counsel read a passage from a medical text regarding a female-specific form of mental illness referred to as "Climacteric Insanity" and asked the witness to comment on its viability in explaining this case. According to the source, climacteric insanity occurred at a particular point in a woman's natural life when,

> instead of passing from the earlier years of married life to the years of a matron's duties ... the patient becomes exacting and querulous, expends her energies in a passion of jealousy, and destroys the home which she has built up with fond care. These unfortunate first steps require a world of patience and most considerate treatment. They indicate a self-consciousness and a loss of control which, unchecked, pass to easily recognisable forms of mental aberration.[29]

Speechly diagnosed Harrop's disconcerting calmness after she killed her husband as a symptom of this particular type of insanity, which was characterized by broad swings of mania and melancholia with underlying features of delusion and depression.

Although Speechly did not wish to confirm that climacteric insanity, a psychotic form of menopause, was the precise condition under which the defendant suffered, he was more confident in his general knowledge as a medical man that she was suffering some degree of mental impairment. He explained, "it is the experience, I think, of every practitioner, that there are times in a woman's life when she feels, sometimes, that she doesn't know what she might do, whether to commit suicide or to commit murder. And they are puzzling, sometimes, those cases – hard to approach. That is, exhausted with the climacteric or the change of life, which is the simpler way of putting it." In a segment of his earlier testimony as coroner, Speechly downplayed the relevance of the "private circumstances of these people," but in his role as "expert" he went on to compare their situation to a "domestic volcano which may erupt at any moment ... the result depending on which of the parties has the most intense mental obsession." He explained to the court that "people like that have what the French call 'a fixed idea.'"[30]

Medical witnesses often incorporated sociological explanations into their opinions and assessments of defendants. In this case, the economic conditions of the Harrop family were considered important in order to understand the events leading up to the murder, as well as to comprehend the inferred mental instability of the defendant. Common sense seemed to dictate in this and other cases that exposure to long-term domestic stress and poverty would naturally alter one's reasoning ability.[31] Knowledge about domestic life and conjugal obligation, in turn, influenced the doctor's professional interpretation of psychiatric doctrine in a way that was specific to the circumstances of Harrop's case, and indeed to the determined character of Harrop herself. The process of interpreting responsibility and mind-state through discourses of gender, class, and domesticity will be revisited in more detail later on, but it also serves here as an excellent example of the interplay between expert and common-sense knowledges.

The trial judge pressed the issue of insanity further and asked Speechly to clarify if the "peak" of this climacteric condition could be considered a "disease of the mind." In cases where insanity was formally raised as the defence, witnesses were often asked to (re)phrase, (re)enter, and (re)constitute psychiatric evidence into a form of legally recognized language. In this case, "disease of the mind" was a term that would satisfy the legal definition of insanity, but "climacteric insanity" was not officially recognized terminology. Speechly confirmed that only if the state caused mental deterioration, which it "very often" did, would a person be compelled "to do a thing that was totally insane."[32]

The common-sense-inspired medical theory that a woman's behaviour is inextricably linked to her reproductive biology was evident in this menopausal explanation for what appeared to be an irrational act of violence. Other psycho-sexual explanations offered at trial suggested that her "insane" behaviour was the result of her refusal to have sexual relations with her husband, therefore disturbing her "mental balance." Counsel for the defence also added that the emotional stress caused by irregular menstrual periods and fear of pregnancy could perhaps have induced a mental break; however, he was unable to verify his theory with "medical evidence."

In rebuttal, the Crown called two doctors who were medically qualified and legally accepted as psychiatric experts. Basing their conclusion on their evaluations of her life history and "hereditary facts," both psychiatrists found Frances Harrop to be sane. Dr. Pincock interpreted her unusual calmness to be a lack of empathy rather than evidence of insanity. He described her decision to kill her husband as a calculated act. Although she had recounted to the doctor that she had experienced spells of heightened "irritation," he testified that she was "comparatively cool over the whole situation" and that she "showed no evidence of manneristic or any conduct behaviour ... which appeared to me at all abnormal."[33]

Dr. Alvin Mathers, superintendent of Canada's first "psychopathic" hospital in Winnipeg, also found Frances Harrop legally and medically sane.[34]

His opinion echoed Dr. Speechly's general characterization: he testified that she may very well have been a "hot-tempered woman" with the potential to "explode," but she was also a woman of "refined type" and "fair education" who did not suffer from "disease of the mind." According to Mathers, her chosen response to her "domestic problem" was truly inappropriate, but he "wouldn't call it a disease." He suggested three possible responses to extended periods of "exasperation and torment": one can either accept the situation and live an unhappy life, explode under the pressure in a degenerative rage of violence, or accept a "fatalistic attitude" and resolve the problem no matter what the consequences. The latter response, according to Mathers, best explained Mrs. Harrop's actions.[35]

In the judge's charge to the jury, the supposed authority of expert opinion expressed in the law of evidence was undercut by his instruction to "weigh the witnesses according to your own standards of experience in life." As all juries in the cases I read appeared to be composed primarily of middle- and working-class English-speaking men, ideas about gender identity, morality, and domesticity would have been constituted from their particular social position and "common experience."[36] Frances Harrop's low social position was highlighted throughout the trial and presented to the jury as evidence worth considering in its deciding of the facts and determination of guilt.

The judge further reminded the jury in his final charge that the Harrop family lived an impoverished life with both parents and five grown sons all residing in a small dwelling. He drew the following image in order to make his point clear:

> The husband did not work, had not worked for years. They were all crowded together in close quarters, he sitting around the home most of the time. Had he been out working every day the situation may have been different. The situation, as it is pictured here, must have been one of dreadful living – quarrelling, bickering all the time, apparently. The husband baiting the wife on. She was irritable, quick tempered, harassed by want of money and other things of that sort.[37]

In summarizing the events leading up to the murder, the judge validated Dr. Speechly's common-sense and medical opinion that the Harrops lived in a domestic situation that "might lead to an explosion."[38]

Collectively, the medical witnesses attributed Harrop's behavioural motivation and weakened state of mind to both her biological makeup and her socio-economic circumstances. However, in closing his directions to the jury, the judge surmised, "the state of mind of a human being is a very difficult thing to appreciate ... Just how far this woman was, by her brooding over the difficulties she lived under, and so forth, how far she was drawn off her balance, I don't know."[39] Here we see that, through the adjudication of expert opinion evidence, certain aspects of expert knowledge were taken up as legal fact, and others were rejected. Yet, at the same time, common sensibilities about the nature of women and domesticity were consistently reaffirmed. Frances Harrop was found legally responsible for murdering her husband, but as we see here, the narrative processes through which responsibility was assigned were deeply rooted in middle-class Anglo-Christian assumptions about married life, gender roles, and feminine nature, and introduced as legal fact through the opinions of legally qualified medical experts.

Experts, Law, and the Appeal to Common Sense

The apparent clash between legal doctrine and psychiatric theory on criminal responsibility surfaced in Canadian criminal trial proceedings throughout this period as judges routinely reminded juries that the law was neither interested in nor obligated to entertain psychiatric theories of criminality or insanity. Although the doctors in Harrop's case were permitted to testify at great length as to whether she was in control of her mind, her emotions, and her behaviour, their evidence did not strongly support the case because the states of mind they described did not constitute a "disease of the mind" and therefore did not meet the legal requirements of an insanity defence. Not only did legal and psychiatric authorities often disagree on the particulars of insanity in individual cases, they also fundamentally disagreed on the role experts should/could play in criminal courts. For instance, according to one legal scholar, professional arguments generally reflected the feeling that the use and presentation of medical expert testimony in criminal cases were "not only imperfect" but also burdened by the "serious evils which tend to bring the medical profession into disrepute."[40] Some legal men seemed frustrated by the very nature of the adversarial process, which itself opened the way for psychiatric experts to testify. They also seemed frustrated by the fact that counsel often selected experts without regard for their specific qualifications or professional standing, so long as "the expert so selected is willing to give an opinion in favor of that side of the case."[41]

Many medical men disagreed, however, arguing that experts provided a much needed lens of objectivity and clarity to the legal process. According to one psychiatric expert, "when a psychiatrist becomes [an] expert in criminal courts, he assumes a clearly definite part and one of high responsibility before society. He is selected with the utmost confidence, to throw light on a difficult, ambiguous and obscure case."[42] From this perspective, therefore, the "mission" of the expert witness was to "instruct the judges, the jurors and the lawyers and to import to them the special learning which is wanted, in order to decide on a problem and to render a definite and final judgment."[43]

Although the debate regarding the role of the medical/psychiatric expert in court has never been theoretically or doctrinally reconciled, in practice psychiatric expert witnesses did, even if indirectly, play an integral role in shaping legal decisions about criminal responsibility and mind-state in capital cases.

At least some legal experts seem to have been well aware that a great deal of discretion was exercised when it came to interpreting the applicability and boundaries of insanity law in order to appease the pleasure of public opinion. The structure and substance of legal proceedings were strongly influenced by the moral and social value that legal decision makers (the executive, judges, lawyers, and jurymen) placed on certain circumstances surrounding the crime, the decided "character" of a defendant and victim, and on the nature and value of expert witness testimony in individual cases. For some, moral judgment (read, common sense) was understood to be an essential characteristic of Canadian law and not something to be reined in. H.B. Spaulding, for instance, outlined the development of British and Canadian law in accordance to public opinion and moral sentiment. In concurring with the position of well-known legal expert Sir James Stephen, who argued that the social function of the rule of criminal law was to support and sanction popular morality, Spaulding posited that "the close alliance between criminal law and moral sentiment is in all ways healthy and advantageous to the community."

On the specific subject of insanity in relation to criminal responsibility, Spaulding told his audience that though the law was very "gradual" in development, it "almost always follows public opinion." Therefore, he surmised, "it is safe to say that the public generally feels that the satisfaction and gratification, which so many people receive from the rigorous and at times harsh punishment of criminals, is a legitimate satisfaction which the law should provide. Until these feelings have changed we can hope for very little advance in the criminal law, and I think there is very little doubt that the only thing that will change public opinion is greater knowledge of the subject more widely held."[44] If we accept that the practices and policies of Canadian criminal law form, at least in part, an institutional representation of popular opinion, we cannot possibly imagine criminal law as separate from the moral climate in which it developed and operated. It follows, therefore, that judicial interpretations of legally recognized mind-states intended to negate, mitigate, or establish intent and criminal responsibility both reflected and validated common-sense understandings of mental deficiency and human nature. The discord between law and psychiatry on the subject of human nature, which often underpinned the adjudication of criminal responsibility, was propelled as much by a perceived alienation between expert and common-sense knowledges as it was by professional rivalry.

Despite routine efforts to distinguish experts and the boundaries of expertise, these lines became at times indistinguishable as legal authorities spoke to and reaffirmed the sensibilities of the jury, the public, and the ordinary man through a common-sense engagement with expert knowledge.

Common-sense interpretations of psychiatric evidence in the courtroom – by witnesses, lawyers, judges, and jurymen – allowed certain theories, or parts of theories, about a defendant's behaviour to be more readily accepted as legal fact. At the same time, alternative representations, including those offered by defendants themselves, were rejected and silenced. This is quite different from what Ruth Harris observed in French courts where the testimonies and confessions of those charged with murder were readily incorporated into psychiatric and legal accounts of the facts of a particular case. This led Harris to conclude that the role of the defendant was quite important in the creation of responsibility discourse. For instance, she explores the way in which defendants' narratives of themselves and their experiences, as expressed through letters, diaries, and other personal documents, were crucial in the initial evaluations made by the court as to whether a medical examination was necessary. These self-reports, or "self-characterizations," were often detailed and subsequently became the basis of both legal and medical determinations of responsibility and motive.

There are some practical limitations, however, to borrowing from Harris' approach to investigate Canadian murder cases. First, our criminal justice system neither relied on nor requested detailed self-reports by defendants. Although the occasional letter of confession or statement of remorse found its way into the case files, their language and handwriting (they were often written by someone other than the accused) make them appear to be extremely filtered. Second, these documents, along with the transcripts of spoken accounts, were not given much weight in trial proceedings. Defendants of questionable character were seen as particularly untrustworthy, and their "stories" were often rejected in favour of alternative narratives introduced by witnesses or, in some cases, abstracted from the evidence by judges themselves.[45]

Further, Canadian trial transcripts show that in some instances the overt psychiatrization of a defendant's behaviour encountered resistance. For instance, a defendant's family history was considered factual evidence only if the psychiatrist's report was substantiated by other family members. Otherwise, reports of past behaviour were viewed as dubious. For example, in the case of Mary Smith, charged with killing her husband in 1935, concerns were raised that she had shammed insanity in order to escape hanging. In the following excerpt from Smith's trial transcript, the judge reproved the psychiatric witness for failing to back up his assessment of Smith's family history by interviewing family members:

> Q: Isn't it the established rule of alienists when they are examining a person as to whether they are insane or not to find out something from their family history, not from themselves, but from their families?
> A: Not always. If I depended on that I would not be able to get anything. I have hundreds of patients where we cannot get the family history at all, but I have to come to a conclusion. I cannot get the family history because there is no family history to obtain ...
> Q: But if it can be done, isn't that the correct procedure?
> A: It is a good procedure if you can get it.
> Q: And it could have been done in this case if you had taken the time. It could have been done?
> A: If I had gone to Duck Lake ...
> Q: And got the family history.
> A: If the Agent of the Attorney-General had instructed me to do that and given me my expenses I would have done it.[46]

This process of measuring the validity of expert testimony through lay corroboration seems to have been fairly routine, and it was one way in which common-sense knowledge could limit the boundaries and content of expert knowledge.

However, the judicial appeal to common sense and lay validation seemed to frustrate psychiatric experts who also routinely attempted to position themselves and their profession above the rudimentary impressions of ordinary folks. As early laws on expert evidence suggest, and as some experts themselves claimed, the presumption behind legally engaging specialized knowledge and experience on the subject of mental capacity was that expert knowledge constituted a truth that somehow transcended common-sense knowledge. Therefore, psychiatrists who were interested in participating in criminal law cases often saw themselves as doing battle with the common sensibilities of ordinary men, as well as with the law, for the authority to decide the issue of criminal responsibility.[47]

Dr. Charles Kirk Clarke was particularly confident about his ability as an expert, and the ability of psychiatry generally, to see above and beyond the limited realms of law and common sense when it came to determining mental capacity and legal culpability. As he put it, "any one who takes the trouble to study practical psychology in a Canadian penitentiary, will be astounded at the want of regard for the subject of responsibility shown by our law, law founded on what is speciously termed good common sense, when uncommon sense was really required in its proper development."[48] However, because Clarke was also well aware of the law's appeal to common sense, he was careful not to distance himself or his profession too far from the hearts of "average men." In a strong urge for law and medicine to "bury the hatchet" and work toward a more productive relationship, Clarke defended his professional brethren as elite thinkers who nonetheless had their feet firmly planted in common sense: "Many people assert that asylum physicians are faddists and theorists, but it can safely be asserted that the man who does best work in a Hospital for the insane is not the so called heaven born genius or theorist, but a broad minded practical man of common sense so dearly beloved by the average Briton."[49] He further suggested, however, that if common sense were to be the "requirement in forming an opinion of responsibility in cases of mental defect," it was reasonable to assume – "in the interests of humanity" – that common sense "backed by long experience and special education is likely to give more satisfactory results."[50]

The importance of common sense to legal decisions was recognized, at least by this Canadian psychiatrist, to the extent that it influenced the way in which he expressed and exercised his position as an expert. The emergence of a distinct criminological discourse in Canadian law and psychiatry during the early twentieth century reflects a continuation of a trend that Joel Eigen observed in England during the eighteenth and nineteenth centuries. As Eigen points out in his analysis of British cases, the trial process introduced a "range of innovative ways of conceiving the mind that challenged, directly and indirectly, the fundamental notions of legal intentionality and self-control." Accordingly, Eigen suggests, "medical theorizing about madness shifted, too, often keeping legal considerations of accountability very much within its sights."[51]

Although medical men were supposedly called to offer their specialized knowledge on matters of science deemed beyond the understanding of "ordinary men," the final assessments of legal facts and the subsequent validity of a particular witness's testimony were established according to the common-sense experiences of jurymen and not according to claims of a particular witness's expertise. In several instances, theories regarding criminal behaviour that fell outside the common experience of fact-finders or the wording of the law were omitted from legal consideration or found inadmissible. But again, as Harrop's case demonstrates, the process of simultaneously selecting and omitting certain aspects of what experts were saying constituted a salient fusion of common-sense and expert knowledges.

The judicial appeal to common sense and popular opinion on the issue of responsibility was also the perceived stumbling block for those experts who protested the lack of weight given to their testimonies in court. The resolution of the conflict between what experts said and what courts were inclined to accept as being true would, according to Douglas Walton, depend on the prior acceptance of the source of expert knowledge by all parties involved in the decision-making process, as well as a general agreement regarding the weight of evidence accorded to the source.[52] This seems logical enough, given the doctrinal recognition of the value of expert opinion evidence, particularly in insanity cases. It may have been, as so many historians have reported, that professional bravado, not the nature of the law itself, accounted for the battles over the role and authority of expert evidence in criminal cases. But on a dialectical level, much more was going on than simple professional or political claims over the right to regulate the boundaries of insanity.

The general concern among legal officials was that relinquishing decision-making power over mind-state, and hence responsibility, to experts would challenge not only the law's commitment to common-sense knowledge but the essential role of the jury and the authority of British law in Canada. So, why allow expert testimony in the first place? What legal purpose did experts serve? And what difference did their testimonies make in cases where mind-state was raised as an issue? Looking to the more subtle nuances of trial deliberations in Harrop's case, and in cases to be examined in upcoming chapters, suggests that although underlying professional tensions provided the bedrock for rules outlining the use of expert testimony, the routine practice of engaging psychiatric knowledge (itself a construct of the social context in which it emerged and was practised) actually (re)affirmed, rather than challenged, common-sense knowledge.

Experts frequently used scientific language to articulate their opinions and observations, but the essence of what they were saying about the nature of women and men, their classifications of "character" or criminal "types," and the influence of social-economic circumstances on a given individual's ability to reason were hardly the result of cutting-edge psychiatric discovery. As the many letters written to the minister of justice to oppose Frances Harrop's death sentence suggest, it was also just common sense for those living in Canada at that time.

During a scientific age, when objectivity constituted legal truth and experts claimed to be objective, the legal appropriation of certain kinds of expertise outwardly cast the law as also objective, while not disturbing underlying Anglo-Christian sensibilities. Through the judicial process of decision making, certain kinds of arguments or forms of inferences were abstracted from expert evidence that further justified and supported a legal outcome as being based on factual evidence. It is important, therefore, to distinguish between the ways in which law kept experts at arm's length and the ways in which narratives of expertise were drawn in. Here, the (re)constitution of expert opinion evidence as legal fact gave the impression that common men sometimes accepted expert opinion, when in fact expert knowledge was, for the most part, (re)affirming the sensibilities of popular opinion.

The artificial divide between expert and common knowledge is implied in Tony Ward's suggestion that the "challenges of experts to legal and common-sense assumptions sometimes constitute an advance towards a more adequate understanding of the issues at stake in a trial" by bringing in sociological factors that successfully combatted "orthodox medical and legal individualism." He cites, for example, the introduction of "shell-shock," used by doctors to describe the mental effects of trench warfare during the First World War, as an example of how some psychiatric discourses were able to offer a more "coherent explanation of psychosomatic symptoms than competing medical and military discourses," resulting in the rescue of several alleged "cowards" and "deserters" from the firing squad. This argument is consistent with Alan Norrie's position that "some forms of sociology or social psychology offer a better – more complete, less distorted – understanding of human agency than the 'decontextualization of madness' effected both by law and by orthodox psychiatry."[53] Following this point, I would agree that the judicial appeal to common-sense knowledge, *through* expert knowledge, indeed served to contextualize and give meaning to the negotiations of criminal responsibility. But it did so without disrupting dominant distorted ideologies about class, gender, and race difference.

Conclusion

Michel Foucault once argued that crime came to be an important issue for psychiatrists because it provided a "modality of power to be secured and justified." He describes, for instance, the "fictitious" creation of "homicidal monomania" as an "insanity which is nothing but crime."[54] According to Foucault, legal authorities willingly adopted the medical diagnosis of monomania in order to explain and understand the nature of what otherwise appeared to be motiveless criminal behaviour. The assumption here is that power was achieved through the production and legitimation of expert knowledge, and that those without power – including women, the poor, and non-white individuals – were regulated through the production of knowledge, and by the knowledged. The concepts of medicalization and psychiatrization, which emerged in part from Foucault's interpretation of the history of French psychiatry, have been accepted by contemporary social historians, for the most part, as historical fact. However, there is evidence in capital case files to suggest an uncertainty about the power of psychiatric knowledge in Canadian criminal law.

In examining the records of capital murder cases, we can trace the flow of criminological thinking throughout and around the adjudication process, and in doing so we can better appreciate the rather symbiotic, perhaps even co-dependent, relationship between expert and common-sense knowledges on the subject of criminal responsibility. We can see, for instance, how common-sense knowledge about human nature was deeply entrenched in the doctrines and practices of law, psychiatry, and politics – even if on occasion the value of common sense was contested by certain legal experts, psychiatrists, and politicians. We can also see in some cases the way in which professional and expert knowledges, and the language of scientific notions of determinism and mental degeneracy, worked their way into common-sense discourses.

The relationship between law and psychiatry, experts and ordinary men, expertise and common sense has been the subject of scholarly investigation for centuries.[55] Contemporary medical-legal scholars, such as Joel Eigen, Janet Tighe, and Ruth Harris, describe instances of co-operation between psychiatric experts and legal authorities in England, the US, and France respectively, while others, such as Andrew Scull and Roger Smith, describe the relationship as an ongoing battle of ideas and egos founded in a long-standing contest of professional one-upmanship. Further still, Nigel Walker argues that medical men dreaded the thought of entering the legal process. He characterizes the expert witness as a reluctant participant rather than an opportunist, like a "wrestler who is compelled to box" in a "contest ... for which he is not trained."[56]

In an effort to locate the Canadian expert witness within these larger scholarly and historical debates, I think the most that can be said is that it depended on the particular case at hand. As Frances Harrop's trial and conviction illustrate, Canadian murder trials individually provide evidence that both supports and contests many of the general claims historians have made about the role of the expert and the nature of medical-legal discourse. But collectively they show how social explanations intermingled with scientific reasoning to produce complex courtroom narratives about responsibility, which then influenced the legal process in many different and contradictory ways. Although the official laws of insanity and definitions of criminal responsibility were not seriously challenged by expert theories on the cause and nature of mental deficiency, the *interpretation* of insanity law and the variable *meanings* of responsibility in Canada were quite permeable and open to a range of factors not always specified by law.

Case file evidence regarding the questionable authority of the psychiatric expert and the persistent judicial appeal to common sense does not dispute the basic concept of medicalization: rather, it points to the importance of context in evaluating the form, substance, and weight of expertise, and the specific social-institutional dynamics that produced and ordered differing versions of responsibility knowledge. Psychiatric theory clearly worked its way into and was influenced by the legal process, but this did not necessarily occur through the straightforward doctrinal approach of engaging expert opinion evidence to inform judges and juries on issues deemed beyond the common knowledge of ordinary men. The legal qualification of certain medical witnesses as experts and the selective taking up of expert opinion evidence were determined within the specific common-sense and circumstantial frameworks of each trial, not on the presumption that experts possessed a privileged knowledge status. Although professional status was often important in getting a doctor's opinion legally qualified as expert opinion in court, it did not guarantee that his testimony would be considered valuable or even relevant to decisions about responsibility.

As the next three chapters unfold, we shall see that much of what might be considered psychiatric evidence actually came through the testimonies of non-expert witnesses: neighbours who testified about spells and odd behaviour, police officers who described psychotic episodes, lawyers who introduced medical concepts, and relatives who testified about other relatives locked away in mental institutions. It appears, therefore, that *what* was said, and the way in which it was articulated, were usually far more important than *who* said it.

4

Negotiating Responsibility in Law's "Marketplace": Beyond the Insanity Defence

As we have seen, the trial and post-trial stages of the criminal justice process brought together various forms of responsibility knowledge that differed in both content and meaning.[1] Murder trials, in particular, were the sites where important discussions and decisions around social pathology took place and where the tensions and concerns of a historical moment were unfurled and put on display. The coming together of competing knowledge forms sometimes caused friction between legal actors who were each in their own way, and for their own reasons, trying to make sense of a particular case. However, as much as murder trials were about making sense, and spectacle, of a terrible crime, they were also about finding appropriate resolutions within the moral boundaries of Canadian law and society.

In the legal arena, as well as the social, decisions about individual responsibility were largely based on assessments of the accused person's state of mind – before, during, and after the crime. I am not at all suggesting that this was a bad thing. Arguably, we ought to be concerned about an individual's ability to appreciate the nature of his or her actions at the time a crime was committed. My critique is not, therefore, directed toward the ideals of the law: rather, it is directed toward the nature of law and legal processes. In order to understand some of the ways in which responsibility was negotiated through narratives of mind-state, it is useful here, I think, to invoke Michael MacDonald's description of the various discursive "marketplaces" in which "insanity" has historically been bartered.[2] MacDonald suggests that, within these political and ideological spaces, "compromises" were struck between "expert knowledge" and "lay knowledge."

In the previous chapter, for instance, we saw the ways in which psychiatric experts often battled with legal decision makers and each other on the boundaries of mental disorder and (ir)responsibility. We saw the ways in which legal decision makers engaged with various theories on motive and mind-state as they were represented in the opinion evidence of expert witnesses, in the testimonies of lay witnesses, and in various forms of public response. We also saw the ways in which some members of the public reacted to legal decisions and reported psychiatric diagnoses as they, too, struggled to make sense of horrific events that took place in their communities. We saw, in these sites of negotiation, how the continuous coming together of different knowledge forms shaped the legal decision-making process.

Legal-history literature on insanity law tends to draw primarily from legal doctrine and reported cases in which insanity was the formal defence. This approach is very useful for documenting official decisions and applications of the law, but it misses some of the more subtle processes that shaped the production of knowledge on insanity (broadly defined) and informed the larger socio-political significance of legal decisions about criminal responsibility during this period. One goal of this chapter is thus to show that though the insanity defence was perhaps the most obvious legal marketplace in which discursive exchanges over the issues of mind-state and responsibility took place, it certainly was not the only one. I suggest we might learn something important about the cultural meaning of "insanity" by paying attention to other judicial dealings with the subject of mental capacity, including cases in which insanity was *not* the official defence.

Below, I touch on the various points at which the question of mind-state could be raised and examine the laws of insanity themselves. I then excavate the contentious professional battles over "insanity" and insanity law. I look at the post-trial commutation stage and the defence of provocation, two other procedural/doctrinal marketplaces within which standards of criminal responsibility were routinely contested, negotiated, and classified through assessments of the accused's mental capacity.[3]

I then consider the power of narrative in legal decision making, with the understanding that certain criminological narratives provided important discursive marketplaces within law. Here, I consider the effects of appropriating scientific/expert knowledge and the implications of certain socio-political events on interpretations of criminality. In particular, I look at how the conditions of war and poverty were seen to produce mental deficiency in certain vulnerable individuals, and how the perceived mental effects of war and poverty worked their way into evaluations of criminal responsibility.

We have already seen that the *idea* of degeneracy provided a conceptual framework for articulations of criminal responsibility and mind-state, and that it fluctuated to reflect the concerns of the day. Degeneracy was expressed as the affliction of certain human types and an alarming condition of society as a whole. The conditions leading to degeneracy, such as growing up in poverty, could be identified as a reason to grant mercy. Yet, the same conditions could be identified as reasons for harsh punishment. This suggests that decisions regarding the appropriate role of law during times of national instability were not a matter of standard policy: rather, they were formed on a case-by-case basis and clearly reflected the current political climate.

I end this chapter by analyzing the narrative qualities of responsibility knowledge through an examination of the ways in which popular, legal, and medical assessments of mental capacity relied upon representations of character and citizenship. In cases where character, sometimes described as "disposition," was identified as an important factor, both women and men were measured according to masculine British sensibilities about what it meant to be of respectable class, citizenship, and moral character. During this period, notions of British citizenship and the biological politics of national identity were very much tied up in perceptions of character and subsequently informed the production and ordering of responsibility knowledge.

Collectively, the case studies selected for this chapter highlight some of the socio-political and legal dynamics that brought together various knowledges about criminality and human nature in order to resolve the legal question of guilt, establish moral responsibility, and determine an appropriate sentence. Various social and professional institutions – including religion, academia, medicine, law, and the family – produced politically informed theories about human nature and social idealism that both supported and challenged one another. Mothers who wrote letters to the minister of justice, begging him to spare the life of another mother sentenced to death, interpreted the meaning of the trial's outcome differently from politicians who expressed discomfort with the idea of executing a woman, or psychiatrists who testified that the defendant was not of sound mind, and hence not criminally responsible. It is necessary, therefore, to consider the many narratives of criminality and mind-state that formed representations of responsibility in each case and to recognize how specific historical contexts and/or professional interests shaped not only the rules of judicial negotiation but in fact the very marketplaces in which negotiations took place.

Sites of Negotiation: To Insanity and Beyond

According to early legal texts, a plea of insanity could be formally raised at three points during the judicial process. If we also include the point at which the police laid the charge, there were theoretically four stages where the question of insanity could be introduced. Evidence brought in at the point of arrest is important because case documentation reveals that the impressions of the arresting and investigating officers were usually taken into account during pre-trial, trial, and post-trial decisions about the mental capacity of an accused at the time the crime took place. During the pre-trial stage, the legal question was whether an accused was mentally fit to stand trial. If the accused was found fit, the question moved to whether she or he was insane at the time of the crime to a degree and nature that would establish a lack of guilty intent, or *mens rea*. If an accused was found guilty and legally responsible at trial, the appeal court could still overrule a guilty verdict and substitute a verdict of "not guilty because insane," or the more common wording, "not guilty by reason of insanity" (ngri).[4]

Medical-legal literature published before 1950 indicates that insanity was not often raised in criminal cases. If insanity was raised as a legal defence, it was usually reserved for murder cases, where a guilty verdict meant a mandatory death sentence.[5] Unfortunately, *Criminal Statistics* does not show how often insanity was raised in murder cases between 1920 and 1950; nor does the official record show how often a verdict of ngri was rendered at trial. Court statistics gathered on murder charges during this period included a category titled "detained for lunacy" that probably included individuals found unfit to stand trial as well as those found ngri at trial. Although there were no distinct statistical categories for pre- and post-trial detainment for lunacy, the record does indicate that of the 1,443 individuals charged with murder between 1920 and 1950, 180 (12 percent) were "detained for lunacy."

The commutation stage was the final point in the criminal justice process at which mind-state was again considered. If a guilty verdict was not appealed, or if it was upheld on appeal, the focus during post-trial deliberations moved from the question of guilt (guilt being proved at trial) to whether sufficient evidence of insanity or mental deficiency had been raised before, during, or after the trial to warrant commuting the mandatory death sentence to life in prison. Later on, I show how decisions about criminal responsibility during the post-conviction stage often (re)introduced expert opinion evidence along with lay opinion on the mind-state of condemned individuals. It seems that during the commutation stage, where legal officials were not bound by the rules of evidence on expert witness testimony, they may have given more weight to the opinions of certain psychiatric experts.[6] Again, a distinction must remain clear between the way in which legal officials dealt with psychiatric experts and the way in which various forms of expert knowledge were taken up.

In capital murder cases, the majority of discussions regarding the defendant's mind-state were in fact not in the context of a formal insanity defence. This makes perfect sense, given that those cases in which an insanity defence may have been used successfully would not be included in this collection. Every case in *Persons Sentenced to Death in Canada* represents someone who was found both guilty and sane, and who was sentenced to death. Therefore, it is impossible to approach anything like a comprehensive study of the insanity defence in Canada using only these case files. However, what we can learn from these files is how the legal question of mental capacity was routinely dealt with in ways other than through the laws of insanity.[7] Where I do examine how the issue of mind-state was raised and negotiated through the laws of insanity, I am particularly interested in the effect of tensions between law and psychiatry regarding how that law ought to be interpreted and applied. And given that the defence of insanity and other legal defences of mind-state were usually reserved for cases of murder, it may first be helpful to understand more generally how the law was structured to accommodate defences to murder.

A "murder," according to the *Criminal Code* of the day, occurred only if the person who caused the death of another person(s) intended to do so.[8] Each legal defence designed to negate or diminish criminal responsibility therefore spoke directly to the issue of intent and the question of *mens rea,* or a guilty mind. The exception is self-defence, which was/is understood to be an intentional but justified act. Long before the period covered by this book, in the English case of *R. v. Tolson* (1889), Judge J. Stephen raised the following concerns with respect to the differing legal meanings of *mens rea* in criminal law: "'Mens rea' means in the case of murder, malice aforethought; in the case of theft, an intention to steal; in the case of rape, an intention to have forcible connection with a woman without her consent; and in the case of receiving stolen goods, knowledge that the goods were stolen. In some cases it denotes mere inattention. For instance, in the case of manslaughter by negligence it may mean forgetting to notice a signal." Judge Stephen argued in his decision that it was "confusing" and "misleading" to classify so many states of mind under one name, cautioning that to an "unlegal mind it suggests that by the law of England no act is a crime which is done from laudable motives, in other words, that immorality is essential to crime."[9]

The logic here is rather circular, but essentially sets out that an individual could not form rational intent without *mens rea,* where *mens rea* was evidenced by rational intent, foresight, or knowledge.[10] Therefore, in order to be held criminally responsible for murder, or to have their actions legally "justified," defendants were required by law to be in a rational mental state at the time of the crime. This seems fair enough, but as Jonathan Glover has observed, "how far from the truth is any view that merely identifies responsibility with some mental state from whose absence one may suffer." According to Glover, disagreement among decision makers regarding the meaning of criminal responsibility and the determination of an individual's mind-state reflected conflicting moral attitudes and responses toward the circumstances of a particular criminal act or actor, as well as "different views about how men should be treated in various situations." He suggests that disagreement, particularly between law and psychiatry on the basic elements of legal responsibility, is not simply about differing understandings of the "concept" of responsibility but also reflects competing ideas about punishment. As Glover put it, "our attitudes towards people and what they do are influenced by our knowledge of them and their situation. But we are not forced by any facts, even the truth of determinism, to modify our attitudes. It is up to us to choose which considerations to accept as excuses or mitigation."[11] In other words, the practice of law, along with the negotiation of responsibility in criminal cases, was very much a human process, a process propelled by the routine, creative exercise of moral judgment and situational (re)evaluation. During the inter-war and post-war period in Canada, there was a decided lack of consensus on how and by whom criminal responsibility ought to be established.

Negotiating Power: Law, Psychiatry, and the Defence of Insanity

Since 1843, the legal test for insanity in Canada has been defined by the M'Naghten rules, set out following the British case of *R. v. M'Naghten* and adopted in section 19 of the *Criminal Code of Canada*.[12] According to the rules, as laid out in the *Criminal Code*,

> 19. No person shall be convicted of an offence by reason of an act done or omitted by him when labouring under natural imbecility, or disease of the mind, to such an extent as to render him incapable of appreciating the nature and quality of the act or omission, and of knowing that such an act or omission was wrong.
> (2) A person labouring under specific delusions, but in other respects sane, shall not be acquitted on the grounds of insanity, under the provisions hereinafter contained, unless the delusions caused him to believe in the existence of some state of things which, if it existed, would justify or excuse his act or omission.
> (3) Every one shall be presumed to be sane at the time of doing or omitting to do any act until the contrary is proved.

From the moment of their introduction, the rules have been the subject of much criticism, primarily regarding the vagueness of terms such as "wrong," "nature and quality," "appreciation," and "knowing." During the early twentieth century, medical experts strongly voiced their frustrations over the narrow legal definition of insanity as a disorder of reason.[13] Certain psychiatrists in Canada and the United States wanted the definition revised to reflect what they considered to be a more progressive medical model. But more importantly, they wanted medical experts, not legal officials, to author any revisions to the law.[14] Some doctors who favoured reform proposed even more drastic legal action: namely, the total abolition of insanity as a legal defence in criminal cases.

Medical experts who pushed for new insanity laws argued that a more precise medical definition would go a long way to eliminate the ambiguity of insanity law. They also hoped that a medical definition would prevent the embarrassment many medical witnesses reported experiencing in court at the hands of lawyers who manipulated their testimonies to fit the outdated and, in the doctors' view, unsophisticated understanding of the scope and nature of insanity. The more skeptical medical men, however, did not see how any sanctioned definition of insanity, no matter who devised it, would eliminate the inevitable courtroom battle into which psychiatric experts were repeatedly led. Some proposed that the issues of insanity or mental deficiency ought *not* to be introduced at trial and ought *not* to be tied to the legal question of guilt. Rather, evidence with respect to a defendant's state of mind, some argued, should be reserved for discussion after the trial and only in relation to sentencing.[15]

This particular call for legal reform, where the jury would decide only on the question of guilt and have nothing to do with determining a defendant's state of mind, popped up from time to time during the first half of the twentieth century and was the subject of some debate during the 1953 *Royal Commission on the Laws of Insanity as a Defence in Criminal Cases*. Each time, however, it was rejected by legal experts as an option. Perhaps this request for a change in procedure was rejected because such an initiative would not only have undermined the fundamental role of the jury but would also have required substantive revisions to the law. As it stood, determining legal "guilt" required establishing both *actus reus* (did the individual commit the act?) and *mens rea* (did the individual mean to commit the act?). Evidence of insanity went directly toward establishing *mens rea* and therefore could not be easily separated from the question of guilt.

The ongoing strain between legal and medical experts on the subject of insanity definitely bent the processes through which mind-state was questioned and responsibility was decided in Canadian criminal cases. The role of the jury, and the (in)ability of jurymen to decide on matters related to mind-state using their "common sense," concerned both legal officials and psychiatrists. The function of the jury was to decide on facts brought out in evidence, where expert opinion was considered evidence toward fact.[16] Even though jurymen during this period were predominantly of British heritage and selected from the upper, middle, and working classes, psychiatrists, lawyers, and even laymen were still concerned that the typical jury was not intelligent enough to make *right* decisions. In addressing the "many complaints raised against the jury system," legal expert H.B. Spaulding argued that "the faults of the jury system are not so much inherent in the system itself as in the law with regard to jurors, which excludes from liability to service on juries the more intelligent and better trained members of the community."[17] Although the question of *who* was qualified to make decisions about the fact of a defendant's mental capacity was always an issue, it became more or less urgent according to the specifics of a case, the nature of the legal defence, and/or the stage of the trial process at which the subject of mind-state was raised.

During this time, the law specified three mental conditions as constituting insanity: a "disease of the mind," "imbecility," and "delusion." Evidence constituting a clear, observable case of mental "disease" or "idiocy" seemed to be readily agreed upon by medical and legal authorities. However, the qualities and parameters of categories such as "imbecility" and "delusion" were points of strong contention. Imbecility was particularly ambiguous, as both a medical diagnosis and a legal classification. According to Spaulding, imbecility was intended to describe individuals who were deemed "defective" rather than diseased. He further pointed out that in law, the term "defective" was typically applied to those born without proper reasoning faculties and who would never recover, whereas those suffering under a "disease" of the mind might recover their reason at some point in the future.[18] This differs, however, from the common law interpretation of insanity, which did not recognize those "diseases of the mind" that were considered temporary.

In an article entitled "Canadian Criminal Law in Regard to Insanity," Dr. Charles Kirk Clarke pointed to some of the other challenges involved in bartering with the law for an agreeable definition of imbecility: "No one doubts the irresponsibility of idiots, but when it comes to the question of imbecility we are on a battleground where law and medicine are widely at variance, simply because Canadian law is hampered by the stern sense of what is called, in our determination to be loyal to imperial interests in everything, British justice ... In the absence of a standard man with whom to make comparisons, abstract definitions prove difficult to manage." Clarke, who seemed to imply that psychiatry managed to function independently of imperial interest, called for the law to fix the standard of criminal responsibility. However, he did not trust politically motivated Canadian lawmakers, or ignorant jurymen, with the task.

Clarke agreed with the general legal argument that it was not necessarily the jury system but the "common sense" of common jurymen that obstructed justice in cases involving the insane. He seemed frustrated about the persistent old-fashioned ideas of what he termed the "uneducated classes," who failed to recognize that "Jack is not as good as his Master in forming an estimate of a person's mental condition or measuring his responsibility." Clarke also lamented the reluctance of criminal law agents to acknowledge the skill required to determine criminal and moral responsibility. He argued that it was an assignment far "too complex" for "twelve excellent jurymen who are chosen, not so much for their intelligence and ability to grapple psychological problems, as for their inherited Anglo-Saxon quality called common sense." Clarke explained to the legal community that "if it is a difficult thing for physicians who are dealing every day with imbeciles, to form a just estimate of their responsibility," then "how absurd it is to suppose that a judge, lawyer and jury can settle the question in a few hours."[19]

In his other writings and public addresses during the early twentieth century, Clarke repeatedly ranked the insights of the psychiatric "expert" and the "expertise" of psychiatry well above the common sense of "ordinary men." Yet, as I argued in the last chapter, documentary sources in capital case files suggest a dialectical and ideological relationship between "expert" and "common sense" knowledges whereby the routine legal engagement with psychiatric knowledge actually helped structure and reinforce, rather than challenge, the judicial appeal to common sense. The imbedded paradox in medical-legal discourse about the role of expert knowledge and the strong judicial appeal to common-sense knowledge can be observed in different forms, as we shall see later on. The point I am making here is that although psychiatrists frequently bewailed that the insanity defence was both ambiguous and inappropriate, it was precisely the definitional ambiguity of the rules that allowed decision makers considerable breadth when it came to interpreting and applying the law. In other words, it was the ambiguity of the insanity defence that enabled experts to testify in court in the first place.

In capital cases, lawyers' decisions to use the insanity defence appear unpredictable but certainly not haphazard. Of the sixty-six cases analyzed in this study, nineteen (29 percent) included a formal plea of insanity.[20] Without knowing how many individuals charged with murder were able to successfully plead insanity – success meaning that they were found not guilty because insane – or what factors constituted a successful defendant and defence, I am unable to draw conclusions regarding the general nature and practise of the insanity defence. However, within this small sample of unsuccessful insanity trials, some interesting observations can be made. In turn, these observations provide some insight into the legal interpretation of insanity law and the broader cultural meaning of responsibility knowledge within the social, moral, and political climate of the day.

For example, insanity was most often the official defence in those capital cases where the defendant's motive for a murder was unclear or deemed questionable. When a motive appeared obvious to the court – such as lust, heated emotion, or want of money – efforts seemed to go toward establishing evidence to mitigate responsibility through alternative legal defences such as provocation. However, this did not always lead to a commuted sentence or reduced charge. As we will see in Chapter 6, women who killed their husbands for money or to take up with another man were often treated more harshly than were women who appeared to kill in the heat of a domestic quarrel. The method used by a defendant to kill his/her victim(s) was also important. On the one hand, if the method appeared excessive or particularly violent, it was often interpreted as a loss of reason or control and therefore as evidence of mental abnormality. On the other hand, less physically violent methods, such as poisoning, were typically seen as methodical or cowardly. Case file evidence suggests, then, that there were many influences on legal application of insanity law, including shifting theories about criminality and moral interpretations of the offender's behaviour and circumstances. If indeed it can be established that assessments of motivation, and therefore responsibility, seemed to follow very closely with the moral sensibilities of law and psychiatry as well as with the common sensibilities of the public, we ought to be paying attention to how those sensibilities were constituted.

Beyond the Insanity Defence

It certainly makes sense for historians who are interested in the nature of insanity discourse to look to insanity defence cases in order to document the legal constructions of mental deficiency and criminal responsibility. However, assessments of mental capacity were also central in cases where insanity was not the official defence. Canadian judges did not require counsel to plead "insanity" in order for defence to argue that mental deficiency was the cause of a defendant's behaviour. In fact, the majority of courtroom discussions regarding mind-state took place outside the insanity defence, enabling judges, lawyers, and witnesses to debate and evaluate mental deficiency without having to adhere to the narrow language restrictions of insanity law.[21] Outside of the insanity defence, through the adjudication of other legal defences, and during the post-conviction stage, limitations on language were relaxed to some degree. Within this more open marketplace, alternative representations of mental deficiency that did not satisfy a proper insanity defence were up for negotiation. In this legal marketplace, as in other legal marketplaces, there formed a knowledge about the responsible person, which, despite an official verdict of guilty in each case, (re)established that certain types of people were inherently less or more responsible than others.

For example, in 1920, the remissions report on the trial of Marie Anne Houde (Gagnon) opened colourfully as follows:

> The Accused is a French-Canadian, thirty years of age, and was charged with the murder of her step-daughter, Aurore Gagnon, ten years old. The very nature of the crime – Aurore was ill-treated, beaten and tortured by her step-mother, from August 1919 until 10th February 1920, when she died as

> a result of the wounds inflicted upon her – aroused great indignation, and public feeling, especially in Quebec, ran very high ... Defence [counsel] ... admitted that Aurore died as a result of the wounds inflicted upon her by the accused ... and repeatedly qualified the behaviour of the prisoner as atrocious and monstrous, and entered a plea of insanity.[22]

Transcripts from Houde's trial indicate that, of the three expert witnesses who testified for the defence, only one supported the official defence of insanity. Meanwhile, seven experts (including one of the original defence witnesses) testified for the Crown, each of whom claimed that Houde was sane during the months in which she tortured her stepdaughter. In the eyes of medical and legal authorities, Houde was officially sane and guilty of murder. However, on the basis of her gender and supporting theories about the negative mental effects of consecutive pregnancies, there were several ongoing debates, both in and out of the courtroom, regarding her actual level of criminal responsibility.

The official verdicts of "guilty" and "sane" brought by legal authorities and several medical experts in Houde's case did not displace the strong opinion from some members of the public, given the decided "horrific" nature of her crime, that she "must have suffered some form of insanity." According to one newspaper comment, Houde was an "abhorrent and loathsome freak."[23] Her actions, this citizen reported, were either those of "a depraved female beast in human form, or a human imbecile."[24] The idea that she acted intentionally or with a "normal mind" was, by this and other accounts, beyond comprehension.[25] In the end, it appears that government officials may have agreed with this assessment of the situation because her death sentence was commuted to life in prison. The mitigating factors of gender and pregnancy (she was reportedly pregnant at the time of the trial) were not relevant to the question of guilt at trial but were seriously considered during the post-trial commutation stage and probably influenced the final decision to grant mercy.

In several ways, Houde's case typified the manner in which responsibility was (re)negotiated at different stages of the judicial process and simultaneously articulated through a number of legal and non-legal classifications of mind-state. The insanity defence was certainly one legal site where issues around a defendant's state of mind were raised and adjudicated. However, other conditions of mind, such as that caused by the conditions of pregnancy, also provided a discursive space in which standards of criminal responsibility and mental capacity were reasoned and ordered.

Material brought to the attention of the minister of justice during the commutation stage of Houde's trial came from many sources and included a wide range of opinions. Petitions and letters from the public, the defendant, and the defendant's relatives were sent to the minister alongside psychiatric evaluations, police reports, newspaper articles, and unofficial accounts written by the trial judge and lawyers. Collectively, these documents told several stories that simultaneously cast Houde as a degenerate female monster and confused mother.[26] The Canadian Prisoners' Welfare Association, for instance, submitted to the minister that "any woman who has gone through the process of maternity under such circumstances has some special claim to leniency, whatever her crime."[27]

No one writing to the minister in support of clemency for Houde suggested that the guilty verdict was unwarranted, or that she should not be duly punished, only that she should not be hanged. And certainly not everyone agreed with the portrayal of Houde as a mother in need of sympathy. One newspaper editorial reported, "The argument of the Prisoners' Welfare Association that 'there is no thought of allowing the woman to go unpunished' is illogical, inconsistent and ridiculous because she is either deserving of the full penalty of our law or no punishment at all, and the evidence supported by competent scientists states she was in full possession of her normal senses when she committed the hideous and infernal brutalities she did."[28]

In another letter, Thomas Vieu, a member of the House of Commons, argued, "it is true that four Crown expert witnesses declared that in their opinion she was compos mentis ... It is very hard to believe that a woman compos mentis would commit such abominable acts." Vieu further reminded the minister that the defendant "was pregnant a number of times; as a matter of fact, she was almost constantly in a state of pregnancy, and that alone is sufficient to unsettle the nervous condition of a woman."[29] Although the issue of insanity was legally rejected at trial and a guilty verdict delivered, the question of Houde's mind-state and the degree of moral responsibility to which she should be held remained points of negotiation through to the post-conviction stage. It was often within these more flexible judicial spaces, outside the courtroom and beyond the insanity defence, that conflicting narratives about responsibility and mind-state were synthesized.

The ways in which standards of mind-state and degrees of responsibility were negotiated in non-insanity cases show the cultural and contextual specificity of legal responses particularly well. In the absence of a formal insanity plea, lawyers frequently introduced theories about mental deficiency into legal arguments to establish *diminished* responsibility. Here, various psychiatric explanations, which would have been formally excluded from the definitional language of the M'Naghten rules, were solicited from medical and lay witnesses before the court and further reinforced through judges' interpretations of the laws of evidence and expert testimony. Diagnoses such as moral imbecility, partial insanity, temporary insanity, and uncontrollable impulses were regularly incorporated into trial proceedings despite the fact that they were not formally recognized defences in Canadian law, and diminished responsibility was not a legally recognized concept.[30]

Despite legal standards for admitting evidence, the trial process provided an open forum for evaluations of human nature and responsibility. The presumption that responsibility could be, and was, diminished by certain states of mind was sanctioned through the adjudication of evidence regarding the specific effects of passion, provocation, fear, and other "natural" reasoning deficiencies. Although evidence to establish these conditions often reflected similar forms of language seen in medical-legal discussions about insanity proper, terms such as "delusional," "insane jealousy," "blind madness," "moral imbecility," "loss of control," "mental spells," and "stupor" typically did not constitute the grounds for a legal defence of insanity. Therefore, a defendant's criminal responsibility could be mitigated due to low intelligence, congenital imbecility, degeneracy, irrational past behaviour, or any number of medically/socially recognized signs of mental defectiveness, without the legal plea of insanity ever being raised.

Lawyers often called psychiatrists to testify as expert witnesses in non-insanity cases in order to help draw the boundary between legal insanity and other forms of mental deficiency. The Crown would typically use experts to discount theories of mental deficiency, whereas the defence would direct expert opinion evidence to show that although a defendant may have known her actions were wrong in the legal sense, enough evidence nevertheless existed to suggest that she was not in complete charge of her mental faculties. Even if evidence did not satisfy the laws of insanity and render a verdict of not guilty at trial, it sometimes prompted a recommendation to mercy from the judge and jury and kept the subject open for (re)negotiation during the post-conviction stage.

The way in which variable standards of criminal responsibility were applied in each case was not obvious in official decisions about *guilt.* Instead, responsibility knowledge was articulated through, and represented in, judicial recommendations to mercy, the partiality of public petitions and letters, newspaper reports, unofficial letters between court officials, medical reports, and post-trial conversations about the appropriateness of the death sentence. Popular, legal, and medical evaluations of criminal responsibility and mind-state were never totally unified in the courtroom, where decisions about guilt depended upon the judicial selection of particular narratives as being more plausible than others and the knowledge forms that were applied to make sense of the circumstances at hand. Therefore, the conceptual boundaries between full responsibility, diminished responsibility, and not criminally responsible were both temporary and artificial in that they were drawn, erased, and redrawn according to the symbolic value placed on the characteristics of each case and at different stages of the trial process.

Medical men, legal officials, and lay witnesses offered opinions about numerous states of mind – such as passion and provocation – that were also evidenced by a loss of control but nevertheless fell shy of fully negating responsibility. Consider, for instance, the case of William Monchuk (1938), charged with murdering his three neighbours with an axe. Separate trials were held for each of the three victims: Mr. Seabright (who had been in constant dispute with the defendant over property boundaries), Mrs. Seabright, and their daughter. The defence in each case was provocation. At the trial for the murder of Mrs. Seabright, the judge did not permit defence counsel to introduce evidence regarding the specific mental effects of provocation on Monchuk's ability to form intent, because it was technically Mr. Seabright, not his wife, who allegedly provoked the defendant. The judge claimed "that arguing the defendant was in a state of provocation in Mrs. Seabright's case would legally constitute a defence of insanity."[31]

However, the judge did permit defence counsel, in the absence of the jury, to submit "for the purpose of the record" that all three murders were committed while the defendant was in a state of provocation. He further suggested, perhaps in anticipation of an appeal, that it should be for the jury to decide "whether an ordinary, reasonable man would, in their opinion, regain his power of self-control" after killing his antagonist, Mr. Seabright, in order to form the intent to kill the wife and daughter. The trial judge agreed that perhaps Monchuk was not in a reasoning state of mind when he "lost total control" and began wielding his axe but stuck by his direction to the jury that the proposed defences of provocation in the cases of Mrs. Seabright and the daughter were not legally sound. The strict application of the law of provocation seen in this case was not typical of other cases where provocation was entered as a defence. For instance, in cases of domestic murder, the application of provocation law was quite liberal: evidence of generally unhealthy domestic situations was seen as logically provoking.

In Monchuk's case, the question of mind-state as related to provocation was never seriously considered at the trial level, and he was found guilty on all three charges of murder. However, the point made by defence counsel "for the record" regarding the nature of provocation later became the primary line of inquiry and the driving issue of the appeal process. After the trial, the attorney general independently requested that the defendant's "mental background" be assessed. Monchuk's mental capacity was subsequently diagnosed as generally "unbalanced," and the doctors' reports included terms such as "loss of control," "bad temperament," and "uncontrolled passions." None of the medical men who examined Monchuk would verify that he was legally insane, but all acknowledged the mental effects of being provoked as relevant in their assessments of criminal responsibility.

If Monchuk's trial had taken place after 1962, when degrees of murder were introduced in Canada, his charge probably would have been classified as non-capital murder, which did not carry a mandatory death sentence. Also, as the appeal decision in this case indicates, a better argument regarding provocation and a reduced charge to manslaughter would have been made. Because there was no doubt as to whether Monchuk killed his three neighbours, and insanity was not considered a viable defence, the jury's decision on all three charges was guilty.

However, on a series of appeals, the Supreme Court reversed the three murder convictions and ordered Monchuk retried on three charges of manslaughter. His new defence counsel for the appeal process, J.C. McRuer, a prominent Toronto lawyer who later authored an influential report on mental disorder and the criminal trial process, argued that the defendant did indeed suffer a significant mental breakdown as a result of being provoked by Mr. Seabright to the extent that all three murders were caused by the same mental break.[32] After the court decided to reduce the three murder charges to manslaughter, McRuer made the following statement: "This man Manchuk [sic] has undergone the agony of three murder trials ... He has been months in the death cell. All arise from the same outburst of mind. We can't allow the process of criminal law to be a tortuous process that outrages our sense of humanity."[33]

Although McRuer presented Monchuk as an unfortunate victim of external forces and the judicial system, other accounts of the defendant's behaviour linked evidence of situational provocation to his natural tendency as a "high strung character" to be easily provoked. For example, in a letter to the chief remissions officer, Monchuk's original defence lawyer, who also worked with McRuer on the appeal, explained his client's "illogical" and "unbalanced" state of mind: "My experience with Monchuk has been that he is completely irresponsible in any discussion of this case ... I do feel that he is completely irrational on this topic and I am so impressed with that view that I would be concerned about accepting instructions from him without some such examination by a qualified psychiatrist ... Monchuk is, of course normally a very high strung character and the long course of the dispute over the line fence can readily be understood to have struck a highly responsive chord in his sentimental make-up."[34] In much the same way that narratives of insanity reflected an Anglo-Christian notion of mental disorder, other mind-states, such as provocation, which were intended to diminish individual responsibility, were also strongly influenced by culture and class biases. In the cases of Elizabeth Tilford and William Monchuk, we can also see that, when the formal structure of insanity law was not in place, a wider range of interpretations was possible, and fewer restrictions were laid on the kind of evidence that could be introduced.

As we saw in the case of Elizabeth Tilford, a guilty verdict in criminal law did not necessarily precipitate corresponding or unified representations of criminal responsibility. Rather, the negotiations continued throughout the commutation process and, in Tilford's case, ended with a decision in favour of clemency. Also, in some cases where provocation was introduced as a defence in order to reduce a charge from murder to manslaughter, legal interpretations of the emotional and cognitive nature of being "provoked," and the expected (in)ability of a particular defendant to control his/her passions in provocative situations, were often grounded in essentialist ideas about class, race, and gender difference. Despite the fact that Canadian law did not recognize defences of "diminished responsibility" or "temporary insanity," evidence introduced to establish provocation and loss of control nevertheless mimicked the language of an insanity defence and, hence, seemed to function in some cases as a defence of temporary insanity.

The link between human nature and human behaviour was constantly (re)negotiated and (re)inforced by legal officials who routinely articulated their arguments, opinions, and judgments regarding the state of a defendant's mind using popular versions of scientific/psychiatric knowledge. Below, I take this one step further and consider how the specific conditions of war and poverty shaped the content of criminological knowledge and influenced socio-legal interpretations of responsibility. In the cases that follow, we continue to see the legal promotion of psychiatric knowledge throughout capital case deliberations, further supporting my argument that although judges often formally rejected the opinions of particular psychiatrists, they often reaffirmed the *premise* of psychiatric expertise on human nature in their interpretations of the law. One way of observing the effect of psychiatric knowledge on processes of legal decision making and, indeed, on the formation of common-sense knowledge is to map out the content, meaning, and consequences of particular narratives. I take this direction in the remainder of the chapter.

"Unhealthy" Environments: War and Poverty

The numerous letters, petitions, official reports, and newspaper commentaries found in most case files offer a unique and valuable insight into common-sense thinking on matters of criminality, criminal responsibility, capital punishment, and the social role of law. These historical documents also illustrate the influence of broader social/political concerns on each author's interpretation of the case at hand. For instance, those writing with respect to cases during the 1930s and early 1940s frequently referred to the effects that economic depression and hardship could have on mental stability and, therefore, on the level of criminal responsibility that should be assigned to the accused. Information regarding the impoverished living conditions of an accused was typically not offered to the court as an independent factor to be considered in decisions about guilt. Rather, circumstantial information was indirectly received through the opinion evidence of medical witnesses and the testimonies of lay witnesses in assessments of mind-state, motive, and intent. Also, letters received by the minister of justice from the public often cited material circumstances as important to understanding the true nature of the crime and, hence, what the appropriate response should be.

For example, when Dina Dranchuk was convicted for the murder of her husband in 1934, members of "The Women's Auxiliary to the Unemployed Men's Association" wrote to the minister in protest of the scheduled execution of the Edmonton woman. The secretary of the Calgary branch explained, "we do not hold with murder by any means, but as a body of women who understand women's problems, especially in these days of meager relief quotas, we do not think that the extenuating circumstances which drove the woman to commit such a rash act were fully taken into consideration at the time of the trial."[35] In the same case, the author of a petition claiming to represent the views of the "Women's Section of the Canadian Labour Party" argued that ample evidence had been submitted to the court to show that Mrs. Dranchuk's reasoning ability had been negatively affected by her husband's "brutal treatment," which, when "combined with abject poverty," produced "an abnormal condition of mind."[36]

Ideas linking economic hardship to mental capacity were common in the language used by lay observers to make sense of murders committed during this period, and were also reflected in the language and sentiment evoked in medical and legal assessments of criminal responsibility. In Dranchuk's case, her lawyer, E. Clare Darling, followed up a recommendation to mercy from the judge and jury by writing the minister of justice to offer his "representations" of the case. He argued that the accused was "suffering from a belief of injustice," explaining that her adverse circumstances "culminated in a period of frenzy which induced the act resulting in the death of her husband." Darling went on to say that medical experts who testified on behalf of both the Crown and the accused "supported this viewpoint, although, possibly or even certainly, not going to the extent of that degree of insanity which could justify an accquittal [sic] of the accused."[37] In light of his client's dire living conditions and questionable mental stability, Darling requested that the minister consider a prison term for her, rather than execution, arguing that this was not a case in which "the extreme penalty of death should be exacted."[38] In this case, it seems that perhaps the plea from her lawyer and the expressed will of some members of the public did influence the executive's decision. In the end, Dina Dranchuk's death sentence was commuted to life in prison.[39]

Although observers did differ in their interpretations of Dranchuk's case and in the precise language they used to account for her murder of her husband, no one seemed to dispute the fact that living in impoverished conditions caused, at least temporarily, a dysfunction of her mind. Still, the significance attributed to the relationship between criminality and "abject poverty" clearly reflected both the interests and the social position of the author(s). Some texts were written from the perspective of personal experiences of economic hardship, whereas others expressed a more general political concern for the state of the nation. This provides some clue as to how Canadians generally imagined crime during this period. The theory that one's character, or constitution, was weakened by exposure to an "unhealthy" environment may also have been widely understood. This is suggested, for instance, in a letter written in support of clemency for Annie Rubletz (1940), a nineteen-year-old "girl" convicted for the murder of her infant.

Following the trial, a local teacher who knew Rubletz for many years described her as the "unhappy product of a very bad environment." Rather than showing "criminal tendencies," the teacher argued, she displayed the behaviour of someone of "weak character." In his letter, he explained that Annie Rubletz's "home was of the poorest and her parents of a low moral and mental caliber ... She is one of a family of not less than fifteen children, none of whom was at any time, so far as I knew them, properly fed or clothed."[40] Letters written in support of Rubletz reinforced the sentiment that otherwise healthy individuals could become defective when exposed to unhealthy environments, and also that morally defective individuals produced unhealthy conditions and threatened society as a whole.

Similarly, the author of "British Justice in Canada," a newspaper editorial in the *Prairie Citizen,* expressed concerns about the link between crime and the country's dire economic state: "It is quite easy to see that the majority of crime is caused by our economic conditions, which for the majority of our people means starvation in the midst of plenty. If more of our natural wealth that we produce each year was put to better use, such as more homes for these unfortunate girls and free education, we would in a very large measure reduce our crime record."[41] In an effort to "rouse public opinion" regarding the Rubletz case, this anonymous writer made a strong appeal to "every right-thinking citizen," including "social and welfare workers and church members and church organizations" who believed in "practical christianity [sic]," to "rise up" against "barbarism" and demand an investigation into her case. The author claimed that during "war time" it was important to show not only Canadians but "the world at large that we are fighting barbarism in the war and in our everyday lives ... 'Justice with mercy' should be our slogan if we are to make the British Empire a thing to be proud of."[42]

However, there were counter-interpretations of the Rubletz case. One writer in particular proposed harsh treatment and warned of the dangers of "coddling criminals." Although some viewed Rubletz as a victim of her circumstances and in need of protection, others saw her as morally "tainted" and a danger to the health of society. Writing from Regina, Saskatchewan, a Mrs. E. Eaton criticized "sob sisters" and the many other "hysterical writers" who blamed the men/fathers in cases like those of Rubletz. She suggested that blame be put on the real problem, prostitution: "Prostitution is rife in small towns in Sask [sic], as young girls are seen soliciting men on the streets. In the case of Annie Rubelietz sterilization would be an answer, as according to the paper she had given birth to an illegitimate child in Regina before ... We must let justice triumph throughout Canada and forget this sob sister stuff."[43] Although we can observe contrasting interpretations of the relationship between crime and environmental conditions, the general assumption that material conditions were relevant to understanding and explaining criminality was nevertheless unshaken in this case.

References to the perilous consequences of unhealthy environments pertained not only to the state of one's domestic situation but to the state of the nation as well. As the *Prairie Citizen* writer pointed out, fighting the "barbarism" of poverty and crime was necessary, particularly during times of war, to uphold the authority and perceived superiority of the British Empire and British law. In this case, therefore, the appropriate role of the rule of law was seen by some as tempering "justice with mercy." For Annie Rubletz, cries for mercy from the public were predominantly represented through narratives of wartime. In another letter to the editor, this time in the *Regina Leader-Post,* a woman writing from Moose Jaw, Saskatchewan, who simply identified herself as "Another Mother," wrote that "there is enough bloodshed going on in the world now, without any hangings of girls."[44]

The case file of Annie Rubletz also provides evidence of the politics of capital case file dispositions, in particular of the law's appeal to public opinion. For instance, included in the file was a single page with five different newspaper clippings arranged together. It was compiled by Arthur Davies from Moose Jaw, Saskatchewan, and addressed to Hon. Ernest Lapointe, the minister of justice. At the top of the page, Davies wrote,

> Dear Sir
> I have cut these letters from the Leader-Post of Friday 18th. Public opinion seems to be in favor of clemency in this case. In a Democracy some notice should be taken of Public Opinion. In fairness I am sending one letter opposed. I have already sent you my appeal for clemency.[45]

The sampling of newspaper clippings was subsequently received and signed by the remissions officer, who, for some reason, drew a large X through the single article that opposed clemency. Perhaps this was to signal to the minister that the letter opposing clemency was not indicative of the general trend in public opinion. The murder charge against Rubletz was eventually reduced to a charge of concealment of birth, for which she was convicted and sentenced to one year in prison.

The consideration of environmental conditions (domestic, social, and economic) in assessments of criminality, alongside the specific characteristics of each case and the position of the author, is also evidenced in a letter written by Mary L. Kennedy to the minister of justice in support of clemency for Frances Harrop (1940), the woman convicted for the murder of her husband who was introduced in Chapter 3. According to Mary Kennedy,

> Men have no idea what that woman's life was: trying to be the best kind of mother to her five sons; trying to manage and to work for their welfare against terrific odds; to hold the home together. Mr. Minister, surely Canada can afford to give this woman her freedom for the sake of those five young men, sons whom she has given to her country and ours. They need her: she has had a life of punishment, notwithstanding all her well-doing. So many valuable lives are hourly going out of the world in this war time; numberless homes being devastated. Her life is specially valuable. Let us build up this home for the sake of these young men, who will make all the better Canadians in gratitude for governmental leniency.[46]

Evaluations of an individual's home life and the state of the country's political environment could influence the way in which a particular criminal act was understood and provide much of the subtext to legal, medical, and lay decisions about criminal responsibility. Within this context, narratives of the *nature* of criminality itself consistently reflected a preoccupation with the constitution of certain individuals, as well as with the constitution of the Canadian citizenry.

Citizenship, Character, and the Biological Politics of Identity

The notion of British citizenship, and the obligations and privileges that came with being a British citizen in Canada, were established through the selective processes of national identification, as well as through the selective practices of social actors to identify themselves in the context of their social world. By the 1920s, Anglo-Canadians were beginning to fully embrace the task of identifying and managing the morally weak and "feebleminded" while at the same time identifying themselves as healthy "Canadians." By this time, the technologies of genetic theory had been redirected from agriculture to human reproduction and presented to the public as a legitimate solution to a range of social "disorders," marking the birth of a new biological politics in Canada.

In his 1919 article titled "Genetics: The Science of Breeding," W.L. Lockhead, a Canadian botanist, reported on the eugenists' proposed "measures for improvement of the race." Lockhead's suggestions for race betterment included the following: "more stringent marriage laws; sexual segregation of defectives; stricter control of immigration; and measures of sterilization of dangerous defectives."[47] Perhaps not surprisingly, "dangerous defectives" were identified by reformers as products of the poor, uneducated, and non-Anglo immigrant classes, who also represented the bulk of prison and asylum populations. It was also about this time that the United Farmers of Alberta called on the government to draft legislation "providing for the segregation for life of the feeble-minded and to study the feasibility of implementing a sterilization program."[48] Then, in 1924, under the slogan of "democracy was never intended for degenerates," the United Farm Women of Alberta pushed the campaign into high gear and put the Alberta *Sexual Sterilization Act* into action.[49] British Columbia followed suit in 1933 – the same year in which Nazi Germany launched its own campaign for racial hygiene – with legislation sanctioning the sterilization of defectives and the mentally ill.[50]

Following the First World War, organizations such as the Dominion Council of Health, the Canadian Council of Child Welfare, the National Council of Women, and the Canadian Social Hygiene Council ambitiously distributed the message across Canada suggesting that the quality of the country's citizenry was in danger.[51] As "respectable" Canadian citizens were becoming increasingly concerned about the social and private lives of the dangerous classes and the perceived threats degenerates posed to the health of Canada, messages reinforcing the traditional ideals of British Canadian citizenship were popping up in the case files of those on trial for murder.

A common feature in capital case file texts during this period was the claim that the practice of hanging represented a blow to "Canadian civility."[52] Others argued, however, that capital punishment was a necessary evil put in place to protect Canadians from dangerous "foreign elements." For example, in response to the case of Harry Rudka (1922), identified as an unemployed Romanian immigrant and convicted for killing two men in a brawl, several newspaper articles made reference to the threat of "foreigners." A report in the *St. Catharines Star* claimed that "human life is of no consequence" to "foreigners who at every turn smash Canadian law" and are able to get away with murder.[53] Even Rudka's lawyer, in a post-trial letter to the justice minister, made reference to the "rather bad foreign element in this Country, particularly Thorold, Niagara Falls and Welland."[54] The ideals of civility and Christianity seemed to constitute the essence of what some Anglo citizens counted as Canadian identity. It therefore makes sense that narratives of criminality commonly produced representations of murder and murderers as the manifestation of an evil or uncivilized force.

When William Schmidt (1944) was charged along with three other men for torturing a woman who refused to hand over her money, the judge told the court that "it is almost unbelievable that this act of savages could be committed in this year 1944 in a Christian country."[55] At the same time, however, the fact that Schmidt was a "Canadian citizen" by birth became an important issue in his defence. In a letter to the chief remissions officer following the trial, Schmidt's lawyer made the defendant's citizenship status known and established Schmidt's sense of nationalism by noting that prior to the unfortunate incident, he made five attempts to enlist for service overseas.[56]

Chapter 5 will more deeply explore the racialized processes that informed responsibility knowledge, but here I make the point that, when certain social actors identified themselves as *Canadian,* and as Canadian *citizens,* these identity politics tended to reflect the way in which they understood particular cases and therefore the way in which they expressed their views about criminality and responsibility. The cultural and conceptual boundaries of British identity were maintained by taking stock of the constitutional makeup of Canadian citizenry, and also by keeping one eye on what was going on in the rest of the world. For instance, case files compiled during the thirties and forties contained several references to Nazism as the embodiment of evil. In 1941, when Frank Patrick was sentenced to death after strong evidence of insanity, one observer made the point that "only Nazis make a practice of killing the insane."[57] Another drew the comparison between Nazism and what it meant to be Canadian by claiming that "Hitler might do this and never flinch – but surely not Canadians."[58]

One particularly revealing letter in Frank Patrick's file shows the intricate way in which ideas about racial and national identity combined with theories about human nature and environmental conditions to forge a meaningful account of his case and of criminality in general. Following the conviction of Patrick, who was identified in official records as a forty-year-old Ukrainian, the Reverend Jules Pirot wrote to the minister of justice in order to express his views on the case. He began by reminding the minister that, because the jury had access to newspapers during the trial, they would surely have known that the victim was the wife of a "soldier" overseas. As a result, Pirot wrote, "it could be presumed that they were prejudiced against the accused."[59] He then pointed out that the accused lived in "one of the wildest parts of Saskatchewan" where there were only "a few settlers, all poor, without a church, without a school."[60]

As a lay witness called to testify during the trial about Patrick's state of mind, Pirot pointed out that as a child the accused was always "abnormal, insane and violent," and more importantly for legal purposes, that he was "unable to understand any distinction between right and wrong in the moral field." He added that the psychiatrist who had previously testified that Patrick was legally "sane" later "seemed to be distressed" about his testimony and regretted his conclusion before the jury.[61] Although Pirot's ultimate wish was for the minister to see his way to ordering a new trial, he hoped that

Patrick would at least be treated with mercy so it could not be said that "in Canada we hang insane persons." His plea for mercy, Pirot alleged, was not just for the accused but also for "his many children and relations, all of them nice people and respectable citizens of Canada."[62] In concluding, he implored, "Honorable Sir, for thirty seven years I have worked in the West among foreigners, trying my best to make them good Christians and good citizens under the protection of our laws. I hope the decision you are going to take will confirm them in the tenets of my teachings."[63] The letter was endorsed by a recommendation from the chief remissions officer that mercy was indeed warranted in this case; as a result, Frank Patrick's death sentence was commuted to life in prison.

Criminal Characters and the Ideals of British Citizenship

As several of the cases we've seen so far indicate, implicit in the language and idealism of national identity and British Canadian citizenship was the moral concept of "character." According to legal doctrine of the time, a defendant's "character" was not relevant in the trying of a criminal case. The 1936 edition of Sir James Fitzjames Stephen's *Digest of the Law of Evidence,* a standard legal text in England, the United States, and Canada, stipulated that, "generally," an individual's "character is deemed to be irrelevant" in courts of law. However, article 57 of his chapter entitled "Character, When Deemed to Be Relevant and When Not" provided an escape from the "general" rule regarding character by restating its relevance as follows: "In criminal cases, the fact that the person accused has a *good* character is deemed to be relevant; but the fact that he has a *bad* character is deemed to be irrelevant, *unless it is itself a fact in issue, or unless evidence has been given that he has a good character, in which case evidence that he has a bad character is admissible.*"[64] Therefore, evidence regarding the character of a defendant was, in practice, legally relevant and admissible so long as the defence raised the issue – which counsel usually did in cases of murder.

"Character" was defined in British common law as an individual's "reputation," *not* "disposition." However, the fictitious distinction between disposition as an inborn characteristic and reputation as a socially acquired characteristic was contradicted in the doctrinal requirement that evidence regarding character could not be given "of particular acts by which reputation or disposition is shown."[65] In practice, the legal guidelines set out for dealing with the issue of "character" provided no real evidentiary limitations in the courtroom or during commutation decisions. Given the extraordinary attention paid to character assessments in capital cases, the rules seem rarely to have been followed. In Canadian murder trials, "disposition" was not distinct from "reputation," and evidence of "bad character" was not stifled or legally restricted in any meaningful way. Historians are therefore provided with plenty of material for understanding the role that character assessments played in legal decisions and the processes through which character was established in criminal law.

Very generally, it could be said that the reputation and disposition of a defendant (male or female) were consistently measured against the masculine British Anglo ideal of what it meant to be a good citizen. British "character" was central to the adjudication of responsibility in Canada; it not only symbolized the optimum standard against which women and men before the law were held but also the socio-political identities of most judges, juries, and experts. Although psychiatrists and some lawyers often complained about the quality of jurors, judges routinely appealed to jury members, as men of respectable class and character, to apply to their common wisdom and reasoning power in their duties as fact-finders and decision makers. We can see this, for instance, in the closing statement of the judge in the trial of James McGrath (1931). Before sending the jury off to deliberate, the judge empathized with the jurymen in their difficult task of deciding the fate of a fellow British subject, who was charged with stabbing his wife twenty-five times:

> No doubt, gentlemen, you are full of sympathy for this unfortunate man. We all are. There is no question about it. We sympathize with him in the fact that he got himself into this position. But we cannot be governed – we must not be governed by sympathy ... You may return to the jury box with a verdict of "Guilty" with tears running down your cheeks, your hearts filled with pity, but you have sworn to do your duty ... Do not again I say, be influenced by sympathy. That element is strong in every breast, but the jury box is no place for it. With pity in our hearts and our souls filled with anguish we can elate our manhood by doing a duty imposed upon us by our ideals of British citizenship.[66]

The ideals of British citizenship and masculine Anglo character formed the essence of moral responsibility in Canada and helped give meaning to both the language of criminal law and the science of criminality. For instance, it seems that the defence of insanity may have been applied/interpreted differently in some cases, or for some defendants, than in others.

Of the seven identified British men in these case studies, six entered a formal plea of insanity, as did three of the four defendants (two men, one woman) who were classified as Indian. However, a qualitative difference existed between the arguments/evidence for insanity/mental deficiency in the trials of British defendants and those of defendants deemed "racially" inferior. In the few cases of Aboriginal men, an insanity plea was introduced by legal counsel not as a *defence* but as a judicious means of explaining, and confirming, the presumed natural violent tendencies of "Indians." Conversely, in trials of British men, insanity was argued by counsel more in the traditional style one would expect of a legal defence. Indians who behaved in an insane manner were seen as manifesting the innate wildness assigned to them by European ideas regarding savages. Thus, their behaviour, though unacceptable, could not spring from madness. By contrast, British men who pleaded insanity tended to be constructed, both in and out of the courtroom, as *real* madmen.

The overrepresentation of convicted British and Aboriginal defendants who pleaded insanity contrasts with the relatively small number of European defendants who attempted the insanity defence – only four of the twenty-four represented in this sample. Similarly, only one of nine condemned French Canadians entered a defence of insanity. However, because nearly all individuals sentenced to death for murder in Canada were poor, most simply could not afford the cost of effective legal representation in an insanity trial. These general observations regarding the use of insanity as a defence in capital cases may not prove to be statistically meaningful, but when read side by side, they do reveal the complex racialized processes inculcated in the practices of law and in evaluations of responsibility, mental deficiency, and character.

The artificial tying-up of racial inferiority/superiority with mental capacity had serious implications when it came to interpreting insanity law. Although the M'Naghten rules included provisions for circumstances in which a defendant suffered "natural imbecility" as well as a "disease of the mind," the medical-legal concept of *disease,* as an anomalous state, was often neutralized during the trial process by presumptions about *natural* mental degeneracy.[67] Trial transcripts suggest that a formal insanity defence was likely to be entered if the defendant's violent behaviour was deemed *unnatural* for his or her prescribed class and character type; irrational violence was not considered by legal authorities to be a natural trait of British men of good class and character.

Anglo-Canadian assumptions about identity and human nature shaped interpretations of criminality in quite obvious ways but also shaped the more subtle ways in which responsibility was negotiated. During the trial of Sarah Jackson (1920), a thirty-five-year-old woman charged with shooting her husband, Dr. Loggie, a prominent psychiatrist, testified that Jackson was "a woman of low moral type, of distinctly animal nature, a woman of uncontrolled passions and sexual nature ... As well ... she had animal instincts, and I would deduce ... that she might be a woman who in stress of circumstances ... might be governed by unreasoning fear of an animal kind."[68] Although the expert's blatantly sexist testimony may have appeared scientific and therefore objective to the jury, the subtext of his diagnosis, which was revealed in letters written after the trial, was that her weak-minded proclivities developed from living in the "North Country," while her husband was off hunting for weeks at a time, leaving her alone in the company, and under the influence, of local "half-breeds." The presumption here was that the degenerative effects of "race" were not just inherited through blood but also through association. Social and political preoccupations with racial borders and blood purity in Canada during this period were cultivated through the practices of law and psychiatry and further nurtured through efforts to maintain the racial quality and dominance of British citizenship.

The representations of Sarah Jackson as a white woman who associated with "half-breeds," or William Monchuk as a "high strung" man who lost control and killed his neighbours, show how "character" was legally constituted according to a number of interrelated factors that then influenced the way in which responsibility and mind-state were understood. The legal constitution of character *types* – according to the degrees of significance placed on nationality, gender, occupation, race, sexual and domestic practices, temperament, appearance, religion, political affiliation, and reputation or predisposition for drinking/vices/swearing (to list a few) – provided flexibility in the way in which responsibility was evaluated from one case to the next.

Consider, for instance, how terms such as "passion" and "control" incited particular meanings in the characterizations of particular "types" of defendants. In the case of James McGrath (1931), the man charged with stabbing his wife twenty-five times, the trial judge flatly rejected the formal insanity defence entered by the defendant's counsel and advised the jury to do the same. However, he did not entirely discard the psychiatric expert's opinion that the accused was overtaken by "extreme passion" to the point that his behaviour resembled a wild animal's. In his charge to the jury, he explained that "extreme passion" did not constitute insanity in this case, because "men must control their passions."[69]

The idea of losing control of one's passions was a predominant theme of the Canadian murder trial during this period. Passion, if unchecked, could lead to all sorts of nasty and socially undesirable consequences. Deeply rooted in English Protestant philosophy was the idea that passion was a dangerous impetus for unreason and madness.[70] However, the precise dangers and nature of passion, and its relationship to madness, were interpreted largely through narratives of character. Not all men were expected to be in control of their passions – but respectable white men were – and women, by and large, were presumed to be naturally passionate and unreasonable to some extent. Recall, for example, the expert witness at Sarah Jackson's trial who testified that she was "a woman of uncontrolled passions" and "governed by unreasoning fear of an animal kind."[71] "Wild animal" imagery continued to be fairly common in early-twentieth-century theories of insanity even though the "wild beast" test had been put aside in the mid-nineteenth century as an unsophisticated and outdated legal measure of criminal responsibility. (The wild beast test was intended simply to show that, if a defendant was so bereft of reason that he understood the ramifications of his behaviour no more than did an infant, a brute, or a wild beast, he would not be held responsible for his crimes.) However, the symbol of unbridled wildness was often introduced during the trial process, infused with culturally/politically generated sexism and racism.

During the trial of George Dvernichuk, a Ukrainian immigrant charged with killing his sister-in-law's family of five in 1930, two asylum doctors who had observed him in custody reported that the apparent lack of motive for Dvernichuk's extreme behaviour indicated some form of mental derangement, but not insanity.[72] The medical experts described his clinical symptoms of sudden "hysteria"; for their part, legal officials highlighted his questionable character and racial predisposition for bad "temperament" and social dissent. The police report, for example, noted that the accused, "like all members of his race," demonstrated communistic tendencies and, as a "typical foreigner," maintained a poor work ethic. Unlike in the case of James McGrath, extreme "passion" and unreason in Dvernichuk's case were not interpreted as behaviour necessarily out of character or unnatural. Like Sarah Jackson and William Monchuk, he was perceived as an unreasoning "kind" rather than simply as an individual who had behaved unreasonably.

So, despite the superficial similarities between the trials of McGrath and Dvernichuk (insanity was rejected as a viable defence, and both were hanged), the legal understandings of the particular mental effects of an extreme emotional break were quite different in each. McGrath's state of passion, or loss of control, was interpreted as his failure to uphold the standards of Anglo manhood, whereas Dvernichuk's loss of control (re)confirmed elitist presumptions about the naturally crude behaviour of south-eastern European immigrants. Both were deemed bad characters, but of quite different types.

Conclusion

The case studies provided in this chapter demonstrate that judicial discussions about insanity often extended well beyond the doctrinal requirements of the insanity defence and incorporated fundamental concerns about character, citizenship, and British justice. The inter- and post-war period between 1920 and 1950 is well documented by Canadian scholars as also being preoccupied with the biological politics of social hygiene, national identity, and human degeneracy.[73] In this context, "insanity" was much more than a legal defence and a psychiatric diagnosis: it was a way to explain and order social disorder, which otherwise, in the realm of common sense and everyday experience, defied reason. In the courtroom, cultural knowledge about insanity and insane people mixed to produce what Joel Eigen described as "something rather more combustible than the sum of its two volatile parts."[74]

In cases where insanity was not the defence, we see that legal and popular rationalizations regarding the internal and external causes of mental deficiency and abnormality nevertheless often borrowed the language and structure of a formal insanity plea, as well as psychiatric knowledge on the nature of insanity itself. However, the arguments of lawyers and testimonies of witnesses (lay and expert) were not bound by the narrow doctrinal requirements of insanity law. By looking at a number of different legal sites, or marketplaces, where the issues of mind-state and responsibility were negotiated, we can see that each had its own conventions, which in turn helped establish the parameters of responsibility knowledge in each case. In other words, the marketplace(s) in which a defendant's state of mind was taken up would define, to a large extent, which narratives of mind-state and responsibility were deemed both plausible and possible.

The specific legal context in which a defendant's mind-state was addressed (such as the stage of the judicial process and/or the type of defence entered at trial) also determined who had more decision-making power – experts, juries, or legal officials.[75] This chapter established that although psychiatric theories during this period linked crime to degeneracy and mental deficiency, the proliferation of psychiatric knowledges and growing efforts of some psychiatrists to find a professional space in the criminal justice system did not necessarily increase their authority. Much early professional literature suggests that the forensic psychiatric expert and the judicial use of psychiatric expertise made a very shaky start in Canada. However, in reading capital case files, we see how professional tensions between law and psychiatry – rooted in a fundamental disagreement about the definitional parameters of mental capacity, decision-making authority over the matter of criminal responsibility, and the intense need to appease public opinion – often helped form the bedrock of the negotiation process.

A tremendous amount of crossover existed between insanity defence discourse and other legal and non-legal categories introduced to established mental deficiency, and between common sense and expertise. In cases where mind-state was raised as an issue, the interpretation of the law and the nature of evidence admitted to establish mental deficiency fluctuated according to the decided characteristics of each case and each defendant. The routine and somewhat less restricted negotiations of criminal responsibility through more flexible legal categories, such as passion and provocation (and as we'll see in later chapters, self-defence), embodied a strict Anglo perspective on human difference, which in turn provided the language and meanings of responsibility knowledge. I explore these themes further in the next two chapters, where I consider how medical-legal representations of responsibility were articulated through interdependent hierarchical narratives of race, gender, and domesticity.

5
The Racialization of Criminal Responsibility

Expert and common-sense knowledges about racial degeneracy are well represented in Canadian capital case files. Although Canadian legal historians have demonstrated that the meanings of "race" and representations of "racism" fluctuated over time and within specific social and institutional contexts, case file evidence nevertheless shows that racialized constructs of character, class, and gender behaviour were consistently deployed to socially, legally, and medically designate individuals on trial for murder.[1]

As Appendix A-1 indicates, 86.5 percent of the defendants represented in this analysis were assigned an identification of race, ethnicity, and/or nationality by court officials. Legal references to "ethnicity," "nationality," and "origin" seemed to imply the same hierarchical meanings as more explicit racial designations such as "coloured" and "Indian." Each capital murder case file contains a standard Department of Justice document that provided the chief remissions officer and the minister of justice with summary information about the case and the accused. Jail officials were responsible for filling out the department forms, which included a list of questions regarding the defendant's age, place of birth, nationality of mother and father, religion, literacy, and occupation. In Table 1, we see a significant overrepresentation of individuals from south-central and eastern European countries – particularly from the Ukraine – who were convicted for murder. Several non-Anglo defendants were legally classified by the determined race or nationality of their parents, even if they themselves were born in Canada. As Kenneth Avio has shown, and this sample confirms, racial/ethnic identification seemed to generally influence the likelihood of execution but according to several different logics.[2]

The question I address in this chapter is not whether race was an issue in the deliberation of capital cases. Clearly it was. Several Canadian scholars have provided historical evidence of the interconnectedness of nation building, racism, and criminal law practices. I will examine, instead, how processes of racialization differed from one case to the next, and how race did,

Table 1

Racial identification of individuals convicted for murder

%	Official racial identification
35.0	South-central/eastern European (Galician, Russian, Ukrainian, Italian, Polish, German)
13.5	British (English, Irish, Scottish)
13.5	French Canadian
7.5	Black ("Coloured," "Negro," "American Negro")
7.5	American
7.5	Aboriginal ("Indian," "Half-Breed")
4.5	Canadian
1.5	Chinese
12.0	Unspecified

Notes: Identification was assigned by police and/or court officials. Total percentage exceeds 100 because some individuals received more than one designation.

and did not, come into play in efforts to establish criminal responsibility. Just as interpretations of degeneracy, mental fitness, and expertise were determined according to the context in which they were understood, the sociopolitical meanings of "race," and racial designations, also differed from case to case.

In Chapter 4, I demonstrated how introducing evidence of mental defects and aberrations, without entering a formal insanity plea, effectively broadened the range of evidence admitted at the trial and post-trial stages of the judicial process. This evidence often included expert and lay opinions on the relationship between race, criminality, and degeneracy, or feeblemindedness. The racialization of criminological knowledge and the production of criminological knowledge *through* narratives of racial identity provided particular meanings to the legal concept of free will – some people's wills being freer than others – and provided the language to articulate perceived natural standards of criminal responsibility in Canadian murder cases. Common-sense-cum-expert theories about racial difference and hierarchy were inherent in the ideas of mental deficiency and in turn (re)affirmed through legal procedures of establishing criminal responsibility. "Race" was not simply a factor in legal decisions about a defendant's mind-state: rather, racist ideology helped define legal, popular, and psychiatric representations of normalcy and degeneracy.

In *"Race," Rights and the Law in the Supreme Court of Canada,* James Walker describes changes in the "common sense" meaning of "race" in Canada up to the 1950s. Walker explains that the concept of race, as a measurable natural/scientific quality that justified discrimination and white domination during the 1920s and '30s, had lost its "scientific validity" by the 1940s and '50s. In a word, it became unfashionable to be overtly racist. "Racism," according to Walker, came to be understood as a cultivated attitude rather than a natural occurrence, and in the view of the populace, the character of the mind was no longer determined by biology/race. But, as Constance Backhouse points out, and this research to some extent confirms, changes in the "new thinking" about race and racism during this period were "more semantic than substantive."[3]

Capital case file evidence clearly shows that racism did not disappear from legal discourse. Similarly, medical discourse on standards of mental capacity certainly continued throughout the first half of the twentieth century to draw scientific validity from "known" theories about racial difference. However, a discernible shift also occurred in what counted as knowledge about race during this period. In particular, during the 1940s, language around citizenship, national identity, and mental hygiene tended to repackage essentialist ideas about race in a way that only seemed "new." Therefore, tracing the meaning of race and its relationship to the meanings of mental capacity, degeneracy, and responsibility is not easy. It is also not appropriate to make it the subject of broad historical description. Racial designations were unevenly applied and highly contestable, just as theories about human nature and mental illness were continually (re)defined and contested.

In reading capital case files as cultural texts, we can see that, as a discursive concept, race was intrinsically tied up with other constructs such as gender, sexuality, character, civility, and criminality. In other words, race knowledge cannot be understood as separate from the larger cultural and political processes through which it was formed and informed. By examining the cases of racialized defendants against the broader systems of racism in Canada, we can make out how common-sense thinking about race was articulated in law and, again, how single historical events drew meaning from broader historical contexts. In particular, this contextual analysis reveals how race knowledge, or at least what counted as knowledge about race, shifted to reflect emerging national concerns about social purity and the effects of war.

Differential Meanings of "Race" in Legal Decision Making

Within a general climate of social, political, and economic insecurity – fuelled by the ideas of degeneration, eugenics, mental hygiene, and Eurocentrism – the origin, nationality, and/or racial identity of individuals on trial for murder were meaningful. The specific social, political, and economic "problem" of feeblemindedness in early Canada was outlined in a 1936 report titled "A Brief for the Sterilization of the Feeble-Minded." The report was prepared for the Association of Ontario Mayors Annual Conference by Dr. William

Hutton, president of the Eugenics Society of Canada and medical officer of health in Brantford, Ontario. In his analysis of the situation, Hutton characterized the feebleminded as

> people with the capacity and abilities of children ... They appear to the casual observer to be persons of usual capacity, but they require supervision, for they suffer from arrested development of the mind, and they are incapable of competing on equal terms with their fellows ... In times of economic crisis they are among the first to require public assistance. They often live in conditions of extreme squalor. Indeed, persistent unsanitary surroundings are an evidence of the presence of the feeble-minded ... We misunderstand them to our own undoing, and fail to recognize that it is to their benefit as much as to our own for the intelligent electorate to control their reproduction.[4]

Although Hutton did not mention race in his report, it surely did not take much imagination in the minds of Canada's "intelligent electorate" to associate the identification of the weaker "classes" with the presumed characteristics of the weaker "races" in order to justify regulatory initiatives in the name of what James Walker refers to as "imperial responsibility."[5] In what follows, I chronicle the variable meanings of "race" in representations of criminality and mind-state through an analysis of three racialized categories: the Indian, the coloured, and the immigrant. In each case, race played out differently. However, through the adjudication of mental capacity and criminal responsibility in each case, white male supremacy was routinely affirmed.

"Indian Hanged"

Characteristics associated with savagery, and presumed to be typical of Aboriginal peoples and their way of life – as uncivilized, immature, ignorant, illiterate, unclean, and unsettled – were also recognized signs of degeneration and mental deficiency. Those who were identified as "Indian" or "half-breed" were viewed in and out of the criminal justice system not as individuals but as representatives of a racial collective. Anglo judges, lawyers, and juries had a common-sense notion about what it meant to be "Indian" and understood certain behaviours to be stock characteristics or "customs" of the "Indian race."[6] This can be seen in the trial of Albert Le Beaux (1921), an "Esclave Indian" charged for the murder of his wife and infant son on a reserve in Fort Providence, Northwest Territories.

While trying to establish the limits of normal behaviour between non-Aboriginal married couples, defence counsel in this case asked Crown witness the Reverend Father Le Guen, a priest working at a nearby mission, if it was generally "an uncommon thing for a husband to beat his wife." The witness declared that it was "rather unusual" and only "sometimes seen."[7] Le Beaux's lawyer hoped to show that past episodes of domestic violence were the result of an abnormal mind. However, in his re-examination of the same witness, the Crown began his line of questioning with a brief and unsubstantiated reference to "the habit of the Esclave Indians to beat their wives."[8] This casual observation by the Crown regarding the domestic life of Indian couples had nothing to do with the actual question posed to the witness, which was to establish how long he had lived in the area and how long he had known the defendant.

No evidence was offered to support the Crown's spontaneous claim regarding the nature of conjugal relationships among the Esclave; and the fact was never contested. The practice of wife-beating was easily taken up as "uncommon" within civilized communities but "customary" within Native Indian communities. Similarly, when defence counsel suggested that in fact Le Beaux's wife had killed their baby and then killed herself, the Crown asked two witnesses, the reverend father and the doctor who had examined the bodies, if they had "ever heard of Indians, either male or female, committing suicide." Both witnesses assured the court that to their knowledge suicide was not an Indian custom.[9]

The "low mentality" and "uncontrolled passions" of Native Indians were also not issues for lengthy legal debate – these were understood by Canadian legal officials to be natural characteristics. For instance, in his report to the secretary of state, the trial judge recommended mercy solely on the grounds of Le Beaux's naturally diminished mental capacity. He concluded, "considering the low mentality of the Accused, (an ignorant Esclave Indian), who, except for violent fits of temper at different times, has otherwise shewn good behaviour, I think that his sentence should be commuted to life in prison."[10] Case file evidence suggests that the standard of responsibility for Indian defendants was low, and not something that needed to be determined legally because it was determined by nature. Le Beaux's presumed diminished mental capacity was not directly discussed during the trial; it was simply introduced by the judge in his final report as a matter of fact and common sense. This sentiment was further supported in a letter to the minister of justice from a local bishop, who, from his "own personal knowledge," was convinced that Le Beaux should not be hanged because he obviously suffered from a "violent passion" that had caused him to lose control.[11] However, the remissions officer, who first received the letter, disagreed with the bishop and explained to the minister in his summary report that since the judge's recommendation for mercy was not "supported by any sufficient reason," the law should be allowed to take its course.[12]

Following the trial, the focus in Le Beaux's case shifted from the question of individual responsibility to an intense concern for the public and political impression that would result if an Indian from a particularly contentious region of western Canada were hanged at that moment. For example, in response to allegations that the murdered infant was actually the child of a missionary who seduced Le Beaux's wife, the jury prepared and read a statement in court before the delivery of their guilty verdict: "We as a Jury wish to express our condemnation of immorality among the White men and Indians and are desirous of seeing the Indians given to understand that any such cases will be investigated by the Crown. This comes from a desire to see a high standard of morals maintained in opening this new country."[13] After the trial, Crown counsel also explained in a letter to the minister the undesirable political impression that a commuted sentence would leave in the northern community. Reaffirming the authority and role of British law and the privilege of white men in western Canada, he reported, "the two Mounted Police Officers and all the white-men I have talked to think it will have a bad effect, both among the Indians and Whites, if this murderer is not executed ... I cannot conceive of a case less deserving of commutation of sentence than the present one – and I am convinced that a very bad impression of Canadian law and justice in this far-north country would result if the law is not allowed to take its course."[14] In the end, despite recommendations for mercy from both the judge and jury, the law was allowed to take its course, and Albert Le Beaux was executed. Surely an impression was made.

The social and political significance of certain racial designation seemed to be so well understood during this period that one need only to associate with a member of an undesirable "breed" in order to be affected/infected by his or her degenerative nature. When Sarah Jackson pleaded self-defence following the shooting of her husband in 1920, the trial judge put aside evidence of previous domestic violence as well as expert testimony about her "uncontrolled passions, sexual nature, animal instincts and low moral type," and urged the jury to consider the more likely motive that Jackson, a white woman, simply wished to get rid of her husband, also white, "in order to be free to live with her paramour, an Indian."[15] Common-sense knowledge regarding the psychological effects of Jackson's illicit association with an "Indian" was expressed in various letters from the public in support of commutation. In one letter requesting "great leniency," Mr. H.C. Reynolds, Esq., expressed his outrage at Jackson's husband for subjecting his white wife to such dangerous and wild living conditions. The concerned citizen theorized that "leaving her alone surrounded by Halfbreeds without the necessities of life her mental condition deterriated [sic] and she no doubt became helpless prey to any person and no doubt was largely influenced by them ... Here she was surrounded by men of low moral type, in the wilds of the West far removed from human civilization threatened by an immoral Husband. What human life could endure such a strain no less a nervous woman impelled and swayed [by] any isolated suggestion which might arise from any quarter."[16]

The image of the "wild" North and the degenerative influence of the "wilderness" have been a popular narrative in Canadian history and storytelling culture, one that persisted well beyond the period covered by this study. For instance, a 1962 novelette entitled "In the Wilderness" and published in a popular magazine told of the trials and peril of a "devastatingly pretty" young white schoolteacher working at a government school on an Indian reserve in the Canadian "North Country."[17] Although the teacher found pleasure in the shy, simple nature of the Indian children (feeling compelled to feed and clean them), she lived in constant fear and unrest in the foreboding wild. An element of danger loomed when the local Indian agent warned her to lock her door, and rumours began to stir about a stranger on the reserve. Then, one stormy night, when she forgot to lock the door, the stranger found her:

> The man stepped briskly into the room. I had to step back quickly to avoid his bumping into me ... "You don't ask me in, I come anyway," he said softly. I was confused and terrified. I could see clearly, now, that he was an Indian. He was handsome, taller than most Indians. His hair was dark and crisply curling, unlike the straight hair of the Indian. His skin was deeply tanned and the cheek-bones were high but not markedly so. His eyes were a brilliant, burning blue! A blue-eyed Indian! But he was Indian; I'd lived here long enough to recognize the characteristics. Then I said what proved to be a very stupid thing. "You're Indian!" He stood staring at me for what seemed an eternity. He said solemnly, "My father white man, French-Canadian! My mother Indian!" His eyes burned into mine. I had made him angry![18]

Further into the story, we are told that the stranger is a half-breed named Pierre who had just been released from the Provincial Hospital for the Insane, where he was being treated for his "psychopathic tendencies" and "delusions about being a white man." On that frightful night, Pierre terrorized the teacher by asking her to dance and telling her that she was to be his. The young teacher fainted at the threatening prospect, and Pierre ran off, soon to be recaptured and returned to the hospital.

Meanwhile, word of her encounter with the strange Indian got back to her fiancé, Jess, a law student. Jess wrote his wife-to-be in order to express his deep disappointment over the fact that her "purity" had been soiled and to explain that they obviously could no longer be married: "Our love had been so beautiful so pure, Jess wrote, a priceless thing! This awful thing that happened to me, and he was sure it had happened, was horrible, tragic! I'd been entirely blameless, he knew, but our love could never be the same again. Surely, I would understand? It was hard for him, too, he went on. He'd been working so hard to make a future for us and now this!"[19] Although this tale is told in a fanciful and idealized way, it echoes the earlier stories from the archives and shows the resilience of popular knowledge regarding what supposedly happened to women, particularly white women, who lived in the wilderness, and in close proximity to "half-breeds."

The fact that Sarah Jackson lived and associated with "uncivilized men" of "low moral type" put her own character into disrepute and provided a platform for theories about her acquired degenerative state. Nellie McClung, suffragist and pro-sterilization activist in Alberta, also wrote to the minister about Sarah Jackson, whom she evocatively described as "a woman from the north country." McClung did not see Jackson's condition as a lost cause, however, arguing that despite her "low grade of intelligence" and "undeveloped mentality," it was possible, if her sentence were commuted, "that under proper discipline and influence she may repent of her evil deed and develop into a better citizen."[20]

Theories about racial inferiority and diminished responsibility were common among white officials and public observers, but they were also aware of the symbolic effect judicial decisions may have had on Indian communities. The complexity of race discourse, simultaneously constituted as scientific, political, and common sense, is well demonstrated in the 1944 case of Paul Abraham, a twenty-four-year-old "half-breed" charged with the murder of his wife in Cherhill, Alberta. In a scathing letter from the secretary of Indian affairs to the chief remissions officer, written at the latter's request, the circumstances of Abraham's crime and the question of his state of mind at the time were subsumed in a nationalistic account of the unstable and uncivilized "Indian situation" in Alberta. The secretary wrote, "people of mixed blood in northern Alberta have predominately [sic] Indian characteristics, both physiologically and psychologically, and usually live the Indian mode of life ... The murdered woman was the daughter of ... the chief of a tribe of Chippewa Indians, numbering about 250, ... who are of a primitive type and who present a special problem to this department. They are, in fact, the only group of Indians in Alberta who are not in treaty with the Government and who have no reserve."[21] He went on to explain, from his experience in the intemperate northwest parts of Alberta, that "Indians, perhaps more than others, are prone to repeat crimes of violence." He further drew the remissions officer's attention to a particularly important feature of the case – "the fact that the murdered woman was the wife of the accused." The secretary reported that "out of 65 cases of homicide by Indians since 1928 recorded by this branch, the victim in 20 cases was the wife or common-law wife of the accused." He attributed this phenomenon of spousal murder to the "old aboriginal idea that the husband has power of life and death over his wife and can exercise it at his caprice." The secretary claimed there was a need for "stern law enforcement" in order to "disabuse Indians, and those of Indian blood, of this vicious predilection."[22]

The fact that the remissions officer solicited a report from the secretary of Indian affairs is noteworthy, particularly since the information provided was then included in the remission report and used to shape the representation of Abraham's case to the minister of justice. Although evidence does not suggest that the soliciting of such reports was typical in capital cases, it shows the general authority of the remissions officer's "expertise" in selecting and omitting information put forward to adjudicate each case. The observations made in the secretary's letter and subsequently restated in the official summary report were further supported by a report filed by the commissioner of the RCMP. By the commissioner's account, Abraham was "an illiterate" and "subject to violent moods." He deduced "from the evidence available" that "Abraham committed the murder during a violent fit of temper caused by what might be termed ordinary domestic friction. His illiteracy would no doubt have some bearing on the matter plus the mode of life followed by these people, it being not uncommon for Indians and half-breeds to beat their wives."[23]

Abraham's violent temper was recounted by several witnesses during and after the trial. Defence counsel called Dr. Randall McLean, superintendent of the provincial mental hospital at Ponoka, Alberta, to testify about evidence heard at trial and offer his opinion on Abraham's mental condition. Although McLean had not personally examined the defendant, he was confident, from expert evaluation of the lay evidence, that there was "good reason" to believe Abraham suffered "mental abnormalities."[24] The medical expert described a number of possibilities, including epilepsy, palsy, amnesia, and delusion, which could account for the defendant's "impaired judgement." However, he was unwilling to support a full defence of insanity by testifying that at the time of the crime, Abraham did not appreciate what he was doing or know that it was wrong. He would only say that "epileptics are likely to be very bad tempered and have poor control of their tempers."[25] This is suggestive of the ways in which definitions of mental abnormality often echoed derogatory racial descriptions, since "Indians," too, were presumed to have poor control over their tempers.

It does not appear from the evidence that the scientific account of Abraham's behaviour was seriously considered by fact-finders at any point during the trial. The doctor's testimony was not revisited in the final charge to the jury, in which the trial judge dismissed insanity as a viable defence. The remissions officer pushed the issue a little further, however, and requested that Dr. Harvey Clare, who had "acted as a psychiatrist for this Department for a great number of years," examine Abraham following his conviction.[26] Clare subsequently reported that Abraham was "definitely not suffering from any mental impairment." He was firm in his conclusion that it would be "unreasonable" to think that Abraham's mind was "not functioning normally when he committed the crime for which he now stands convicted."[27]

Despite the expert opinion of Dr. Clare, it appeared that the most valued "expert" on Paul Abraham's state of mind was actually his own father, who told authorities that his son's mental state was normal at the time of the crime and that there had never been anything wrong with his mind in the past. In his letter to the minister, the secretary of Indian affairs illustrated the importance of this kind of lay knowledge in assessing certain standards of responsibility and accounting for violent behaviour: "There is nothing in our records to show that there was anything in the conduct of the murdered woman that could extenuate her husband's crime. On the other hand it appears that he was the aggressor in their quarrels and had threatened her on many occasions. His excuse, as reported by the police, that he was influenced by Indian medicine, was discounted by the Indian interpreter, and from my own knowledge I would say that there was nothing to it; his further excuse that he was of feeble mind was discounted by his own father."[28] In his "Condensed Summary" of the case, the remissions officer did not offer a direct opinion on whether Abraham should be executed. However, the manner in which he organized and presented trial and post-trial evidence regarding mind-state in his report to the minister clearly suggested that he did not object to the law taking its course in this case.

The use of the insanity defence in cases involving "Indian" and "half-breed" defendants was often precarious. Evidence brought forward to establish past episodes of violence or irrational behaviour was often countered with arguments suggesting such behaviours were not abnormal but typical "Indian characteristics." Also, the issue of individual responsibility in cases involving Indian defendants was often overshadowed by efforts to appease racial tensions and sedate political unrest. However, the strong political interest in using judicial actions to send the correct message to the correct people did not seem to penetrate the general public to quite the same degree. The news coverage of "Indian" trials was scarce compared to that of others. Perhaps this was because little needed to be said. When Paul Abraham was put to death, a tiny newspaper notice in small type briefly and poignantly announced "Indian Hanged."[29]

Racial designations used to legitimize British rule and white supremacy persisted well into the war and post-war periods, in which the scientific validation of racism continued to pervade the language of criminological knowledge. Although "race" did not exist as a legal category, and despite the law's well-managed image as non-discriminatory and objective, race did matter in the deliberation of capital murder cases.[30] When Mary Smith, a "half-breed," was charged in 1935 with killing her husband, a British soldier, the judge pointed out the couple's racial differences on the first page of his report to the minister of justice. The deceased, he reported, "was a returned soldier and an Englishman by birth. The accused, *on the other hand,* was a native of the prairies and was what is known as a half-breed, having both Indian and French blood in her veins."[31] Likewise, in the case of Joseph Proulx, charged with the murder of a fifteen-year-old girl in 1945, the remissions officer opened his summary report for the minister by identifying "the prisoner" as a "French half-breed, 17 years of age." He added that Proulx was one of fourteen children and that "none of his family appears to be bright and their standard of education is described as poor."[32]

Racial designations and essentialist characterizations were typically placed within the first few lines of the remissions report, setting a powerful image against which the facts of the case were to be considered. For Mary Smith, the remissions officer's identification of her as a "half-breed" and her husband as an "Englishman" was significant – it warned of the dangers and consequences of mixing blood in both birth and marriage. And in the case of Joseph Proulx, it reaffirmed knowledge about the natural relationship between racial and intellectual inferiority.

"Unsuitable Examples"

The processes of racialization that characterized the adjudication of "Indian" cases are quite different from those that emerge in cases of other racialized defendants. For instance, where the defendant was simply identified as "coloured" or "Negro," there did not seem to be the same concern for political avowal, or even for a precise identification of origin or nationality. For instance, Benito Pasquale (1926) was reported in four different court documents as "Costa Rican," "Porto Rican [sic]," a "Mexican," and "a colored man from Jamaica."[33] However, he was officially identified in the remissions report, "from his appearance," as Costa Rican with a mix of "Indian and Negro blood, with the Negro strain predominating."[34] Despite Pasquale's ambiguous racial classification, the colour of his skin dictated a particular view of his behaviour and had a strong impact on the medical and legal assessment of his mind-state and natural culpability.

Pasquale was convicted in 1926 for the murder of a white nurse who tended him while he was in a BC hospital for rheumatism. Believing she had given him a poison pill that made him crazy, he slashed her throat from ear to ear with a razor when she came in to check on him. During the trial, three expert witnesses testified regarding the question of insanity. One found Pasquale sane, the second found him insane, and the third concluded that he may or may not be insane. Due to the inconclusive nature of the medical evidence, Dr. Harvey Clare was asked by the minister of justice to examine Pasquale following the trial.

Clare visited Pasquale on three occasions at the jail and found him, physically, to be "a very poor specimen of a human being." Clare reported that, besides having bad social manners, the prisoner was

> the lowest type of human being that I have ever examined for mental disease. Insanity is a change from the normal but I think this man is in his normal mental condition. It is very far removed from the normal of a native of our country but I think that he is a normal citizen in the place where he was born [Jamaica]. These people are ignorant, superstitious, childish, uneducated, revengeful and very impulsive ... I do not think this man is insane at the present time and do not think we have any proof that he was really the victim of delusions or hallucinations when he committed the act.[35]

Although medicine and law were tools that authorities could use to manage those perceived to be socially "dangerous," legal officials did not seem to view the execution or commutation of a black person as a suitable example for *lessons* of the law in the same way that certain Aboriginal accused were. For instance, when Louis Jones was convicted for the murder of his estranged wife in 1927, his lawyer, John Mahoney, wrote the following testimonial to the chief remissions officer regarding Jones' character: "I want you to take into consideration the general character of the half white. I admit that it is not up to standard, but they are usually people of very strong passions and feelings, possessing a good deal of the white mans [sic] vanity and pride, without the mental qualities to offset them."[36] And to establish the relative social and political insignificance of Jones' case, the lawyer further pointed out that "at this moment there is hardly anybody in Halifax who would bother noticing the fact if the sentence were commuted to life imprisonment. So far as the public is concerned: 'this is just another nigger.' I think on inquiry you will find that extending clemency to this man will have no effect on the public one way or anther; and if he is hanged it is all the same. He is not regarded as a suitable example at all."[37]

The racist ideology that the mixing of blood caused degenerative effects had long been the subject of scientific research programs in Canada and the United States. In an article titled "Psychological Traits of the Southern Negro with Observations as to Some of His Psychosis," published in a prominent North American psychiatric journal, Dr. W.M. Bevis discussed his findings on "the insidious addition of white blood to the negro race" and its effects on the latter. According to the doctor, "if the original white parent were always even an average representative of his race, mentally and morally, the hereditary effect upon the more or less mulatto offspring would naturally be that of improvement of the traits and mentality of the colored race, but unfortunately the white man by whom this fusion of blood starts is most often feeble-minded, criminal, or both ... The race may have gained in an intellectual way but not in a moral."[38] Bevis further described "all negros" as naturally lacking initiative, uninterested in education, and too interested in sexual matters, crime, and vice. Black women were described as "promiscuous" from a "remarkably early age," with a low moral sense toward gratifying "their natural instincts and appetites."[39]

Bevis interpreted essential socio-cultural differences as evidence of psychosis and mental deficiency. For instance, he cited the irrational "fear of darkness," obvious "cowardice," and "constant reiteration of stories of the ante-bellum system of patrol of the plantations, of ghosts and the impressive nocturnal performances of the Ku-Klux-Klan" as evidence of "noctiphobia" (fear of the night) perpetuated by the delusional effects of the unhealthy Negro preoccupation with "superstition." Evidence of racial inferiority and naturally diminished mental and moral capacity was further confounded, according to the doctor, by the deep "conscious or unconscious wish of every negro to be white" – not unlike Pierre, the "insane Half-breed" from the popular fiction story. Signs of natural excitability of the "Negro race" were documented from observations of their worshipping practices, which were depicted as the "occasional grunt, groan, or exclamation ... with the continuous motion of the congregation, increasing in volume as the service progresses until a point is reached where their emotional fervor reaches its climax in wild disorder." This wild disorder, reported Bevis, was "only a step away from the manic phase of a manic-depressive psychosis or a catatonic excitement."[40]

Although there were clear similarities between the medicalized language used to characterize both "Indian" and "coloured" defendants as overly passionate and mentally stunted, the legal, political, and cultural meanings ascribed to each racialized group, as well as each defendant, differed significantly and contrast the differing histories of slavery and colonization.

Returning to the case of Louis Jones, we can observe the way in which cultural beliefs around race mixed with concerns about sexuality and social order to produce particular interpretations of responsibility, criminality, and mental deficiency. According to official records, Jones and his wife separated because she had been unfaithful to him. When she left their home and moved to another city, he followed her, claiming he had forgiven her and was prepared to "take her back." She refused to return and angrily informed him she was having a sexual relationship with someone she considered his "better." Almost immediately after his wife's confession, he stabbed and killed her. Jones' defence was not guilty on the grounds of extreme provocation causing him to have no recollection of the actual killing. According to his counsel, "the words which this woman uttered to this man ... were of such a character" that any "reasonable man" would be so provoked to "lose control of himself and commit this act."[41]

An insanity plea was never officially raised in Jones' case, and when Dr. William Forrest, the jail physician, attempted to answer a question from the Crown about the defendant's mental condition, defence counsel entered into a lengthy debate with the judge regarding the ability of any doctor to comment on such a thing. He argued that "no man is an expert" on another man's "conscious recollection" and that it was for a jury to decide whether "those words were so provocative" that they had an effect on Jones' mind.[42]

In assessing the viability of the defendant's claim that he was provoked, the trial judge, in his final charge to the jury, cited the nature of the victim's language as evidence of her bad character. The judge found her words to be so vile that he questioned the defendant's account of the events leading to the murder, doubting that any "woman ever used language like that." After the trial, Jones' lawyer responded to the judge's presumption that *all* women were incapable of such language in his letter to the chief remissions officer. He argued, "it is evident that [the judge] has no acquaintance with the coloured race. I have found this language very popular among this class of people."[43]

The lawyer further pointed to the relevance of certain conjugal prerogatives, racial tendencies, and the general insignificance of the crime: "No matter what the man's record was, this woman was his wife. They had had their troubles it is true, but what else are we to expect between people of this class ... Jones was exceedingly jealous of a woman who was his own property and was regarded as handsome and something to be desired. There is no great public principle involved in this case such as the case of shooting an officer. It is a row between husband and wife."[44] The central importance of race in judicial deliberations, and the power of the law to reinforce racial difference as a social fact, are well demonstrated here. In his letter to the remissions officer, the defence counsel cautioned, "this colored fellow may have had a fair trial, but for the reasons I have given he has not had what is popularly called a fair show."[45]

Once the trial was over, the jury foreman disclosed that he "disliked niggers because they are niggers." The lawyer expressed to the remissions officer that the juryman's "decided feeling towards all niggers" was a reflection of the sentiment of "most whites here [Halifax]."[46] Despite evidence of racial prejudice, the jury did recommend mercy for Jones. However, we might speculate as to whether the decision regarding mercy was perhaps based, at least in part, on theories about the questionable character of the victim. In the end, neither the judge nor the remissions officer supported the jury's recommendation for mercy. Jones was executed with no report of public hue and cry.

The legitimation of racial subordination through medical-legal processes was, and arguably continues to be, an integral part of Canada's social-cultural matrix. Although these cases show that Aboriginal people and other people of colour had quite divergent experiences, there was commonality in the language used to medicalize cultural and physical differences to be packaged as evidence of unreason, which, in the process, defined what it meant to be a reasonable white man. However, the artificial construct of the moral superiority and mental hygiene of the English-speaking Anglo race did not hinge solely on skin colour or the presumed natural inferiority of "other races"; it was also deeply rooted in a fear of the gradual degeneration of the race's own "pure" stock.

"Defective Immigrants" and "Diseased Classes"

Case file evidence suggests that the testimonies of psychiatric experts were not always privileged in criminal courts. However, some asylum doctors did become increasingly influential in the medical and public sectors during the early nineteen hundreds. Political and popular speculation about the devastating effects of unregulated immigration encouraged, and was supported by, scientific programs of eugenics, social deprivation, and the presumed proliferation of feeblemindedness and criminality in Canada. In 1916, Dr. Charles Kirk Clarke published, along with many other pieces on the subject, an article in the Canadian *Public Health Journal* titled "The Defective Immigrant," to warn of the future burden society would assume if the government continued to permit the "Old World" to dump its "defective and diseased classes on Canadian soil."[47] Clarke was not interested in identifying particular types of mental illness for clinical purposes (advancing psychiatric treatment within asylums): rather, his ambition to "build a great nation" using only the "best materials" appears to be primarily economic and political. To encourage his program, Clarke proposed that "the inspection of immigrants should be lifted out of the slough of practical politics and placed in the hands of scientific men."[48]

Later, in 1933, Dr. H.A. Bruce, then the lieutenant-governor of Ontario, reported that the Canadian population had doubled between 1871 and 1931, yet the prevalence of mental illness had increased six-fold.[49] The blame for the estimated near-crisis level of mental illness in Canada was placed squarely on the influx of "defective" and "feeble-minded" immigrants that Dr. Clarke had warned about nearly two decades earlier.[50]

In the political climate of early-twentieth-century Canada, racial categories that grew out of scientific discourse combined with what Ian Dowbiggin refers to as "a visceral suspicion of foreigners."[51] These social-scientific ideas about "the immigrant" worked their way into the courtroom through the testimonies of psychiatric experts such as Drs. Clarke and Bruce, as well as through common-sense understandings of the country's well-publicized immigration and mental hygiene problem. Foreign-born whites, and those of foreign-born parentage, particularly from southern and eastern European countries, were routinely classified as weak-minded or socially degenerate.

If they did not speak English clearly, were unemployed, or exhibited any reluctance to fully "Canadianize"[52] themselves, immigrants were routinely classified as illiterate, ignorant, and mentally underdeveloped. The reputations of some immigrant populations for drunkenness and violence often preceded them, and in court, evidence regarding mental competence tended to (re)affirm perceived defects in racial character rather than indicate mental "disease."

When George Dvernichuk (1930), a Ukrainian immigrant, shot his sister-in-law's family of five at close range, the detective at the scene of the crime made note in his report of the defendant's particular brand of "bad temperament." According to the police report, "he had shown, like all members of his race, a leaning towards a socialistic or communistic order of society, despite his being a resident of Canada for over 30 years ... He was typically foreign and disliked hard work. Only working when there was substantial material gain. He was very clean about his person, but smoked and drank considerably."[53] The detective opined that, "although Dvernichuk often suffered violent fits of temper ... he was fully aware of what he was doing." His impulsive, "morose," and "selfish" behaviour was not interpreted as necessarily out of character in any way, and the casual mention of his "reputation of being cruel to dumb animals" – a classic indication of mental derangement in psychiatric literature – was further evidence that he typified his "race."[54]

No psychiatric experts testified at Dvernichuk's trial regarding his state of mind at the time of the shooting, although he spent three weeks under observation at the mental hospital at Ponoka, Alberta. While Dvernichuk was under observation at the hospital, Dr. E.H. Cooke, the medical superintendent, documented that he was "a man of quick, irritable, uncontrolled temper, and such symptoms as he has exhibited during observation in this hospital, in our opinion, are of a definitely hysterical nature and not dependent on any discoverable organic disease." In a footnote, Cooke added that one of Dvernichuk's sisters, diagnosed with dementia praecox, had been a patient at the hospital since 1919, and that his "father and two brothers drank very heavily."[55] A formal plea of insanity was not introduced during the evidentiary proceedings; however, basing his approach on characterizations of Dvernichuk's poor work ethic, his draw toward communism, his violent fits of anger (described as bordering on "hysteria"), his apparent inability to assimilate – along with reports of headaches, epilepsy, and a glass eye – defence counsel argued in his closing statement to the jury that the defendant was indeed mentally defective and therefore not fully responsible.[56]

Also at issue, both during and after the trial, was the defendant's apparent lack of motive, a factor that often inspired an insanity defence in cases of murder. However, the judge determined in Dvernichuk's case that two possible motives did, in fact, exist: revenge and money. Lay witnesses testified at trial that his sister-in-law inherited a substantial sum of money when her father died. The judge theorized that Dvernichuk was angry and probably believed the inheritance should have gone to his wife (the diseased sister) instead.[57]

Through processes similar to those seen in the trials of "coloured" and "Indian" defendants, racial descriptives were consistently reiterated as evidence of mental fitness and used as guidelines to either establish or mitigate criminal responsibility. White men who were considered to be of questionable character were also subject to similar processes of racialization, although the language and underlying meanings were somewhat different. As I will show more thoroughly in the next chapter, evidence of uncontrolled passions, fits of anger, unemployment, drinking, and wife-beating was also used in cases of white men to establish a deviation from "normal" behaviour. The difference, however, is that evidence of such behaviour among white defendants was more likely to be legally and medically individualized and interpreted as real insanity than to be seen as confirmation of a naturally lower standard of heredity and civility. Also, as I demonstrate in the next chapter, degrees of "whiteness" and qualities of "character" were defined largely through discourses of class, gender, and region.

While George Dvernichuk was still under psychiatric observation following his trial, a tiny memo scribbled on Department of Justice stationery was passed from the deputy attorney general to the minister of justice that simply stated, "public opinion would be outraged if death sentence were commuted."[58] In a climate of considerable political pressure, and due to the decided absence of "medical evidence given one way or the other as to sanity or insanity," Dvernichuk was found fully responsible and hanged.[59]

Public opinion also weighed strongly in the deliberation of Catherine Tratch's case (1924), but this time it swayed in support of commutation. Women convicted for murder, regardless of racial designation, were typically characterized as infantile and weak-minded. The exceptions to this rule were women who killed their "good" husbands for illicit love or money. However, this characterization evoked a particular meaning in cases of racialized women that would further remove them from full citizenship. As with immigrant men, the standards for responsibility and normality for immigrant women were low and therefore more easily met. Gendered language also helped structure the meaning of racist discourse about criminality and responsibility.

Tratch, a thirty-eight-year-old "Galician" woman, poisoned her husband by putting strychnine in his whisky.[60] According to J.H. Currie, a local notary public and insurance agent who claimed to know Tratch and "the Ruthenian people" quite well, the idea to kill her husband came from "her big strong neighbor, a leader in the community" who showed her "attention which she [could not] resist." Her accomplice, Currie surmised, artfully gained control of her "untrained mind" and convinced her to do away with her husband. In her "almost childish mind," she had fallen in love with the scoundrel and merely "followed out [his] instructions."[61] Public outcry ensued when her conspirator, considered to be the brains behind the crime, was acquitted, leaving Tratch, a mother of eight, convicted for murder.

Defence counsel offered a variety of sociological and cultural explanations for Tratch's behaviour in a letter written following her trial, while at the same time affirming his own position as a full citizen and member of the dominant "race." From his personal observation of Mrs. Tratch, J. Harvey Hearne determined that she was not insane exactly, but did not have "the regard for the husband that is usual among people of our race." Hearne further explained that the defendant, a victim of her "greatly undeveloped mind and by reason of her being uneducated and by reason of her marriage at so young an age" (fourteen years), was "really not a woman who would act upon her own initiative."[62]

However, the trial judge was much less convinced by evidence of the defendant's weak mind and urged government authorities to ignore the considerable public pressure to commute the death sentence, which he felt was "based on ignorance of the evidence."[63] According to the judge, Tratch acted in accordance with the cold-blooded nature of her race: "The murder was deliberate and cowardly, and in its results brutal. There is not one redeeming circumstance ... So far as I can see, the only things in her favour are (1) that she is a woman; (2) that she is a Galician, and that her environment has created in her, as among many belonging to this race, an indifference to the value of human life."[64] Further impressions regarding public sentiment and evidence to establish the mental weakness of Catherine Tratch were offered in a letter from C.W. Stewart, MP for the Humboldt district. In his letter to the chief remissions officer following Tratch's conviction, Stewart included an excerpt from another letter written by an unidentified resident of Rosthern, Saskatchewan, where the crime took place, to the local secretary-treasurer of council. According to the unidentified writer, Tratch, although "physically a fully developed woman," was by nature "mentally ... a child that could be easily influenced and led astray ... The public was greatly surprised and the general feeling among those interested in the case is very high. Taking the above into consideration I would ask you to make a vigorous representation to the minister of justice on behalf of this unfortunate and weak-minded woman."[65] In his effort to "throw more light upon the attitude of the community affected,"[66] Stewart determined in another letter sent directly to the minister of justice that, although there was no evidence of a miscarriage of justice in the Tratch case, "nor was there evidence of insanity," he was "personally convinced" that Tratch was "not wholly responsible for her action."[67] Stewart's message as a representative from the community appeared to be fairly effective. In fact, the same excerpts from the unidentified writer's description of the defendant, which first appeared in Stewart's letter, also appeared in the final remissions report to the minister of justice. The remissions officer began his summary of the case with the following declaration: "Your attention may be drawn at the outset to the claim that the accused 'mentally is a child who could be easily influenced and led astray.' The under-signed is inclined to the opinion that there is very much in the material on record to support such a view. According to the information obtained from reliable sources and considering the petitions so numerously signed on behalf of this condemned woman it appears that the community sentiment is favourable to the exercise of clemency."[68] He then proceeded to outline the facts of the case, highlighting the importance of the "popular verdict" where her accomplice was concerned and the unfairness of the trial judge in not recommending mercy for the "unfortunate woman." Although we cannot be certain, it seems likely that the views of the remissions officer and represented members of the public would have been taken into account when the minister and his council commuted Catherine Tratch's sentence to life in prison. She was released after fourteen years.

Understanding the intimate relationship between constructs of racial order, social purity, and sexuality is crucial to understanding the meaning of "race" within a particular case. Women of various racial and ethnic backgrounds were racialized in ways different from those for men and from each other. But overall, most women were rendered less responsible than their male counterparts. Still, there are a few exceptions. For example, when Tommasina Teolis, a forty-five-year-old Italian woman, conspired in 1934 with two men, also Italian, to kill her husband for insurance money, she was considered by the judge to be at least as responsible for the crime as were the two men who actually committed the deed. As he put it to the jury, "have you sufficient proof that the accused, Tommasina Teolis, was aware of the crime to be committed, that she counseled it, approved of it, that she participated in it with thorough knowledge? If you have, she is responsible to the same degree as her accomplices, and perhaps more so than the other accomplices, Gagliardi and Donafrio, who would then have merely carried out her orders in execution of the plan prearranged between herself and Gagliardi."[69]

Her state of mind was never raised as an issue, and she was executed along with both of her accomplices. In this case, the character of her husband, "a poor old man" who had "worked all his life to save a few pennies for his family," was very important. Although race and gender were not explicit issues in the deliberation of her case, the evidence and the events leading up to the crime, including evidence of her "intimacy" with one of the co-accused, Leone Gagliardi, and her negligence as a wife and mother, make it clear that Teolis threatened the Christian ideal of domestic life and natural gender roles.[70]

Racialized women were overwhelmingly constructed, both in and out of the courtroom, as ignorant, childlike, and weak-minded, yet in these cases they were not found legally insane. Social/political concerns for racial purity and domestic order mixed variably with ascribed characteristics of race, sexuality, and gender to help inform and define legal interpretations of responsibility.

Conclusion

Although insanity law did not alter during the first half of the twentieth century, representations of criminal responsibility, mental defectiveness, and human deficiency were quite flexible and derived their particular meaning from different forms of cultural knowledge as well as the immediate circumstances of each case. Racism was deeply encoded in the language and meanings of criminal responsibility and cannot be fully understood in general terms or within a single theoretical framework. To sift out the complexity of these processes requires coming at the issue from different angles and analyzing it within different contexts. The Canadian murder trial is only one site of interrogation, but it is a particularly illuminating site.

Historically, the Canadian criminal justice system, through the indoctrination of racially neutral language and the selective appropriation of "expertise," has tried to present itself as objective. But these neutralizing processes have only furthered the cultural myth that race was not a factor in legal decisions. As Constance Backhouse observed, "'race' does not appear as a recognizable legal category of classification between 1900 and 1950."[71] However, various legal categories, including insanity, self-defence, and provocation – along with non-legal classifications such as ignorance, immaturity, weak-mindedness, and loss of control – were deployed by judges, lawyers, and medical witnesses in capital cases to help mitigate responsibility, lend meaning to violent behaviour, and establish the inherent character of defendants. Standards of mental capacity were subsumed in "scientific" theories that linked racial inferiority to a range of behavioural tendencies and predispositions. I have shown, for instance, how "Indians" and "half-breeds" were characterized as naturally violent and predisposed to moral indiscretion. Violence between Native Indian women and men was interpreted as evidence of savage character or simply as a ritual of Indian custom. On the other hand, respectable white men, and to a lesser extent women, were expected to know better. From their positions of privilege, white judges, juries, police officers, doctors, and government officials took as common knowledge the vile language and character of blacks, the habits of drunkenness and communistic leanings of southern European immigrants, and the natural sexual perversities of all non-Anglo women (as well as Anglo women who kept company with men of questionable character).

The central point of this chapter, therefore, has been to lay bare some of the ways in which legal measures of states of mind and criminal responsibility hinged on constructs of racial difference, constructs that were forged by a strong common-sense understanding of British authority, national identity, and white supremacy. The very ideas of degeneracy, eugenics, and moral/mental purity became inherent in the definitions and meanings of various social and individual descriptives that made articulations of, and decisions about, criminal responsibility possible.

6
Murder between "Wives" and "Husbands"

The language of early-twentieth-century courtrooms, supporting legal records, letters, and newspaper reports promoted a culturally informed and primarily middle-class understanding about the inherent nature of certain *types* of people. The cases analyzed thus far provide many examples of routine references to the "well known" and "typical" characteristics of certain "classes," the duty of jurymen to "impose the ideals of British citizenship," and the perpetual (re)casting of idealized masculine and feminine roles in formal and informal representations of responsibility knowledge.[1] As the trial and post-trial analyses of individual capital cases have shown, one of the most significant factors in making sense of a murder case was the relationship between victim and offender.

In this final chapter, I examine the dynamics of murder committed in domestic situations to show how those who killed their spouses were consistently measured against and interpreted through an idealized commonsense notion of Anglo-Christian domestic life. In cases of spousal murder, criminal responsibility and evaluations of mind-state – including whether mind-state was even considered – were negotiated through a series of moral judgments about the conjugal obligations of "a husband" and "a wife" and the willingness or ability of both defendant and victim to meet the determined standards of their sex, race, and social position. These cases also show the way in which specific forms of knowledge about an accused, as a particular *sort* of wife or husband, were produced through idealized standards of acceptable, or disreputable, domestic life.

The cases examined below include those in which murder was committed between married, common-law, or co-habiting heterosexual partners. Excluded from this grouping were cases in which the victim or offender was identified as a "girlfriend" or "boyfriend," or in which the couple did not occupy the same domestic space. Spousal murders make up a significant portion of my sample. Of the twenty-three women whom I studied, fourteen (61 percent) killed their husbands or common-law spouses. And from my sample of forty-three men, eleven (26 percent) killed their wives or common-law spouses.

My objective here is not to compare cases in which husbands killed their wives with those in which wives killed their husbands, although some noteworthy differences are mentioned. Instead, I point specifically to how Anglo-Christian ideologies, which informed the prevailing common-sense wisdom about the rules of domesticity and conjugality, provided legal, expert, and lay observers with the language and conceptual frameworks to make sense of murder committed within domestic spaces, and how this common-sense wisdom reinforced particular expectations and classifications of "wives" and "husbands." Given that every spousal murder case in my sample involved poor and lower-class couples, and given the privileged status of those in positions of judicial authority, an analysis of murder between wives and husbands also chronicles the distinctly class-based nature of judgments about conjugal discord and obligation.

Representations of Conjugality and the Domestic Space

A range of institutions and individuals interested in promoting the Anglo-Christian notion of conjugality helped shape and reinforce a utilitarian "expertise" about normal/natural domestic behaviour.[2] Psychiatrists who were interested in the social dangers of criminality were particularly well represented among those social science experts concerned with domestic practices during the pre- and post-war periods in Canada. However, other professionals – including clergymen, politicians, police officers, immigration officials, prison/reformatory officials, school officials, lawyers, and judges – also participated in the regulation of domesticity. Several non-professional groups and individuals such as church organizations, women's leagues, and middle-class urbanites also played an important role in the social, cultural, and political constitution of obligatory domestic roles in Canada.[3] The "cult of domesticity" was, therefore, a ubiquitous concept in essentialist representations of middle-class, Anglo-Christian character and was deeply imbedded in the policies and practices of Canadian law and psychiatry.[4]

Feminist historians have demonstrated the many ways in which law "defined" marital relations through pervasive assessments of gender.[5] However, we need to be cautious in making generalizations about the meaning of legal outcomes in cases involving domestic violence or murder. Terry Chapman, for instance, argues that in early-twentieth-century Alberta, it was rare for a woman to be found "not guilty" for killing her abusive husband. She also concludes that men who abused and killed their wives were typically treated leniently by judges, who assumed that a certain amount of violence was generally "expected" in a marriage.[6] But Chapman's findings do not necessarily prove to be typical. To appreciate the significance and effects of legal decision making in spousal murder cases, it is important to consider the different knowledge forms that came together to produce particular outcomes in particular contexts.

As I argued in Chapter 1, decisions about legal guilt do not adequately reflect judicial, medical, or popular understandings about criminal *responsibility*. Most women found guilty for the murder of their husbands received recommendations to mercy. And in several cases, evidence suggests that women's sentences were probably commuted *because* they had been badly treated by their husbands. Criminal justice records also show that most men who were found guilty of murdering their wives (and there were many) were eventually executed. In particular, post-trial documentation shows that decisions regarding mercy and clemency were not simply based on the legal facts that led juries to find certain defendants guilty but on common-sense and expert assessments of heterosexual conjugal norms. This is a further reminder that we need to look beyond official trial outcomes to appreciate the more nuanced and contingent nature of the criminological knowledge that shaped the meaning of particular historical events, in part through representations of conjugality and gender identity.

For example, spousal murder cases show that domestic hardship and violence were interpreted among middle-class observers as a problem of the "ignorant classes." The adjudication of spousal murder cases, therefore, served to draw class divisions in Canadian society by publicizing that "civilized" and mentally stable husbands did not abuse or kill their wives. However, even those men who were considered prone to abuse their wives, such as "Indian" men and men seen as lacking a moral education, were likely to be held accountable if they went so far as to commit murder. In this sample, five of the eleven men (45 percent) convicted for the murder of their wives received recommendations to mercy from the judge or jury; however, only three (27 percent) were saved from execution.[7] In these three cases, where the death sentence was either commuted or reduced on appeal, evidence was brought forward to establish that the condemned men were essentially good men who had been provoked by the betrayal or "indiscretions" of their not-so-good wives.

For instance, the trial judge recommended mercy in John Boyko's (1947) case due to the defendant's age (fifty-two years), evidence of his peaceful disposition, and the "possibility" that he had been reasonably provoked by his common-law spouse, who had been threatening to leave him for a younger man.[8] Since adultery was perhaps the worst crime a married woman could commit,[9] the narrative of the disloyal wife and the devoted, hardworking husband was a powerful one that could, in some cases, lead to a lighter sentence. It cannot be said, however, that this was a trend. There were several examples where the character of the murdered wife was scrutinized and found to be in bad repute; nevertheless, the husband, for several possible reasons, was executed.[10]

Conversely, women convicted for killing their husbands were typically commuted, acquitted, or given reduced sentences on appeal. As in all murder cases, the outcome of women's cases depended very much on decisions about motivation and evidence of character, their own as well as the victim's. In the few cases where women were executed for the murder of their husbands, the question of mind-state was not raised during the trial, and there appeared to be no history of domestic violence. These cases are particularly interesting because they show the way in which ideals of domesticity and conjugality helped (in)form the representations of certain women as "traitorous" wives who killed in "cold blood" for their own self-interest. The public response to the trial of Marie (Viau) Beaulne, for instance, demonstrates the integration of common-sense Christian knowledge about marriage with dominant scientific knowledge about feminine and masculine nature in decisions about responsibility.

Here, I also consider cases of women and men who killed their spouses in what courts described as a "domestic quarrel." Spousal murders interpreted as acts of revenge, passion, self-defence, provocation, and/or drunkenness – as opposed to the calculated, "cold-blooded" variety – also show the pervasive assessment and (re)inforcement of class and gender status but through somewhat different language. Women's violent responses to "domestic stress" were typically pathologized as "abnormal," whereas the violent responses of men were often interpreted as evidence of masculine "weakness." As a result, men were likely to be executed, rather than pathologized. Competing representations of mind-state, negotiated through and throughout the adjudication of spousal murder cases, reveal a great deal about gender relations during this period. Representations of mind-state in domestic cases also show the ways in which race, ethnicity, age, sexuality, and class designations helped determine what *type* of man/husband or woman/wife a defendant was. Such characterizations, in turn, determined the boundaries of conjugality, decisions about motivation, and judgments about criminal responsibility.

"Traitors" and "Cold-Blooded" Killers: The Worst Sorts of Wives

Of the fourteen women in this study who were convicted for the murder of their husbands, four (29 percent) were executed. Although this seems to support evidence of the general trend in Canada to commute women's death sentences, a closer look at cases where mercy was not granted explicates the nature of hegemonic gender discourse in legal decisions. In every case but one, where a woman was hanged for the murder of her husband, the motive was decidedly money and/or in the interest of pursuing a relationship with another man. And in three of the four cases that led to execution, a male "conspirator" was also charged in the murder.[11] The nature of the relationship between the woman and her conspirator, and the character of the identified conspirator, had a strong influence on expert and legal perceptions of the crime and on attributions of responsibility.

Dina Dranchuk's case (1934) was one exception in which the motive was considered to be money, yet the defendant was granted clemency. However, the circumstances of Dranchuk's case are in keeping with the arguments put forward in this chapter. Case documentation shows a history of "quarrelling" between the husband and wife and evidence that she "believed she was maltreated." Psychiatric evidence was put forward regarding "hysteria," and the judge determined that she was a "very ignorant" woman, one worthy of the jury's recommendation to mercy.[12]

In Tommasina Teolis' case (1934), two male conspirators were convicted and hanged along with her for the beating death of her husband. She was known to be on "intimate" terms with one of the conspirators. Although Teolis did not kill her husband by her own hand, the judge urged the jury to find her as responsible for her husband's death as the two men she reportedly hired to carry out the deed. According to the records, Teolis made a deal with the men that in return for killing her husband, they would receive a share of the life insurance she expected to receive after his death. A general disdain among observers emerged toward the woman/wife who would conspire and coldly kill for what was considered to be a small amount of money, about two thousand dollars. In his charge to the jury, the judge expressed his perturbation that such a "brutal" murder could be committed for mere money: "Gentlemen, one can understand that a man can kill for love, jealousy, anger, but to kill in cold blood ... and all this for a modest sum of money, this is unbelievable, and any person with a heart is revolted by such a crime and refuses any sympathy to its perpetrator."[13] The judge reminded the jury (whom he assumed would not imagine two thousand dollars a sum of money to justify murder), in attributing legal responsibility to the three defendants, that society was also "outrageously violated" by the crime committed, threatened by the idea that a wife would plot the death of her good, hard-working husband for his money. He implored the jury, as "serious men desirous of rendering justice," that it was their duty as enlightened Christian men to deliver justice to the culprits as well as to God and society: "I have no doubt that you will fulfil your duty even though it may be painful. Bear in mind that human justice, like divine justice, punishes always regretfully. It is not revenge that society demands, but simply justice and the reparation of wrongs ... For this purpose gentlemen, you must elevate your mind and during your deliberation keep in mind only justice to be rendered, the evidence to be studied and your conscience to be satisfied, and may Heaven enlighten you."[14] Mental capacity was not raised as an issue in the case of Tommasina Teolis; nor was it raised directly in the cases of the other three women who were hanged for murdering their husbands during this period.

As I demonstrated in Chapter 4, the assumption that one's mind-state could be affected by economic hardship was typically reflected in cases during the 1930s. However, the significance of poverty was offset in this case by the strong evidence of premeditation and calculation. As well, the fact that all three accused were Italian and thus considered naturally hot-tempered seemed to quash any serious investigation into mental competency.

The representations of conjugal and criminal responsibility in women's cases that ended in execution were quite different from those of women who were commuted or acquitted. In these cases, suggestions from the Crown or witnesses regarding a motive of extra-marital relations or want of money were typically overshadowed by evidence of mental or constitutional weakness. Recall, for instance, the case of Catherine Tratch (1924), who fell in love with, and hence under the influence of, her wealthy, charismatic neighbour, who had shown her "attention which she [could not] resist." Evidence offered during and after the trial showed that Tratch poisoned her husband with strychnine in the hope of winning the affections of her co-conspirator. However, the prevailing narrative in this case, and ultimately the mantra of an aggressive clemency campaign, was that she was a "weak-minded woman" who was unwittingly led astray from her marriage by her conniving suitor, who, although arrested, was released shortly after. As I discuss below, differing assessments of a woman's criminality – as the conspiring wife or the degenerate woman – sometimes operated simultaneously in a single case and reflected the social positions of different observers.

An important factor in decisions to commute or execute convicted husband-killers was the perceived character of the murdered husband. Women who killed upstanding men and husbands were likely to be hanged. For instance, when it was discovered that Marie (Viau) Beaulne (1929), a Quebec housewife, had conspired with her lover to poison her husband, collect his life insurance, and quickly remarry, an Ottawa newspaper reporter recounted the judge's strong words of support for the jury's decision to convict the pair without a recommendation to mercy: "The Justice severely condemned the faithless wife, for acting as she did, while her husband, a man in full strength and health, even if he was 60 years of age, was away at the shanties, toiling that he might support her. It was on January 19 that [Mr.] Viau walked 15 miles to his Montpellier home, to return to the comforts his hard work had assisted in acquiring. 'What a welcome!' exclaimed the judge."[15] It was meaningful in this case that Mr. Viau was considered to be a "good" husband. He was a hard-working man who, even in his senior years, supported his wife (considerably younger, at forty-two years) and provided her with a comfortable home. Several cases, including George Dvernichuk (1930) and Frances Harrop (1940), make reference to the men's work ethic as relevant to the establishment of "character." This notion is supported by Angus

McLaren, who also makes the point that a man's character was largely determined by his attitude toward "work."[16]

According to the Ottawa journalist, the judge in Marie Beaulne's case was visibly affected by the task of administering his first death sentence in fifteen years, in what he described to courtroom observers as the most "traitorous" case he had ever tried. As the judge commenced with sentencing Beaulne, he contrasted the decided character of her husband with that of her illicit lover: "You have been found guilty of murder. You have broken your solemn vow to duty to your husband, the man whom you swore fidelity. You loved another man who was not worthy of your husband. You now see what this has done for you. I sincerely pity you and I hope that in the few days that Providence grants you, you will realize the gravity of your crime and seek to repair it in the sight of God."[17] One might consider which "crime" the judge was referring to here, murder or adultery. After hearing the judge's solemn words, the reporter continued, "the woman paled perceptibly and her lips trembled visibly."[18]

Beaulne's accomplice, Philibert Lefebvre, was not only implicated in the death of her husband but also in the "traitorous" crime of domestic interference. After sentencing Beaulne, and as "the courtroom crowded to the doors," the judge proceeded to address Lefebvre. He placed the weight of responsibility for the death of Mr. Viau on Lefebvre, whom he believed "furnished this woman with the means of committing this crime." As for the motive, the judge surmised, "you wanted to get rid of this man Viau and then marry the woman, his wife." The judge told Lefebvre that justice had not been adequately served in this case, because he had killed Viau by poisoning him over two or three days but would have nearly two months in which to make "peace with God."[19]

The legal portrayal of Beaulne as the "faithless wife" added another layer to the story, which evolved from one of murder to that of conjugal betrayal. Beaulne and Lefebvre surely broke the law in committing murder, but perhaps more importantly, they betrayed the ideals of Christian marriage and in the process shook the moral sensibilities of both lay observers and official decision makers.

Certain citizens of Quebec and neighbouring Ontario seemed to agree with the judge's characterization of the Beaulne/Lefebvre case. One commentator wrote to the *Ottawa Journal* that there seemed to be no extenuating circumstances for the "vicious crime of this couple." After all, they freely confessed to the crime and no defence had been offered during the trial, "not even insanity." According to this writer, the two plotted in "cold-blooded deliberation" to end the life of the one man who stood between them. He contemplated that there "might have been some excuse for a crime of passion committed in the heat of a fury, but not for such a sinister, calculated, deliberate, traitorous killing." He further warned those who might be "eager to urge clemency for this couple," or who might romanticize the drama of the lovers' story, that it would be "useless to pretend that they are the stuff of which popular fancy can create heroes and heroines."[20]

However, there were those, particularly from the community of Hull, where the double execution was to take place, who urged clemency for the couple. Middle-upper-class Hull citizens in favour of commutation organized a petition-signing campaign and offered a different telling of the event, which included a survey of the circumstances they felt mitigated criminal responsibility. On 13 August 1929, an article entitled "Are Opposed to Hanging in Hull: Prominent Citizens against Double Execution and Readily Sign Petitions" appeared in the *Ottawa Evening Citizen*. It was intended to represent the voice of Hull's elite community, which was apparently fuming at the prospect of a sordid double execution taking place in its district.

In the article, Mr. Aime Guertin, a Hull county official, argued that capital punishment "should only be exercised in extreme cases where the crime had been premeditated." Guertin reasoned that the full force of the law should not be applied in this case because it appeared, "apart from the findings of the court, that Lefebvre and Viau [Beaulne] are of the ignorant class, without moral sense of the enormity of their crime." At the very least, he continued, "if these unfortunate people must be hanged, the wheels of justice should be turned at Bordeaux jail, instead of Hull."[21]

Although the question of mind-state was not formally raised here, this citizen felt that those in full control of their senses would never display such blatant disregard for civility and the vows of Christian marriage; nor would they have succumbed to such base motivations had they fully understood the consequences of their actions. The suggestion from some Hull citizens that the misguided behaviour of Beaulne and Lefebvre was the manifestation of their inferior "class" is represented in another article that appeared in the same newspaper two weeks before. This provided readers with a list of seventeen reasons for clemency that were forwarded to the minister of justice in the form of a petition.

Except for a brief reference to the general ineffectiveness of the defence counsel and concern that the desired symbolic effect of a double execution would be lost on the backward community of Montpellier, "ignorance" and "class" (of the uncivilized rural kind) were the principal reasons cited by Quebec urbanites for clemency in this case. Listed, for instance, was the fact that Beaulne and Lefebvre were "raised in the wilds," in a district "scarcely touched by civilization" and where "education is as yet in its infancy." Concern was voiced that the two had not received "religious instruction" and had therefore not been "given the chance to develop their intellectual faculties" in order to learn to "subvert their brutal passions" and "natural desires." The lay observer also informed readers that "there are different degrees of responsibility in committing this crime." Borrowing from the language of law, the writer also suggested that no evidence had established that the accused knew the "consequences" or "penalties for their act."

As well as offering general characterizations of the two accused as ignorant rural types, the report stipulated that special consideration be given to the facts that Beaulne had four young children and "is now in a delicate condition" (later proved to be false), and that Lefebvre had "risked his life for four years at the front" and "contributed his share with 'glory and merit' to the winning of the war." Finally, in pointing out the appropriate social role of the rule of law in this case, the author again remarked that ignorance was so prevalent in the rural district from which the couple hailed that "the hanging of this pair would not be an example or a deterrent to others who might contemplate similar crimes." Therefore, life in prison was a much more "suitable" penalty in this case.[22] Supporters of clemency were mindful to position the condemned couple at a safe distance – socially and naturally – from themselves. However, they also seemed to recognize the couple as worthy of sympathy in suggesting that even in their wild and untrained states, this "brute" and this "wife" managed to contribute to society in the only ways they knew – he by going to war and she by bearing children.

References to "the husband" and "the wife" in newspapers and case files were deeply symbolic and carried with them a battery of implied meanings, which writers often tried to explain, so obvious did they appear. In the common-sense wisdom of "respectable" Christian Canadians, certain duties came with each role, and certain boundaries protected the domestic space. Two of the most important rules of domesticity dictated that husbands were to provide for their wives and that wives were not to betray their husbands. Legal responses to the trial of Marie Beaulne and her lover for the murder of her husband were generally those of outrage, a reaction that also seemed to be shared by respectable citizens. Beaulne was pitied as an ignorant and intellectually underdeveloped woman; at the same time, she was demonized as a traitor and cold-blooded killer. But it was through these conflicting characterizations of the defendant as a woman who was "faithless" by nature that she emerged in this narrative as the most dangerous sort of wife imaginable.

"Domestic Quarrels" and Dead Bodies

Murders committed in the heat of a "domestic quarrel" were viewed differently from those that appeared to be calculated and without reasonable provocation. Here the defendant's state of mind was almost certainly raised as an issue, either during trial or during the commutation stage, although psychiatric experts were consulted in only about half of the cases. A formal defence of insanity was raised in seven spousal murder cases, and each time, domestic stress was considered a precipitating factor.

Accused wife-killers who appeared to lack a healthy work ethic, drank habitually, or beat their wives were considered to be weak in character and constitution.[23] They were seen as untrustworthy, ignorant, and not good "husband" material. The women who married them were, therefore, also considered to be of an undiscerning sort with equally questionable characters. They were "brooding" and "hysterical" women who found themselves living in impoverished conditions and in a perpetual state of domestic disharmony.[24] As mentioned above, the idea that living in an "unhealthy" domestic environment could cause mental instability and abnormal violent behaviour was commonly understood and reflected in case file texts. Knowledge about the domestic space in which the accused and victim lived was relevant at every stage of the criminal justice process and was an important factor in decisions about mind-state and criminal responsibility.

Evidence at the trial of Dina Dranchuk (1934), for instance, showed that the domestic life she shared with her husband was "not a happy one." According to the judge, the couple's daily quarrelling was caused by the "failure of the husband to supply his wife with what she considered necessary money. She complained that he did not supply her with the money to buy warm clothing."[25] Two psychiatrists testified that Mrs. Dranchuk, though perhaps not legally insane, did present symptoms of mental abnormality and "hysteria." Dr. Taylor, testifying for the defence, told the court that she was "not normal, mentally," that she "brooded over her obsessions of illness" and "believed she was maltreated" by her husband.

According to Taylor, she struck out at her husband and killed him with an axe without realizing the consequences of her act. From his assessment of the accused, Taylor determined that "she followed a blind impulse, expressing herself in a blind hysteria."[26] Dr. Baragar, testifying for the Crown, made it clear that "she may be suffering from hysteria, but only in a marked degree is this condition treated as insanity." After the trial, the judge reported to the minister of justice that Mrs. Dranchuk, "apparently a very ignorant woman," was "oblivious to all that was going on around her; not once during the trial did she look up or show any sign of appreciating the nature of the proceedings." Given that, by the judge's own account, "the wife was unable to speak or understand English," this detached behaviour in the courtroom is not difficult to explain.[27]

Representations of spousal murders committed within the domestic space combined social-economic explanations with positivist ideas about criminality in a way that naturalized poverty and violence in lower-class, immigrant foreigners' marriages. However, it was also understood that even people of strong constitution could turn mad, if for a brief period, in the face of domestic contrariety.[28] Recall the case of John Boyko (1947), the hard-working man of good character and "peaceful disposition," but also a "foreigner," who killed his common-law wife with a hammer. The court in this case did not take seriously the defendant's claim that he acted in self-defence. It made more sense to the judge that Boyko was provoked to the point of losing control in response to threats from his wife to leave him and marry a younger man. Basing his stance on the "possibility" of reasonable provocation, the judge (but not the jury) recommended mercy, and Boyko's death sentence was commuted.

The use of a provocation defence in spousal murder cases also set up a framework that could reduce estimations of criminal responsibility by jurors, judges, remissions branch officials, and the minister of justice.[29] The emotional state produced by provocation was known to cause, in certain circumstances, a loss of control, insanity, and other forms of mental breakdown.[30] Provocation could function as a defence as well as a motive and was usually considered in conjunction with other emotional states such as revenge, passion, anger, or jealousy. As we have seen, provocation was one way in which a defendant's mind-state could be raised without formally entering an insanity plea, and this proved to be a particularly useful tactic in the adjudication of murder between wives and husbands.

The legal requirements for provocation were stretched and even redefined in cases of spousal murder where the desertion of a spouse from his or her conjugal and domestic responsibilities counted as reasonable provocation. Reasonable provocation could include an array of behaviours and failures, such as repeated drunkenness or sexual promiscuity, failing to provide or keep a proper home, or failing to protect the privacy and sanctity of the domestic space.[31] These indiscretions, or failures, do not easily fit within the *Criminal Code*'s legal criteria of reasonable provocation as produced by "blows, words or gestures," but in the context of domestic murders, they became meaningful and legally significant.

Although provocation was often raised in domestic cases, the meaning of conjugality and the parameters of domestic duty varied for different *types* of heterosexual couples. This translated, therefore, into different medical and legal interpretations of provocation based on hegemonic concepts of race, class, and gender. Recall, for instance, the case of Louis Jones, the "coloured" man hanged for the murder of his runaway wife in Halifax. In Jones' case, a defence of provocation was argued and the seriousness of the crime was diminished in the defence lawyer's account of the event as simply a "row between husband and wife."

The case, according to the lawyer, did not inspire concern from the public; furthermore, he told the minister of justice in a letter that this extreme act of violence was not uncharacteristic between married people of Jones' "class," in which "the wife" was regarded as his "property" and something to be "desired."[32] The boundaries of conjugality and criminal responsibility, as well as the social meaning of the event, were defined in each case according to the perceived position and constitution of victim and accused. This was also evident in the trial of Albert Le Beaux (1920), during which it was suggested that though "wife-beating" was uncommon in civilized society, it was a matter of "custom" among Indians.

Similarly, when Paul Abraham (1944), a "half-breed," was arrested for killing his wife in a "fury," the reporting constable made reference to "the mode of life followed by these people" in which it was considered "not uncommon for Indians and half-breeds to beat their wives." During Abraham's trial (also referred to in Chapter 5), his defence counsel, W.J. Beaumont, cross-examined the victim's father, who was also the chief of Abraham's tribe, regarding the marital "status" of the Indian couple. In doing so, defence counsel drew a line between legitimate/respectable and illegitimate/unrespectable unions:

Q [Beaumont]: Your daughter, she is legally married to Abraham?
A: The old style of the Indian; that is the way they were married.
Q: And how many times can the Indians get married that way? ... Could the woman get married more than once according to your custom? According to the custom of your tribe, of which you are chief, can a woman get married a second time while her first husband is still alive?
A: As long as the husband is living they can live but if the husband dies she can get another husband.
Q: But not unless he dies?
A: Because we get along good.
Q: Your daughter's first husband is still alive isn't he?
A: No.
Q: Doesn't he live at Rocky Mountain House now?
A: No. He is dead ...
Q: You are swearing that your daughter only has two husbands – Jasper Paul and Paul Abraham? Is that correct?
A: Yes, that is it ... She was gone with a fellow and I would not allow her to get married with this fellow and she did not want to get married with him.
Q: Well she never has been *properly* married to anybody, has she?
A: Never ...
Q: Do you believe that it is the law of Canada for a man and a woman to be married in a church?
A: I believe it for the white man, because the white man was given that and he was also given the church.
Q: But it is not the law of the Indian? Is that right?
A: We are using it. God has made his laws. He puts down the rain and the grain grows and we all live from there.
Q [the court]: Is it the law of Canada that the white man be married in a church?

> *A [Beaumont]:* Not necessarily. But that is as far as I can go with this simple type of man.[33]

This exchange provides a good example of the way in which legal interpretations of spousal murder were framed according to Christian values regarding marriage. Beaumont's point seems to have been that, because the Abraham marriage was not a "proper" one (it had not taken place in a church before God), the couple could not be held to the rules dictated by a Christian marriage.

Thomas MacInnes, the secretary of Indian affairs and drafter of the 1910 federal *Immigration Act,* was also interested in the impression the Abraham case would make on the remote Alberta community of Cherhill. He proposed in a letter to the chief remissions officer that the case should be used to "disabuse" the "old aboriginal idea that the husband has power of life and death over his wife, and can exercise it at his caprice."[34] Again and again, the case files reveal the not-so-subtle ways in which elitist assumptions about domestic violence, seen as both a product and a symptom of the ignorance and weakness of inferior classes and races, were legitimized and strengthened through interrogations of the quality and status of the domestic lives of lower-working-class and non-Anglo defendants on trial for spousal murder.

In the same way that constructs of class and race could set the boundaries of "normal" behaviour between wives and husbands, interpretations of defendants' states of mind turned on assessments of the circumstances leading up to fatal domestic quarrels. The culpability of accused murderers depended very much on who killed whom, and, more importantly, why. "Domestic stress" and "provocation" were not gender-neutral concepts, as the trials of James McGrath, Mary Smith, Dina Dranchuk, and Frances Harrop attest. Accounts of responsibility in these cases incorporated common-sense knowledge about what naturally provoked women and what naturally provoked men.

James McGrath's act of repeatedly stabbing his wife was perceived by the trial judge as that of a "mad-man" but not of a legally insane man. He told the jury in his charge that McGrath was "simply giving up on an extreme passion, the act almost of a wild animal."[35] However, unlike in the cases of most women, or non-Anglo men whose "passions" were often articulated in biological terms, the judge in this case determined that the husband's "difficulty ... was that he was unable to support the wife and child and was dependent upon the mother to support them all."[36] As a result, McGrath's failure to control his passion was interpreted as a constitutive failure of his Anglo manhood.

However, explanations of the *circumstances* that gave rise to McGrath's explosive behaviour were based on the married couple's deviation from the common-sense domestic ideal. In fact, much of the theorizing about McGrath's "loss of control" came from non-medical witnesses. For example, in a report written by the constable in charge of the investigation, the defendant's "mental strain" was attributed to the fact that his wife insisted on leaving him and taking away their infant son. According to the constable, this emotional strain was exacerbated by McGrath's financial situation, which prevented him from following her. The constable reported that the defendant's "highly emotional" and "hysterical" state was "no doubt" also affected by the fact that "he had not had sexual relations with his wife for the past eighteen months."[37]

McGrath's mental state was also commented upon at the trial by the coroner, Dr. Arnold Smith. To establish prior instances of abnormal behaviour, the doctor was asked by the Crown in cross-examination to report on an incident in which the accused lost control because his wife "disappeared":

> *Q [the Crown]:* You think that is the reason for his difficulty at that time. There was no doubt in your mind at that time that he suffered from some kind of mental anguish?
>
> *A:* I would say it was extreme mental anguish, yes.
>
> *Q:* And I suppose that condition would naturally weaken a man's will power or a man's ability to throw off, would it not?

Dr. Smith stressed to the court that he was "not an expert psychiatrist" but nevertheless went on to confirm that "there is a tendency to wear down a man's mental resistance by upsets of that kind."[38] The relevance of a healthy domestic life was reinforced here by the common-sense wisdom that a man's mental resistance could be worn down "in such an event as a wife leaving a husband." McGrath's "emotional" disturbance was considered by the judge to represent a weakness in his masculinity – his failed "power of resistance" – brought on by his inability to assume his proper duties and pleasures as a husband.

Although James McGrath was found legally sane, the understanding that he was not in a "right state of mind" when he killed his wife was freely acknowledged by the judge as a matter of both legal fact and common sense. The language evoked in the judicial representation of McGrath's character and state of mind certainly borrowed freely from psychiatric knowledges, yet the court rejected the idea that the case required the specialized knowledge and diagnostic skills of an "expert." According to the judge, it only made sense that anyone who committed such an act "would certainly be in the wrong state of mind"; furthermore, he stated, "I don't think it would take a doctor to tell us that."[39]

Mary Smith, identified in court records as a "Half-breed," shot her husband, a returned soldier and "Englishman," during a heated "domestic quarrel."[40] Although a formal insanity plea was not entered at trial, the basis of her defence was nevertheless that she suffered under a profound mental deficiency. Smith testified on her own behalf that on the night of the murder her husband threatened to beat her, as he had many times in the past. On the witness stand, she recounted the same story she had given to a police officer before she was taken into custody. She told the officer that her husband threatened her and came after her with a gun; they struggled, and he dropped the gun. She kicked the gun under the bed, and after he fell asleep she retrieved it. When he came after her again later that night, she pointed the gun and shot him in self-defence.[41]

However, her first-hand account of what happened was not supported by the forensic evidence, which showed instead that the deceased was asleep when he was shot and that his body was moved once he was dead. Based on this evidence, the judge decided that the more likely "inspiration and motive for the crime" was that her husband threatened to sell their property, take the proceeds, and leave her "penniless." He deduced, "the prospect of him doing this so upset the accused that she took this terrible method to prevent such a thing happening. In any event, under all the circumstances, it appeared that the accused was terribly upset, and was not without considerable amount of provocation."[42] In his report to the minister of justice, the judge drew attention to the fact that Smith did not shoot her husband during their heated argument or in response to the immediate threat of death; instead, she shot him after the argument while he lay asleep. According to the judge, Smith "had taken advantage of the fact that he was asleep so as to make sure that the shot would be effective and that their troubles apparently would be over."[43]

Smith's testimony in court, as recorded in the trial transcripts, seemed to be quite lucid and articulate. Furthermore, according to the judge, she was "the most intelligent witness he had ever seen." However, revealing the significant gap between medical and legal assessments of mind-state and responsibility that often appeared in capital cases, Dr. MacNiel, a psychiatric expert, testified for the defence that she was a "congenital mental defective" who did not possess the intelligence to appreciate the nature of her act.[44] Defence counsel asked the doctor about a "hallucination" Smith reportedly experienced a "hairy man coming to her bed and choking her." She testified that the image represented her fear of her husband, but defence counsel insisted it was either a "condition of hysteria" or "epilepsy." The doctor did not originally offer these two diagnoses in his own evaluation of the defendant, but when defence counsel asked which diagnosis he thought was most likely in Smith's case, he concluded that "her reaction to fear for her life would be that of an abnormal person." The cause, he proposed, could be either "hysteria or epilepsy brought on by her mental defectiveness." The violent context in which the defendant lived prior to the murder was never considered; nor was there an attempt to dispute it as a fact. Instead, it was her psychological and emotional *reaction* to her situation that came under scrutiny and was deemed in the end to be "abnormal."[45]

The medical-legal account of Smith's abnormal state of mind that ultimately led her to lose control and kill her husband was quite different from the masculinized version of McGrath's loss of control. Although not legally excusable, McGrath's actions were nevertheless seen as reasonable. It seemed reasonable to several observers that any man under such stressful domestic circumstances would be provoked to violence. His perceived weakness, therefore, was his inability as a man to control his passions in such trying times. By contrast, Smith's reaction to her domestic circumstances, where fear of physical danger could also be seen as reasonably provoking, was constructed as "abnormal" and therefore excusable.[46]

However, in Smith's case, Dr. MacNiel's "expert" status did not ensure his testimony a position of privilege in the courtroom. The judge was most reluctant to accept the expert's opinion that Smith was mentally defective and not criminally responsible for her husband's death, even though his testimony maintained the common-sense wisdom that women who killed were mentally abnormal. In his report to the minister of justice, the judge downplayed the viability of MacNiel's testimony and reinforced the authority of culturally constituted attitudes regarding marriage, conjugality, and domesticity in legal decisions:

> There was expert medical evidence to the effect that the accused had a mental capacity of a child of the age of eight and a half years. This expert evidence, however, was largely discounted by the ability and mental capacity of the accused, displayed as a witness in the witness box. She showed herself to be a woman of more than ordinary intelligence, and proved herself to be one of the most intelligent witnesses who gave evidence at the trial. It appeared clear, therefore, that she had either fooled the doctors when they were giving her the test examination, or that their examination was not sufficient on which to base a real expert opinion.[47]

When the judge asked the doctor at trial if it were possible that Smith had tricked him into thinking she was insane, he defensively replied, "I don't think so. I have examined a good many people in jails. I have been examining for the Attorney-General's Department for twenty odd years, and I think I have now had enough experience so that I know whether this woman was fooling me."[48] In the end, the judge recommended mercy, despite his reservations about the defendant's character, because he perceived the threat to her personal economic stability, particularly during the depression, as a legitimate cause of provocation. Her husband's threat to desert her, therefore, was taken up as far more disconcerting than his threat to beat her.

The idea that domestic deprivation could drive women to madness and murder coincided with the moral outlook of medical and legal men and their decisions about motivation and responsibility. However, the plight of impoverished wives also concerned the public. After the news of Dina Dranchuk's death sentence, a Mr. Matt O'Reilly urged the women of Alberta to write the minister of justice in support of her clemency: "I have no fault to find with judge or jury, but I have with the women of this province if they do not ask Hon. Hugh Guthrie to reduce the sentence to life imprisonment." O'Reilly went on to state that the women of Alberta were obligated to stand up for other women and families hard hit by the depression, living in dire straits, and staring down madness:

> Knowing the conditions as I do of the north country, where women are on the verge of insanity from looking down empty flour barrels, no clothes, and other necessary things, even to being sick, places me in a position to show that she did not bring out the distress she was labouring under to show what drove her to the rash act. It is common property, and anyone knows that the way relief is pinched out to some, that it discourages a man to ask for it, but the women must do the suffering constantly looking at the poverty that surrounds her. Personally I would not want this woman to hang because of the neglect of others.[49]

It was well understood, according to O'Reilly, that poverty affected men and women differently. Women were apparently driven insane and suffered emotionally and psychologically, whereas men suffered damage to their masculine pride.

However, not everyone was sympathetic to the plight of women during this period, or toward commuting women's death sentences in Canada. For instance, in a stinging letter to the editor of the *Calgary Albertan* signed "A MERE MAN," the writer voiced his frustration regarding the leniency extended to women who killed their husbands. He protested, "dozens of murders have been committed by women in the last 20 years," and "in several cases husbands had their heads hacked off or battered by their wives while they slept, yet hardly one woman has paid the penalty." This writer was particularly concerned about the extreme bias he had been witnessing in the adjudication of Canadian and American domestic murder cases, which was based on the misguided "assumption that a woman, and especially a wife and mother, can do no wrong." Therefore, he continued, "if a man murders his wife, ... he is a brute and must be hanged, but if she murders him, no matter how atrociously, oh, well, he is a brute anyway and brought it all on himself, while she is a downtrodden saint and must be let off. This assumption is totally unwarranted. There are many men whose lives are made miserable by their wives, but if one of them solves the problem as

Mrs. Fusty and Mrs. Dranchuk did, he soon finds himself dangling on the end of a rope."[50]

Some men claimed "discrimination" on the part of justices, but women overwhelmingly came out in strong support of other women who were required to take such drastic actions to end their domestic ordeals. Recall, for example, the case of Frances Harrop, in which the judge cited the "dreadful" living conditions of the Harrop family as the primary cause of her "brooding" and eventual loss of control. The psychiatrist, Dr. Harry Speechly, diagnosed Mrs. Harrop with a menopausal condition referred to as "climacteric insanity," which he claimed had caused her to react in an abnormal and extreme way to her domestic situation. However, the public, particularly middle-class women, felt that the conditions under which Harrop lived and the failures of her husband to provide for her served as ample causes for provocation.

One woman, describing Harrop's husband as "a man lacking in all the attributes which go to make marriage what it should be," claimed that "provocation of the extremest kind" existed in Harrop's case.[51] A letter to the minister from the Home Welfare Association in Winnipeg supported the public's sentiment that Harrop deserved clemency, basing its argument on the following grounds:

1) The crime was committed under great provocation,
2) The woman had been brooding so long that she had become obsessed with the idea that her husband's death was the only way out of all her troubles,
3) The sympathy of a very large majority of Winnipeg women towards Mrs Harrop is very much in evidence.[52]

Representations of the circumstantial or emotional context of spousal murders varied from case to case, but the notion that domestic stress could drive men and women to lose control of their minds – though not necessarily to the point of legal insanity where they could be found not criminally responsible – was constant. Several competing characterizations emerged in the case of Frances Harrop. She was simultaneously seen as neglected by a failed husband, as an insane menopausal housewife, and as a woman provoked by want of money and profound domestic instability. Competing explanations attest to the specificity and diversity of legal decisions in cases of spousal murder (and capital cases in general), but they also reveal the many different ways in which the cult of domesticity was constituted and perpetuated through routine medical, legal, and popular assessments of gender, class, and race during this period.

Conclusion

Spousal murder cases offer telling insights into the state of gender relations at this time and show the way in which factors such as race/ethnicity, age, sexuality, and class designation helped determine what *type* of man/husband or woman/wife a defendant was considered to be. In turn, judgments about a defendant's character helped to shape the discursive and practical boundaries of conjugality, motivation, and criminal responsibility. The specific meanings of conjugality and the domestic space in spousal murder cases were central to the legal task of (re)constructing the events/circumstances leading to murder and ultimately of establishing the culpability of the offender – particularly in cases where the precipitating events leading to spousal murder were described as a "domestic quarrel" or the result of an unfortunate "domestic situation." However, even when evidence of a domestic quarrel was not brought to the foreground, as in the case of Marie Beaulne, lawyers, witnesses, and public observers still offered some commentary on the quality, status, and characteristics of the domestic life shared by victim and offender.

Through processes similar to those in which racialized or poor defendants were judged and classified as particular *types* of people, spousal homicides were classified as a special type of murder case. In each instance, evidence of reputation and character was particularly important, but perhaps more important was the intimate relationship between the victim and the killer, and the obligations bound by that relationship.

7
Concluding Thoughts

The historiographical exercise of arranging and reporting the socio-cultural, political, and institutional meanings of criminal responsibility in early-twentieth-century Canada immediately brings to the fore a clear impression of the sensibilities and concerns of historical observers, those who reported, diagnosed, adjudicated, administrated, or simply wrote about individual cases. However, the personal narratives of those who were actually on trial for murder – how they might have accounted for their own motivations and actions – were systemically silenced and rearranged in these particular case files, largely, I would say, through the discursive processes of truth-seeking and fact-finding. It is unquestionably important that historians seek out and pay attention to the ways in which offenders' self-representations (or counter-representations) challenged and/or contributed to medical and legal decisions.

Finding defendant-centred narratives absent from these judicial procedures and from the case files generally, though infuriating, signals a couple of important things. First, given the marginalized demographic makeup of individuals convicted for murder in Canada, it exemplifies, in a very material way, the privileged role of upper-middle-class Anglo-Christian, and in particular Protestant, ideals in legal decision making. Second, it shows a firm resistance on the parts of legal officials, psychiatrists, and the concerned public to accepting alternative, unknown, lines of reasoning in making sense of murder cases. The primary aim of this book has been to draw out and question the conditions of responsibility knowledge in Canadian criminal law, medicine, and society. In tracing different themes, each chapter revealed some of the ways in which knowledge about criminal responsibility was produced, organized, and legitimized in and through institutional structures, legal procedures, science, cultural representations of identity, and overlapping narratives of mind-state.

In placing the concept of "responsibility" at the centre of this interdisciplinary inquiry, rather than focusing on concepts of "insanity" or "guilt," this book complicates generalized arguments about the role and authority of psychiatric experts, the nature of expertise, and the historical relationship between law and psychiatry. Also, in conceptualizing the notion of criminal responsibility as a contingent cultural product, we must recognize the professional and institutional practices that went toward establishing the boundaries of responsibility knowledge as cultural products. And by extension, we must read the form and content of capital case files themselves as cultural texts in order to appreciate their specific meanings.

Official representations of law may at times suggest that the legal criteria for establishing criminal responsibility were sharply defined and did not accommodate subtle social-cultural shadings or other non-legal factors such as citizenship, gender, and social status. However, this was not the case. At every stage of the murder trial, the accused's life circumstances, ancestry, character, and disposition came under scrutiny. Even when the question of legal responsibility appeared to be settled with the guilty verdict, plenty of room remained for negotiation in determining whether mercy would be granted.

Therefore, we see from the start, with the introduction of Elizabeth Tilford's case, that criminal responsibility was not at all a fixed concept in Canadian law, with clean-cut boundaries and predictable measures. The standards and meanings of responsibility knowledge were (re)negotiated according to the context and circumstances of each case, the character of those involved in the murder, and the concerns and sensibilities of individual legal observers and decision makers. Chapter 2 addressed the issues of "authorship" and "authority" by laying bare some of the long-hidden institutional structures that shaped the production of capital case files and the disposition process. As the primary author of the files, the chief remissions officer played a pivotal role in directing both the official representation of cases and, indeed, the final outcome of some commutation decisions.

This book has also revealed a disjuncture between broadly cast historical and professional accounts of the relationship between law and psychiatry in the West, and the specific ways in which law and psychiatry bumped up against each other in the context of early-twentieth-century Canadian capital murder cases. Although individual psychiatric experts did not seem to improve their professional status by serving as expert witnesses in capital murder trials, the routine linking of law and expert knowledge certainly seemed to perpetuate the appearance of science as a legitimate way of knowing certain kinds of criminals and of law as a neutral fact-finding machine. To this end, I deconstructed, at least in part, the forged divide between *expert knowledge* and *common-sense knowledge* by showing that what counted as expert opinion evidence in capital cases typically served to reinforce, rather than enlighten, common sense. I do not mean that expert knowledge in a broader social-cultural sense was nothing more than common sense in disguise: rather, I propose that an inherent paradox existed in the adjudication of expert knowledge. Through selective appropriation and interpretation, legal decision makers capitalized on the growing popular trust in psychiatry as a scientific authority on criminality, without compromising legal authority over the decision-making process. Most significantly, such an approach did not compromise the Protestant tenets of British Canadian law.

Judicial efforts to qualify certain medical witnesses as experts – some of whom lacked specialization in psychiatry – clearly indicate that the *idea* of expert knowledge was important to legal decision makers during this period. However, due to the very nature of the adversarial system, the limited language of criminal law defences, and the routine selection of certain forms of expert evidence as more truthful than others, the *effect* in the courtroom (and beyond) was essentially a levelling of expert knowledge with common-sense knowledge. Therefore, rather than privileging expert opinion *because* it came from learned experts, judges and juries seemed to privilege only those aspects of expert evidence that most made sense to them.

Courtroom tensions between judges, lawyers, and psychiatric expert witnesses were not unusual during this period, as experts struggled to maintain professional dignity and have their testimonies heard by juries, and judges worked to maintain law's firm grip over questions of mind-state. Yet, in order for experts to be heard by juries and their testimonies to be seen as legally relevant by judges, a necessary synchronization of common-sense and expert knowledge occurred on the basic elements of human behaviour and, in particular, on that of *known* criminal types. Given that judges regularly advised juries to assess all evidence (including expert evidence) equally and according to their own common sense and experience, appealing to that common sense in their testimonies, especially when introducing "new" psychiatric concepts, was in the best interests of experts. Therefore, *what* was said may have been more important than *who* said it.

Although the rise of psychiatric expertise on mental disorders and criminality did not result in changes to Canadian criminal law, judicial attempts to negotiate the boundaries of criminal responsibility did allow room for new ways of identifying and explaining certain kinds of criminals through the appropriation of psychiatric knowledge. As we have seen, the most dominant narratives of criminality to emerge in capital murder cases during the early to mid-twentieth century drew on theories of degeneracy. The *idea* of degeneracy came to be understood as much more than a mere psychiatric classification; it also provided a general conceptual framework for articulations of criminal responsibility and mind-state that could be bent to accommodate the particular concerns and conditions of the moment. Degeneracy was concurrently expressed as the affliction of certain types or classes of individuals, as well as a foreboding condition of Canadian society as a whole.

A number of cases featured elements that were believed to lead to degeneracy, such as growing up poor or in domestic disharmony. In some instances, these were identified as possible reasons to temper justice with mercy. In others, these same conditions became reasons to exercise the full force of the law as an implement of social control – to set an example. Decisions regarding the appropriate role of law during times of national instability were not a matter of standard policy or practice: rather, they were formed on a case-by-case basis and clearly reflected the current political climate.

The trials of Dina Dranchuk (1934) and Frank Patrick (1941) revealed this reciprocal process particularly well, whereby specific social-historical conditions, such as poverty and war, shaped the institutional significance of certain texts, and how the reading of these texts in turn reveals the social-cultural tensions and nuances of the time and place in which they were produced. Although many theories circulated throughout professional and lay communities in Canada and beyond regarding the precise nature and cause of degeneracy and feeblemindedness, the essential idea that degeneracy, in its many forms, *could* mitigate criminal responsibility was rarely contested. The question in some cases, particularly from concerned members of the public, was *should* it?

In recognizing the contextual specificity and shifting nuances in each case, I have argued that assessments of the particular factors that influenced interpretations and representations of criminal responsibility must be considered on a case-by-case basis. Broadly cast generalizations about the relationship between law and psychiatry; the role of law and the psychiatric expert in criminal cases; the political significance of capital punishment; the historical meanings of race, class, and gender; the use of the insanity defence; and/or the meaning of a guilty verdict will necessarily gloss over the important cracks and rough edges in Western medico-legal history. From my perspective, it is only in tracing the contours of the cracks and rough edges that we are able to make out the cultural features of law.

Variations in the conditions of responsibility knowledge, as they are constituted and applied in each case, are not easily discernible in the official documentation of a case and its outcome. We must look beyond reported cases, beyond outcomes, and beyond the most obvious legal sites in order to appreciate the cultural significance of responsibility knowledge and the meaning of specific legal decisions. When we look to alternative legal sites where negotiations of mind-state took place, we can see, for instance, that legal assessments of mind-state were often based on moral assessments of "character." Character, like degeneracy, was a flexible idea that subsumed theories about natural race, class, and gender difference, and acquired meaning according to a range of contextual circumstances. Recall the case of Mary Smith, in which the remissions officer identified the defendant as a "Half-breed" and her husband as an "Englishman" in the first lines of his report to the minister of justice in order to flag the "known" dangers of mixing blood in birth and marriage.

Common signs of degeneracy and/or mental incapacity – such as uncontrolled passions, fits of anger, unemployment, drinking, and wife-beating – were also used to describe the natural tendencies of racialized, sexualized, and similarly "othered" individuals. Post-trial documentation revealed exceptionally well that decisions regarding mercy and clemency were not simply based on the legal facts that led juries to find certain defendants guilty but on common-sense and expert assessments of what was considered normal. For instance, representations of spousal murders committed within the domestic space combined social-economic explanations with positivist ideas about criminality in a way that naturalized poverty and violence in lower-class marriages. However, as the case of Frances Harrop (1940) demonstrated, it was also "known" that even people of the strongest constitution could briefly turn mad in the face of domestic dissention.

In this book, I have imagined responsibility not as a legal fact but as a negotiable idea. And therefore I have cautioned against focusing our critical gaze solely on the formal guilty verdict, which reveals little about the adjudication process and the many shades of criminal responsibility that emerge over the course of a trial and post-trial proceedings. Through these contingent processes of (re)negotiation, the classification of criminal types and the moral/class/sexual superiority of the masculine Anglo-Christian legal subject were reified. The legal site in which a defendant's mind-state was addressed (such as the stage of the judicial process and/or the defence pursued at trial) helped define the boundaries of plausible narratives as well as determine *who* had decision-making power – experts, juries, legal officials, and/or the public. The question of who should have the authority to decide matters of mind-state and criminal responsibility was always an issue in capital cases, and would later become an important consideration in the 1953 *Royal Commission on the Laws of Insanity as a Defence in Criminal Cases,* which marks the end of the period covered by this study.

The 1953 commission punctuated a pinnacle time in Canada's history when questions about the boundaries of criminal responsibility, brewing for well over fifty years, were formally addressed. No substantive changes were made to the *Criminal Code* as a result of the commission, but a number of important debates emerged during the hearings that reflected and were informed by political concerns about the nature of insanity and its relationship to the perceived worsening of social descent and criminality in Canada. The five-member committee, made up of two judges, two psychiatrists, and a prominent businessperson, addressed questions regarding the scope and language of insanity law, the burden of proof, the proposed addition of standards for "diminished" responsibility, and several key factors relating to the legal role and authority of psychiatric experts. My study of the work of commission is ongoing.

This book is in no way a definitive social history of how criminal responsibility was understood and decided in Canadian capital murder cases. It is but one reading of the evidence. I have tried to remain mindful of the perspectives and interests of the many authors and audiences represented in the case files, as well as of my own social position and personal biases in reading, organizing, and presenting the archival sources as evidence. This has not always been easy, given the nature of the material. As I indicated at the start, one need not dig deeply to reveal the influencing attitudes of texts' authors. However, in stepping back from this historical analysis, I am perhaps more struck by its familiarity than by its "new" findings. I note an unsettling sameness between these historical accounts and our current thinking regarding criminality and responsibility. For instance, we continue to psychiatrize women who behave violently or out of step with the traditional heterosexual Christian principles of conjugal and maternal obligation, such as those women who kill their abusive male partners or unwanted children. The thought that these acts may be, in some cases, reasoned and reasonable still falls outside our comfort zone of plausible narratives.

Even the odd valiant attempt by the Supreme Court of Canada to dislodge old ideas and better account for the specific experiences of those accused/convicted of crime have not succeeded in changing these seemingly hardwired codes of interpretation.[1] We have certainly seen this with the medical, legal, and social reification of the "battered woman syndrome" during the 1980s and '90s, and the decision in *R. v. Lavallée* (1990), which stated that the experience of a woman living in violence should be considered when interpreting the meaning of "reasonableness" in the *Criminal Code* definition of self-defence.[2] Similarly, the Supreme Court decision in *R. v. Gladue* (1999) allows for the specific consideration of the particular "circumstances" of Aboriginal offenders when applying the principles of sentencing set out in section 718.1 of the *Criminal Code*.[3] Although these initiatives seem progressive on the surface and hopeful in theory, they have not translated into a significant change in popular attitudes or, in the case of "battered women," lower court practices.

Historically, evidence of the effects of long-term abuse would probably have been used to argue some form of "diminished" responsibility or even provocation in some cases, but it would not have met the legal requirements of "imminent danger" and "reasonableness" in self-defence law. *Lavallée* was supposed to fix that. However, we now know that women who kill their abusive partners have not been successful in arguing self-defence, which would lead to a full acquittal. Instead, psychiatric evidence supporting a diagnosis of battered woman syndrome is often introduced as a plea-bargaining tool in order to have a first-degree murder charge reduced to one of manslaughter. Studies show that since *Lavallée* women have been bartering for a lesser charge and serving jail time, rather than taking the risk of a self-defence claim.[4]

Likewise, social, legal, and political evaluations of the nature and significance of the "circumstances" of Aboriginal offenders remain deeply problematic, particularly because the circumstances that we tend to highlight, and therefore deem most relevant to understanding criminal behaviour, are those concerning violence and substance abuse. This reductionist perspective of the "Aboriginal experience" not only reproduces some of the earlier collective interpretations of "Indian" behaviour – reincarnating an oversimplified Eurocentric understanding of why some "Indians" behave as they do – but also depoliticizes the larger historical issues of colonization, racism, and poverty.[5]

Within Canada's vast but unique cultural matrix, we need to consider and account for the complicated production of criminological knowledges in differing contexts. Variances seen across Canadian cases of women and men convicted for murder between 1920 and 1950, regarding the use, authority, and nature of expert and common-sense knowledges, speak to the importance of diversifying our understanding of the social and legal significance of psychiatric "expertise" in the West. In Canadian capital murder cases, evaluations of mind-state, guilt, and responsibility were often synchronized but never totally unified in the courtroom, where decisions hinged on which narratives were taken up as truthful and which were not. It is necessary, therefore, to expand the way we think and ask questions about how criminal responsibility was/is decided, and by whom.

Appendices

Appendix A-1

Capital case file summary (*N* = 66)

Province			%
AB	Alberta	(7)	10.5
BC	British Columbia	(9)	13.5
NT	Northwest Territories	(1)	1.5
MB	Manitoba	(5)	7.5
NB	New Brunswick	(0)	
NF	Newfoundland	(0)	
NS	Nova Sçotia	(3)	4.5
ON	Ontario	(19)	29.0
QC	Quebec	(16)	24.0
SK	Saskatchewan	(5)	7.5
YT	Yukon	(1)	1.5

Gender			%
F	Female	(23)	35.0
M	Male	(43)	65.0

Age			%
16-19		(8)	12.0
20-29		(17)	26.0
30-39		(17)	26.0
40-49		(10)	15.0
50-59		(7)	10.5
> 60		(3)	4.5
NA	Unknown	(4)	6.0

Racial identification			%
AB	"Indian," "Half-breed"	(5)	7.5
BL	Black ("coloured" "Negro")	(5)	7.5
BR	British	(9)	13.5
CA	Canadian	(3)	4.5
CH	Chinese	(1)	1.5
EU	European (Ukrainian, Polish, Italian, Russian, German, Galician)	(23)	35.0
FC	French Canadian	(9)	13.5
US	American	(5)	7.5
NA	Not identified	(8)	12.0

Occupation (OCCUP)			%
BU	Business	(1)	1.5
FA	Farmer	(1)	1.5
HW	Housewife	(17)	26.0
LB	Labourer	(21)	32.0
OT	Other	(3)	4.5
SO	Soldier	(5)	7.5
TR	Tradesman	(9)	13.5
NA	Unemployed or unspecified	(15)	22.5

►

Appendix A-1

Victim's relation to offender (VOR)			%
BR	Brother	(1)	1.5
CH	Child > 1 yr.	(3)	4.5
FA	Father	(3)	4.5
IN	Infant < 1 yr.	(2)	3.5
KF	Known female	(12)	18.0
KM	Known male	(9)	13.5
MO	Mother	(1)	1.5
PO	Police officer	(2)	3.5
SP	Spouse	(24)	36.6
UF	Unknown female	(4)	6.0
UM	Unknown male	(7)	10.5

Method			%
AS	Assault (beating)	(7)	10.5
AX	Axe	(5)	7.5
HM	Hammer	(3)	4.5
OT	Other	(8)	12.0
PO	Poison	(6)	9.0
SH	Shooting	(27)	41.0
ST	Stabbing	(9)	13.5
NA	Not identified	(1)	1.5

Official motive			%
BR	Brawl (between men)	(4)	6.0
LV	Love	(6)	9.0
MO	Money (insurance or inheritance)	(7)	10.5
OT	Other	(2)	3.5
PV	Emotional provocation (passion, anger, jealousy, domestic quarrel, revenge)	(23)	35.0
RO	Robbery	(9)	13.5
NA	Unknown	(17)	26.0

Legal defence (DEF)			%
DK	Drunkenness	(6)	9.0
I	Insanity	(19)	29.0
NG	Not guilty	(17)	26.0
PV	Provocation	(6)	9.0
SD	Self-defence	(5)	7.5
NA	None/unknown	(13)	19.5

State of mind raised (SOM)			%
C	Post-conviction	(8)	12.0
NA	Not raised	(15)	22.5
T	Raised at trial	(43)	65.0

"Expert" evidence (EXP)			%
C	Post-conviction	(8)	12.0
NA	None	(40)	60.5
T	At trial	(18)	27.5

Recommendation to mercy			%
N	No	(38)	57.5
NA	Not available/known	(1)	1.5
N/Y	No from jury/ yes from judge	(2)	3.5
Y	Yes from judge and jury	(24)	36.5
Y/N	Yes from jury/ no from judge	(1)	1.5

Final known outcome (OUTCM)			%
AQ	Acquitted	(3)	4.5
C	Commuted	(23)	35.0
Died	Before clemency decision	(1)	1.5
H	Hanged	(29)	44.0
NT	New trial	(6)	9.0
RD	Reduced sentence	(3)	4.5
UF	Unfit to stand trial	(1)	1.5

Note: Due to rounding up or down, or because some individuals were included in multiple categories, some percentage totals are greater or less than 100. In some sections, *N* exceeds 66 because individuals were assigned to more than one category.

Appendix A-2

Demographic profile and principal legal features of case files

Year	Province	Name	Gender	Age	Race	OCCUP	VOR	Method	Motive	DEF	SOM	EXP	Mercy	OUTCM
1920	AB	Jackson, Sarah	F	35	NA	HW	SP	SH	PV	SD	T	C	Y	C
1920	QC	Houde, Marie Anne	F	30	FC	NA	CH	AS	MO	I	T	T	N	C
1921	BC	Muskey, John	M	30	EU	NA	KM	SH	BR	DK	T	NA	Y	C
1921	NT	Le Beaux, Albert	M	NA	AB	NA	SP	SH	PV	NG	C	NA	Y	H
1922	ON	Rudka, Harry	M	NA	EU	NA	KM	ST	BR	NG	NA	NA	N	C
1922	AB	Lassandro, Florence	F	22	EU	HW	PO	SH	PV	SD	T	NA	Y	H
1923	QC	St. Onge, Wilfred	M	19	NA	TR	UM	SH	RO	NA	NA	NA	N	H
1923	YT	Joe, Katy	F	NA	AB	NA	KF	NA	NA	I	T	T	NA	UF
1924	SK	Tratch, Catherine	F	38	EU	HW	SP	PO	LV	NA	T	NA	N	C
1924	QC	Dagenais, Alfred	M	31	FC	LB	UF	OT	RO	NA	C	C	N	C
1925	BC	Sowash, Harry	M	25	US	BU	KM	SH	RO	NA	NA	NA	N	H
1925	BC	Debartoli, Alex	M	41	EU	TR	KF	SH	NA	NG	C	C	N	H
1926	BC	Pasquale, Benito	M	50	BL	TR	KF	ST	NA	I	T	T	N	H
1926	QC	Sprague, Emily	F	39	FC	HW	SP	PO	LV	NG	NA	NA	Y	AQ
1927	SK	Schmidt, Valentine	M	50	EU	NA	SP	SH	PV	I	T	T	Y	H
1927	NS	Jones, Louis	M	NA	BL	LB	SP	ST	PV	PV	T	NA	Y	H
1927	QC	McDonald, Doris	F	20	US	HW	UM	SH	RO	NG	C	NA	Y	C
1928	QC	Gaetano, Pepitone	M	44	EU	NA	KF	SH	BR	DK	T	NA	N	H
1928	BC	Chong, Leung	M	29	CH	NA	PO	SH	NA	NG	NA	NA	N	AQ
1929	QC	Beaulne, Marie	F	42	CA	HW	SP	PO	MO/LV	NA	NA	NA	N	H
1929	SK	Carrier, Frank	M	70+	NA	LB	KM	SH	PV	I	T	T	N	C

►

Year	Province	Name	Gender	Age	Race	OCCUP	VOR	Method	Motive	DEF	SOM	EXP	Mercy	OUTCM
1930	AB	Dvernichuk, George	M	44	EU	OT	KM/F	SH	NA	I	T	T	N	H
1930	QC	Poliquin, Antonio	M	27	FC	LB	SP	OT	PV	PV	T	C	N	H
1931	ON	Cambell, Thomas	M	45	NA	LB	FA	AS	PV	PV	C	C	N	H
1931	MB	McGrath, James	M	24	BR	LB	SP	ST	PV	I	T	T	N	H
1932	ON	Beregovenko, Jack	M	60	EU	OT	KM	SH	BR	SD	T	NA	N	C
1933	ON	Antonowicz, W.	M	34	EU	LB/SO	KF	SH	PV	PV	T	NA	N	H
1933	NS	Crawley, Samuel	M	24	BL	NA	FA	AX	NA	I	T	NA	Y	C
1934	QC	Teolis, Tommasina	F	45	EU	HW	SP	AS	MO	NA	NA	NA	N	H
1934	AB	Dranchuk, Dina	F	38	EU	HW	SP	AX	MO	I	T	T	Y	C
1934	QC	Chapdelaine, Beatrice	F	32	FC	HW	SP	PO	NA	NG	NA	NA	N	AQ
1935	ON	Tilford, Ann Elizabeth	F	50	BR	HW	SP	PO	MO	NG	T	NA	N	H
1935	SK	Smith, Mary	F	39	AB	HW	SP	SH	PV	I	T	T	Y	NT
1936	AB	Pogmore, Christine	F	39	NA	HW	SP	SH	LV	NG	NA	NA	Y	C
1936	QC	Brown, Kenneth	M	26	US	TR	UM	SH	RO	NG	NA	NA	N	Died
1937	NS	Farmer, Everett	M	35	BL	LB	BR	SH	PV	DK/PV	T	NA	N	H
1937	ON	Dolan, Frank	M	33	BR	LB/TR	SP	AS	PV	NA	T	NA	N	H
1938	QC	Coutier, Marie-Louise	F	39	FC	HW	SP	PO	LV/MO	NG	NA	NA	N	H
1938	ON	Monchuk, William	M	45	EU	LB/TR	KM/F	AX	PV	PV	T	NA	N	NT
1938	ON	Gunning, William	M	24	BR	LB	KF	HM	NA	I	T	NA	N	C
1939	BC	Wright, R.A.	M	68	US/BL	TR	SP	AS	PV	NG	NA	NA	N	H
1939	ON	Taylor, Jessie	F	50	BR	HW	MO	OT	MO	SD	T	T	Y	C
1940	MB	Harrop, Frances	F	47	NA	HW	SP	SH	PV	I	T	T	Y	NT
1940	SK	Rubletz, Annie	F	19	EU	NA	IN	OT	OT	NA	T	NA	Y	RD

1941	ON	McGuffin, James	M	22	BR	LB/SO	UM	SH	NA	I	T	T	Y	C
1941	BC	Patrick, Frank	M	40	EU	FA	KF	AX	PV	I	T	T	Y	C
1942	AB	Johnston, Chester	M	24	CA	TR	UF	ST	NA	I	T	T	N	H
1942	ON	Kolesar, Edward	M	20	EU	TR/SO	FA	AX	NA	NA	C	NA	Y/N	H
1942	MB	Stasiuk, Rose	F	19	EU	NA	IN	OT	OT	NG	T	NA	Y	C
1943	ON	Kisielewski, Bruno	M	21	EU/US	LB	UM	SH	RO	NG	C	C	Y	H
1943	ON	Zadorozny, Samuel	M	18	EU	LB/SO	KF	OT	LV	NA	T	C	Y	C
1944	AB	Abraham, Paul	M	24	AB	LB	SP	SH	NA	I	T	T	N	H
1944	ON	Schmidt, William	M	29	EU	LB	UF	OT	RO	NA	NA	NA	N	H
1945	MB	Proulx, Joseph	M	17	AB	NA	UF	ST	NA	I	T	T	Y	C
1945	BC	Hainen, William	M	29	BR	SO	KF	AS	NA	I/DK	T	T	Y	H
1946	ON	Dick, Evelyn	F	25	CA	HW	SP/CH	SH	NA	NA	NA	NA	Y	RD
1946	ON	Demeutes, M-L	F	37	FC	HW	KF	AS	NA	DK	T	NA	N	C
1946	MB	McLean, Elizabeth	F	50	BR	NA	SP	ST	PV	DK/SD	T	NA	Y	RD
1947	QC	Boyko, John	M	52	EU	LB	SP	HM	PV	PV	T	NA	N/Y	C
1947	ON	Martin, Charles	M	35	EU	OT	UM	SH	RO	SD	NA	NA	N	H
1948	QC	Beaulne, Adrien	M	55	FC	LB	KM	OT	PV	NG	T	NA	N	H
1948	BC	Weid, Jacob	M	38	EU	NA	SP	ST	PV	NG	T	NA	N/Y	NT
1949	ON	Childs, Dale	M	16	NA	LB	KM	SH	NA	NA	T	NA	N	C
1950	QC	Dube, Leonidas	F	45	NA	NA	CH	SH	PV	DK	T	NA	N	NT
1950	ON	Fosbraey, James	M	27	BR	LB	SP	ST	PV	I	T	T	N	NT/RD
1950	QC	Patenaude, Gervin	M	19	FC	LB	UM	HM	RO	NG	C	C	N	C

Appendix B

Alphabetical list of capital cases with archival references

Name	Date	RG 13 reference volumes
Abraham, Paul	(1944)	Vol. 1641
Antonowicz, W.	(1933)	Vol. 1581
Beaulne, Adrien	(1948)	Vol. 1671, 1672
Beaulne (Viau), Marie	(1929)	Vol. 1555
Beregovenko, Jack	(1932)	Vol. 1577
Boyko, John	(1947)	Vol. 1664
Brown, Kenneth	(1936)	Vol. 1603, 1604
Cambell, Thomas	(1931)	Vol. 1572
Carrier, Frank	(1929)	Vol. 1417
Chapdelaine, Beatrice	(1934)	Vol. 1579, 1580
Childs, Dale	(1949)	Vol. 1684
Chong, Leung	(1928)	Vol. 1547
Coutier, Marie-Louise	(1938)	Vol. 1616, 1617
Crawley, Samuel	(1933)	Vol. 1581
Dagenais, Alfred	(1924)	Vol. 1529
Debartoli, Alex	(1925)	Vol. 1539
Demeutes, Marie-Louise	(1946)	Vol. 1659
Dick, Evelyn	(1964)	Vol. 1661
Dolan, Frank	(1937)	Vol. 1612
Dranchuk, Dina	(1934)	Vol. 1592, 1593
Dube, Leonidas	(1950)	Vol. 1689
Dvernichuk, George	(1930)	Vol. 1564
Farmer, Everett	(1937)	Vol. 1611
Fosbraey, James	(1950)	Vol. 1690, 1691
Gaetano, Pepitone	(1928)	Vol. 1548
Gunning, William	(1938)	Vol. 1618
Hainen, William	(1945)	Vol. 1650
Harrop, Frances	(1940)	Vol. 1625
Houde, Marie-Anne	(1920)	Vol. 1507
Jackson, Sarah	(1920)	Vol. 1509
Joe, Katy	(1923)	Vol. 1526
Johnston, Chester	(1942)	Vol. 1637
Jones, Louis	(1927)	Vol. 1545
Kisielewski, Bruno	(1943)	Vol. 1640
Kolesar, Edward	(1942)	Vol. 1638
Lassandro, Florence	(1922)	Vol. 1523, 1524
Le Beaux, Albert	(1921)	Vol. 1513
Martin, Charles	(1947).	Vol. 1667
McDonald, Doris	(1927)	Vol. 1546, 1547
McGrath, James	(1931)	Vol. 1572
McGuffin, James	(1941)	Vol. 1631
McLean, Elizabeth	(1946)	Vol. 1661, 1662
Monchuk, William	(1938)	Vol. 1607, 1614

▶

◄ *Appendix B*

Name	Date	RG 13 reference volumes
Muskey, John	(1921)	Vol. 1512
Pasquale, Benito	(1926)	Vol. 1538
Patenaude, Gervin	(1950)	Vol. 1690
Patrick, Frank	(1941)	Vol. 1633
Pogmore, Christine	(1936)	Vol. 1607
Poliquin, Antonio	(1930)	Vol. 1564
Proulx, Joseph	(1945)	Vol. 1651
Rubletz, Annie	(1940)	Vol. 1627
Rudka, Harry	(1922)	Vol. 1520
Schmidt, Valentine	(1927)	Vol. 1544
Schmidt, William	(1944)	Vol. 1645
Smith, Mary	(1935)	Vol. 1599
Sowash, Harry	(1925)	Vol. 1536, 1537
Sprague, Emily	(1926)	Vol. 1540, 1541
St. Onge, Wilfred	(1923)	Vol. 1524, 1525
Stasiuk, Rose	(1942)	Vol. 1637
Taylor, Jessie	(1939)	Vol. 1622
Teolis, Tommasina	(1934)	Vol. 1592, 1593
Tilford, Ann Elizabeth	(1935)	Vol. 1598, 1599
Tratch, Catherine	(1924)	Vol. 1528
Weid, Jacob	(1948)	Vol. 1676
Wright, R.A.	(1939)	Vol. 1621
Zadorozny, Samuel	(1943)	Vol. 1641

Notes

Preface

1 Catherine Crawford, "Legalizing Medicine: Early Modern Legal Systems and the Growth of Medico-Legal Knowledge," in Michael Clark and Catherine Crawford, eds., *Legal Medicine in History* (Cambridge: Cambridge University Press, 1994), 89-116; Catherine Crawford, "The Emergence of English Forensic Medicine: Medical Evidence in Common-Law Courts, 1730-1830" (PhD diss., Oxford University, 1987).

2 See, generally, Joel Peter Eigen, *Witnessing Insanity: Madness and Mad-Doctors in the English Court* (New Haven: Yale University Press, 1995); Ruth Harris, *Murders and Madness: Medicine, Law, and Society in the Fin de Siècle* (Oxford: Clarendon Press, 1989); and Roger Smith, *Trial by Medicine: Insanity and Responsibility in Victorian Trial* (Edinburgh: Edinburgh University Press, 1981).

3 Crawford, "English Forensic Medicine," 292. Also see J.E. Goldstein, *Console and Classify: The French Psychiatric Profession in the Nineteenth Century* (Cambridge: Cambridge University Press, 1987), Goldstein, "French Psychiatry in Social and Political Context: The Formation of a New Profession, 1820-1860" (PhD thesis, Columbia University, 1978), Goldstein, "'Moral Contagion': A Professional Ideology of Medicine and Psychiatry in Eighteenth and Nineteenth Century France," in G.L. Geison, ed., *Professions and the State, 1700-1900* (Philadelphia: University of Pennsylvania Press, 1984), 181-222; Harris, *Murders and Madness;* Crawford, "English Forensic Medicine"; M.J. Clark, "The Data of Alienism: Evolutionary Neurology, Physiological Psychology, and the Reconstruction of British Psychiatric Theory, c. 1850-1900" (D. Phil. thesis, Oxford University, 1982); Clark and Crawford, *Legal Medicine;* G.N. Grob, *Mental Illness and American Society, 1875-1940* (Princeton: Princeton University Press, 1983); D. Jack, *Rogues, Rebels and Geniuses: The Story of Canadian Medicine* (Toronto: Doubleday Canada, 1981); S.E.D. Short, ed., *Medicine in Canadian Society: Historical Perspectives* (Montreal and Kingston: McGill-Queen's University Press, 1981); Andrew Scull, *Madhouses, Mad-Doctors, and Madmen: The Social History of Psychiatry in the Victorian Era* (Philadelphia: University of Pennsylvania Press, 1981), and Scull, *Social Order/Mental Disorder: Anglo-American Psychiatry in Historical Perspective* (London: Routledge, 1989).

4 Crawford, "Legalizing Medicine," 90-91, 107. Ian Dowbiggin also suggests that Canadian psychiatrists resented going into the courtroom, in "Keeping This Young Country Sane: C.K. Clarke, Immigration Restriction, and Canadian Psychiatry, 1880-1925," *Canadian Historical Review* 76 (1995): 598, and *Keeping America Sane: Psychiatry and Eugenics in the United States and Canada, 1880-1940* (Ithaca and London: Cornell University Press, 1997).

5 Some clarification is needed here regarding the periodization of the rise of forensic psychiatry. Goldstein, for instance, claims in *Console and Classify* that psychiatry as a profession emerged "almost simultaneously in France, Britain, America and the German lands" although with "distinct national traditions" (5). Here, "America" refers only to the United States. In Canada, psychiatry, as a distinct medical specialization, did not really begin to

gain a professional foothold until the late eighteen hundreds, and psychiatric expert witnesses did not *routinely* appear in criminal trials until close to the turn of the twentieth century.

6 Jennifer Radden, *Madness and Reason* (London: G. Allen and Unwin, 1985).

7 Walter Bromberg, *Psychiatry between the Wars, 1918-1945: A Recollection* (Westport: Greenwood Press, 1982).

8 Janet Tighe, "The New York Medico-Legal Society: Legitimating the Union of Law and Psychiatry, 1867-1918," *International Journal of Law and Psychiatry* 9 (1986): 231, 241.

9 Scull, *Madhouses,* 26, also argued that criminal law in the United States and Britain was essentially unaffected by medical discourse.

10 Smith, *Trial by Medicine,* 3-5.

11 Further on this issue, Joel Eigen documents the privileging of medical opinion in English courts in his essay "I Answer as a Physician," in Clark and Crawford, *Legal Medicine*. See also his and Gregory Andoll's "From Mad-Doctor to Forensic Witness: The Evolution of Early English Court Psychiatry," *International Journal of Law and Psychiatry* 9 (1986): 259-62.

12 Smith, *Trial by Medicine,* 3, 8.

13 Robert Nye applies this characterization to legal authorities, suggesting the law was more powerful as the principle "user" of medical knowledge for social/political purposes. He claims that doctors confined their "actions" to the private sphere until the late eighteen hundreds, when the rise in public concern regarding deviance came to provide a more important state function for experts. See his *Crime, Madness and Politics in Modern France: The Medical Concept of National Decline* (Princeton: Princeton University Press, 1984), 48-49, 335.

14 Eigen, *Witnessing Insanity,* 4.

15 Ibid., 5.

16 Ibid.

17 Nigel Walker, *Crime and Insanity in England* (Edinburgh: Edinburgh University Press, 1968), 246, 246-47.

18 Ibid., 253. For example, Walker points to the creation of "categorical descriptions" and "manias" by psychiatric experts that could subsequently be "slapped" on an accused. He argues that the "more esoteric the name of the disorder the more incapacitating it [would] sound" to the jury (253).

19 Eigen, *Witnessing Insanity,* 6.

20 Sir James Fitzjames Stephen, *A Digest of the Law of Evidence,* 12th ed. (London: Macmillan, 1936), 67-69.

21 See Edward Shorter, *A History of Psychiatry: From the Era of the Asylum to the Age of Prozac* (Toronto: John Wiley and Sons, 1997), and Erwin H. Ackerknecht, *A Short History of Medicine* (Baltimore and London: Johns Hopkins University Press, 1982).

22 Smith, *Trial by Medicine,* 8.

23 In *Witnessing Insanity,* Eigen also argues that the evolving role of the medical expert witness was heavily "bound up" in the changes of that process. In Eigen's words, "the evolving role of the medical witness coincided with a fundamental reconceptualization of the relation between criminal responsibility and madness. Insanity 'became' something very different ... but the role contributed by any one courtroom participant in this critical transformation is bound up with the changing dynamics of the criminal trial itself and ultimately with larger cultural questions concerning human agency. Lawyers and jurors, prisoners and prosecutors complemented, contradicted, and contextualized the testimony of medical experts on a trial-by-trial basis" (6). In some of his smaller-scale works, Eigen better demonstrates the richness of trial evidence and provides further insight into precisely how medical experts used the law to propel themselves out of asylum medicine to a position of judicial necessity. For instance, in both "From Mad-Doctor to Forensic Witness" and "I Answer as a Physician," he examines how doctors' testimonies were received in the courtroom. In both articles, Eigen argues that it became increasingly important for the court to establish the legitimacy of a medical witness' testimony by questioning his credentials and background with a special emphasis on "experience." This is very similar to what Martin Friedland's evidence shows in his *The* Case *of Valentine Shortis: A True Story of Crime and Politics in Canada* (Toronto: University of Toronto Press, 1986).

Chapter 1: Introduction

1 Ed. T. Hammond, Insp. C.I.B., Ontario Provincial Police Criminal Investigation Branch, "Re-Mrs. Elizabeth Ann Tilford," 28 October 1935, 2, Tilford (1935), Library and Archives Canada (LAC), Ottawa, Ontario, RG 13, vol. 1598, file CC437. LAC case file volume numbers are given in Appendix B. All files discussed in this book are from the Department of Justice records (RG 13) at LAC.

2 Ibid., 1.

3 In both the police report and a newspaper article, Tilford is recorded as having nineteen children. See "Mrs. Tilford Should Not Be Hanged," *Observer,* n.d., LAC, RG 13, vol. 1598, file CC437.

4 Ed. T. Hammond, Insp. C.I.B., Ontario Provincial Police Criminal Investigation Branch, "Re-Mrs. Elizabeth Ann Tilford," 28 October 1935, 1, Tilford (1935), LAC, RG 13, vol. 1598, file CC437.

5 Ibid., 2.

6 Ibid.

7 Ibid.

8 Ibid.

9 Ibid.

10 Ibid., 3.

11 Ibid.

12 See "Charge to the Jury" in trial transcripts, 1070, Tilford (1935), LAC, RG 13, vol. 1599, part 3.2, file CC437. Tilford's outburst in the courtroom is also reported in several newspaper articles covering the trial. See, for instance, "Guilty Verdict Found by Jury in Tilford Case," *Montreal Gazette,* 3 October 1935, 1.

13 "Few Hundred Sign Clemency Petition – Number Protesting Death Sentence on Mrs. Tilford Reported Small," *Toronto Mail and Empire,* 27 November 1935.

14 Mrs. M.A. Nicklin, Guelph, Ontario, to minister of justice; Mrs. C. Fraser, Montreal, to minister of justice; Countess S. Fontaine, New York, to minister of justice; and "Mrs. Tilford Should Not Be Hanged," *Observer,* n.d., Tilford (1935), LAC, RG 13, vol. 1598, file CC437.

15 Miss E.S. Warner, New York, to minister of justice; Mrs. Margaret Sim, Hamilton, to minister of justice; Mr. and Mrs. Keill, Fort William, Ontario, to minister of justice; and Robert C. Allan, Cobourg, newspaper articles titled "Letter from Student on Executions" and "Capital Punishment" (publication sources and dates unknown), Tilford (1935), LAC, RG 13, vol. 1598, file CC437.

16 Mr. and Mrs. Keill, Fort William, to minister of justice, Tilford (1935), LAC.

17 According to figures compiled in a report titled "Capital Punishment: Material Relating to Its Purpose and Value," from the Ministry of the Solicitor General in 1965, 125 people were hanged during the 1930s. As reported in Carolyn Strange, "Comment: Capital Case Procedure Manual," *Criminal Law Quarterly* 14 (1998), "in 1931 alone, as the country sank into economic despair, 25 men were executed (out of 32 condemned to death). The previous record – 20 – had been set in 1919: the politically volatile year following the war's close" (190). Strange's article deals with the 1941 publication of the manual.

18 See Strange, "Comment," 190-91.

19 "Mrs. Tilford's Fate Revives Criticism," *Toronto Daily Star,* n.d., Tilford (1935), LAC, RG 13, vol. 1598, file CC437. Part of this article is missing from the file.

20 Mrs. Margaret Sim, Hamilton, to minister of justice, Tilford (1935), LAC, RG 13, vol. 1598, file CC437. Not everyone, however, thought capital punishment was a bad thing. In response to Mrs. Sim's letter, parts of which appeared in a newspaper editorial, Charles D. Stebbing wrote that those who would kill for financial gain, especially a woman who would kill her "lawful husband for the gold which his death would bring her," should not escape the gallows. "Woodstock Murderess," n.d.

21 "Mrs. Tilford Should Not Be Hanged," *Observer.*

22 Trial transcripts, "Charge to the Jury," 1024, Tilford (1935), LAC, RG 13, vol. 1599, part 3.2, file CC437. In an interesting parallel, the Jekyll-and-Hyde analogy was also used in "Mrs. Tilford Should Not Be Hanged." However, in this context, the curious dual personality was suggested as evidence of a psychiatric condition. Reflecting on the facts of the case, the

author surmised, "I find it very difficult to believe that there is not a Jekyll element in this strange woman as well as a perculiarly [sic] atrocious element of Hyde." LAC, RG 13, vol. 1598.

23 Trial transcripts, "Charge to the Jury," 1069.

24 "Killer of Husband Is Hanged Today," *Ottawa A.M. Journal,* 17 December 1935, LAC, RG 13, vol. 1599, part 2, file CC437.

25 In my view, the best critical analysis of the role of the remissions branch and the influence of the chief remissions officer is Strange, "Comment," 184-97.

26 Michael F. Gallagher, for deputy minister of justice, "Memorandum for the Honourable Minister of Justice," 5 December 1935, 19-20, Tilford (1935), LAC, RG 13, vol. 1599, part 2, file CC437.

27 Ibid., 21.

28 I use the term "criminal responsibility" throughout the book to include both legal and moral concepts of responsibility.

29 Patricia Ewick and Susan Silbey, "Common Knowledge and Ideological Critique: The Significance of Knowing that the 'Haves' Come out Ahead," *Law and Society Review* 33, 4 (1999): 1036.

30 Michel Barrett, *Women's Oppression Today: Problems in Marxist Feminist Analysis* (London and New York: Verso Press, 1988), quoted in ibid.

31 Ewick and Silbey, "Common Knowledge," 1036.

32 Ibid., 1037.

33 See, generally, the overview of literature in the Preface. In particular, see the following examples: Carol Smart, "Criminological Theory: Its Ideology and Implications concerning Women," *British Journal of Sociology* 28, 1 (1977): 89-100; Roger Smith, "The Boundary between Insanity and Criminal Responsibility in Nineteenth-Century England," in Andrew Scull, ed., *Madhouses, Mad-Doctors, and Madmen* (Philadelphia: University of Pennsylvania Press, 1981), 339-63, and Smith, "Expertise and Causal Attribution in Deciding between Crime and Mental Disorder," *Social Studies of Science* 15 (1985): 67-98; Robert Menzies, "The Making of Criminal Insanity in British Columbia: Granby Farrant and the Provincial Mental Home, Colquitz, 1919-1933," in Hamar Foster and John McLaren, eds., *Essays in the History of Canadian Law Volume 6* (Toronto: University of Toronto Press, 1995), 274-313, and Menzies, *Survival of the Sanest: Order and Disorder in a Pre-Trial Psychiatric Clinic* (Toronto: University of Toronto Press, 1989); Dorothy Chunn and Robert Menzies, "Gender, Madness and Crime: The Reproduction of Patriarchal and Class Relations in a Psychiatric Court Clinic," *Journal of Human Justice* 1, 2 (Spring 1990): 33-54; Bruce Arrigo, *The Contours of Psychiatric Justice: A Postmodern Critique of Mental Illness, Criminal Insanity, and the Law* (New York and London: Garland Publishing, 1996); Jan Goldstein, "Professional Knowledge and Professional Self-Interest: The Rise and Fall of Monomania in 19th-Century France," *International Journal of Law and Psychiatry* 21, 4 (1998): 385-96; Peter Bartlett, "Legal Madness in the Nineteenth Century," *Social History of Medicine* 14, 1 (2001): 107-31; and P. Susan Penfold, "Drugged, Exploited, Labelled and Blamed: How Psychiatry Oppresses Women," in Susan Boyd, Dorothy Chunn, and Robert Menzies, eds., *(Ab)Using Power: The Canadian Experience* (Halifax: Fernwood Publishing, 2001), 174-84.

34 For studies in the symbolic nature of British law and the social role of the rule of law, see works by Douglas Hay, P. Linebaugh, J.G. Rule, E.P. Thompson, and C. Winslow. D. Hay et al., *Albion's Fatal Tree: Crime and Society in Eighteenth-Century England* (New York: Pantheon Books, 1975). For Canadian examples, see, generally, works by Carolyn Strange, Jim Phillips, and Tina Loo.

35 For examples, see Ewick and Silbey, "Common Knowledge," 1025-41; Mariana Valverde, *Law's Dream of a Common Knowledge* (Princeton: Princeton University Press, 2003); Martin Roiser, "Commonsense, Science and Public Opinion," *Journal for the Theory of Social Behaviour* 17, 4 (1987): 411-32; Michael Salter, "Common Sense and the Resistance to Legal Theory," *Ratio Juris* 5, 2 (1992): 212-29; Robert Ferguson, "The Commonalities of Common Sense," *William and Mary Quarterly,* 3rd ser., 57, 3 (2000): 465-504; Elizabeth S. Sousa, "Lay versus Scientific Knowledge: The Value of a Dichotomy," *European Bulletin of Cognitive Psychology* 11, 3 (1991): 307-21; Edmond V. Sullivan, "Commonsense and Valuing," *Religious*

Education 78, 1 (1983): 5-12; and Bonaventura de Sousa Santos, trans., *Toward a New Common Sense: Law, Science and Politics in the Paradigmatic Transition* (New York and London: Routledge, 1995). Although it may be true that, as Roiser, "Commonsense," put it, the "concepts of commonsense and of public opinion resemble one another quite closely" (414), I consider them to be quite different phenomena. Public opinion can be seen as a collection of individual statements on a subject, which is assumed to be based in large part on common-sense understandings of the subject and its context. Public opinion can be polled and counted; it is subject to "scientific" analysis and interpretation. Common sense, on the other hand, is a more difficult concept to nail down. According to Sousa, "Lay versus Scientific," lay knowledge is much more "confident" than expert or scientific knowledge because it does not require justification or evidence in order to be validated (308-9). Sullivan, "Commonsense and Valuing," offers a more political account of common sense as a reflection of agreement among members of society, which in turn organizes and orders that society (5). Sullivan also suggests that common sense is prone to error, given its lack of scientific basis (10-11).

36 For examples of international and theoretical studies on the anthropology of "race" and race difference during the eighteenth and nineteenth centuries, see Peter D'Agostino, "Craniums, Criminals, and the 'Cursed Race': Italian Anthropology in American Racial Thought, 1861-1924," *Comparative Studies in the Sociology of History* 44, 2 (2002): 319-43; Alan Bearnard, "Anthropology, Race, and Englishness: Changing Notions of Complexion and Character," *Eighteenth-Century Life* 25, 3 (2001): 94-102; Scott Ashley, "The Poetics of Race in 1890s Ireland: An Ethnography of the Aran Islands," *Patterns of Prejudice* 35, 2 (2001): 5-18; Martin Staum, "Paris Ethnology and the Perfectibility of 'Races,'" *Canadian Journal of History* 35, 3 (2000): 453-72; Christopher Herbert, "Epilogue: Ethnography and Evolution," *Victorian Studies* 41, 3 (1998): 485-94; Thomas Strack, "Philosophical Anthropology on the Eve of Biological Determinism: Immanuel Kant and Georg Forester on the Moral Qualities and Biological Characteristics of the Human Race," *Central European History* 29, 3 (1996): 285-308; Hertha Hanson, "Women and Racial Biology," *Lychnos* (1993): 9-33; Douglas Larimer, "Theoretical Racism in Late-Victorian Anthropology, 1870-1900," *Victorian Studies* 31, 3 (1988): 405-30; and John Haller, "Concepts of Race Inferiority in Nineteenth-Century Anthropology," *Journal of the History of Medicine and Allied Sciences* 25, 1 (1970): 40-51.

37 See Ian Hacking's analysis of "interactive kinds" and "indifferent kinds" in *The Social Construction of What?* (Cambridge, MA: Harvard University Press, 1999), 103-23. According to Hacking, "we experience ourselves in the world as being persons of various kinds." For example, "we are affected by the ways in which being female or having a disability are conceived, described, ordained by ourselves and the network of milieus in which we live" (103-4). This is an interactive process. In his interrogation of "madness" as biological or constructed, Hacking says that there is a "constant drive in the social and psychological sciences to emulate the natural sciences, and to produce true natural kinds of people. This is evidently true for basic research on pathologies such as schizophrenia and autism, but it is also, at present, equally true for some but only some investigators who study homosexuality (the search for the homosexual gene) or violent crime (is that an innate and heritable propensity?). There is a picture of an objective to be searched out, the right kind, the kind that is true to nature, a fixed target if only we can get there" (104-5).

38 John F. Mahoney to M.F. Gallagher, chief of the remission branch, 25 November 1927, 3, Louis Jones (1927), LAC, RG 13, vol. 1545, part 1, file CC267.

39 Detective R.C. Rathbone, "Alberta Provincial Police, Report Re: George Dvernichuk – Capital Case," 23 December 1930, 1, George Dvernichuk (1930), LAC, RG 13, vol. 1564, file CC332.

40 James Snell, *In the Shadow of the Law: Divorce in Canada 1900-1939* (Toronto: University of Toronto Press, 1991), 21.

41 Mona Gleason, *Normalizing the Ideal: Psychology, Schooling, and the Family in Postwar Canada* (Toronto: University of Toronto Press, 1999), 4-5.

42 James Walker, *"Race," Rights and the Law in the Supreme Court of Canada* (Waterloo, ON: Wilfrid Laurier University Press, 1997), 6.

43 See Angus McLaren, *Our Own Master Race: Eugenics in Canada, 1855-1945* (Toronto: Oxford University Press, 1990).

44 Here, my analysis of the relationship between expert knowledge and common-sense knowledge is in line with Antonio Gramsci's analysis of power and ideology, in particular his argument that "intellectuals occupy a privileged position in uniting thought with action." According to Gramsci, intellectuals functioned primarily as "educators" who nurtured shared ethical norms but did not impose or invent them. See James Martin, *Gramsci's Political Analysis: A Critical Introduction* (New York: Macmillan, 1998), 52-53. Also see Anne Showstack Sassoon, *Gramsci's Politics*, 2nd ed. (Minneapolis: University of Minnesota Press, 1987), and Showstack Sassoon, *Gramsci and Contemporary Politics: Beyond Pessimism of the Intellectual* (New York: Routledge, 2000).

45 Only men served as expert witnesses in the cases I analyzed.

46 Michael MacDonald, "Madness, Suicide and the Computer," in Roy Porter and Andrew Wear, eds., *Problems and Methods in the History of Medicine* (London: Croom, 1987), 211.

47 I am currently working on a major study of the 1953 commission.

Chapter 2: The Making and Mapping of Capital Murder Case Files

1 Before 1962, there were no degrees of murder in Canada. Therefore, a jury could only find a defendant guilty of murder, not guilty, or not guilty because insane. For studies on the legal concept of responsibility, see H.L.A. Hart, *Punishment and Responsibility: Essays in the Philosophy of Law* (Oxford: Clarendon Press, 1968); Jonathan Glover, *Responsibility* (New York: Humanities Press, 1970); Mary I. Bockover, ed., *Rules, Rituals, and Responsibility* (La Salle, IL: Open Court, 1991); Richard C. Boldt, "The Construction of Responsibility in Criminal Law," *University of Pennsylvania Law Review* 140, 6 (1992): 2245-332; Finbarr McAuley, *Insanity, Psychiatry and Criminal Responsibility* (Dublin: Round Hall Press, 1993); J.R. Lucas, *Responsibility* (Oxford: Clarendon Press, 1993); Tamar Pitch, *Limited Responsibilities: Social Movements and Criminal Justice* (London and New York: Routledge, 1995); and Bernard Weiner, *Judgments of Responsibility: A Foundation for a Theory of Social Conduct* (New York: Guilford Press, 1995). For critical studies of the narratives of moral responsibility within law, see Martha Merril Umphrey, "The Dialogics of Legal Meaning: Spectacular Trials, the Unwritten Law, and Narratives of Criminal Responsibility," *Law and Society Review* 33, 2 (1999): 393-423, and Kimberley White-Mair, "Experts and Ordinary Men: Locating *R. v. Lavallée*, Battered Woman Syndrome, and the 'New' Psychiatric Expertise on Women within Canadian Legal History," *Canadian Journal of Women and the Law* 12, 2 (2000): 406-38.

2 I am expanding here on Patricia Ewick and Susan Silbey's term, introduced in the last chapter, as developed in their "Common Knowledge and Ideological Critique: The Significance of Knowing that the 'Haves' Come out Ahead," *Law and Society Review* 33, 4 (1999): 1037.

3 Tabulated from the record of capital cases listed by year in L. Gadoury and A. Lechasseur, "Persons Sentenced to Death in Canada, 1867-1976: An Inventory of Capital Case Files in the Records of the Department of Justice (RG 13)," (1992), Library and Archives Canada (LAC), Ottawa, Ontario. For reasons both practical and analytical, I chose to look at cases of individuals who were *convicted* for murder. Because I wished to conduct a national study, I looked to LAC, which houses capital case files from across the country in a single collection. A bountiful source of rich archival material, this collection includes every case in which a death sentence was pronounced (although not necessarily carried out), from Confederation to 1976, when capital punishment was abolished in Canada. During this period, every capital case file was sent to the federal minister of justice in Ottawa for review in council. Although he seldom deviated from the recommendations of the trial judge and the chief remissions officer, who wrote a summary of the case for him, the minister nonetheless decided whether a death sentence would be carried out or commuted to life in prison. For Canadian studies on capital cases, capital punishment, and the royal prerogative of mercy, see Carolyn Strange, "Comment: Capital Case Procedure Manual," *Criminal Law Quarterly* 14 (1998): 184-97, Strange, "Mercy for Murderers? A Historical Perspective on the Royal Prerogative of Mercy," *Saskatchewan Law Review* 64, 2 (2001): 559-72, and

Strange, "The Lottery of Death: Capital Punishment in Canada, 1867-1976," *Manitoba Law Journal* 23, 2 (1995): 594-619; Jonathan Swainger, "A Distant Edge of Authority: Capital Punishment and the Prerogative of Mercy in British Columbia, 1872-1880," in Hamar Foster and John McLaren, eds., *Essays in the History of Canadian Law* (Toronto: University of Toronto Press, 1995), 204-41; Kenneth L. Avio, "Capital Punishment in Canada: Statistical Evidence and Constitutional Issues," *Canadian Journal of Criminology* 30, 3 (October 1988): 331-49; and Jim Phillips, "The Operation of the Royal Pardon in Nova Scotia, 1749-1815," *University of Toronto Law Journal* 42 (1992): 401-49.

4 Minister of Trade and Commerce, *Criminal Statistics* (Ottawa: Minister of Trade and Commerce, 1912-25); later Dominion Borough of Canada, *Statistics of Criminal and Other Offences* (Ottawa: Dominion Borough of Canada, 1926-50). This tally is intended only to suggest the general trend in conviction rates and does not include statistics for 1950. Cross-reference with other sources suggests the data in these records may be incomplete. For instance, there is a discrepancy between the number of case files recorded in *Persons Sentenced to Death* and the number of capital convictions reported in *Criminal Statistics*. From 1920 to 1949, LAC has a record of 583 capital case files, but *Criminal Statistics* reports only 559 murder convictions for the same years. This may be explained by the fact that provincial and national record-keeping methods for criminal statistics were not consistent, and systems of gathering and reporting information changed often over the years. So, though *Criminal Statistics* is useful for understanding general trends in rates of conviction and acquittal, it should not necessarily be considered a precise measurement. The record of *Criminal Statistics* shows that of the 1,443 people charged between 1920 and 1950, 180 were detained for lunacy (139 men and 41 women), 704 were acquitted (580 men and 124 women), and 559 were convicted and sentenced to death (537 men and 22 women).

5 I selected the two cases for each year by first drawing a number between one and ten. I drew the number six. I then selected the sixth case in from the beginning of the list of cases for each year, as well as the sixth case in from the end of the list for each year.

6 Incompleteness was determined if personnel in charge of access to LAC records had declared a large portion of a file "missing" or "closed" to public review. However, it is difficult to evaluate with certainty the "completeness" of any file, as I do not know what may have been weeded out over the years or discarded by officials to conserve space or for other administrative purposes.

7 Kenneth Avio, "Capital Punishment," and Avio, "The Quality of Mercy: Exercise of the Royal Prerogative in Canada," *Canadian Public Policy* 12 (1987): 366-79.

8 See Strange, "Comment," 184.

9 Ibid.

10 In a brief 1998 article, Bruce MacFarlane, QC, describes how, while working as assistant deputy attorney general in charge of federal prosecutions, he came across the 1941 booklet in some "long-forgotten" Department of Justice files in Ottawa. For a verbatim reproduction of the booklet in its entirety, see Bruce MacFarlane, "Instructions to the Executioner," *Criminal Law Quarterly* 14 (1998): 178-83.

11 Ibid., 181.

12 Strange, "Comment," 185.

13 The next government publication regarding the remissions branch's duties did not come until 1956 – the same year a report on capital punishment was released. However, even in this more elaborate report, there is little information about the prerogative of mercy and capital case file dispositions. See Canada, Department of Justice, *Report of a Committee Appointed to Inquire into the Principles and Procedures Followed in the Remission Service of the Department of Justice of Canada* (Ottawa: Department of Justice, 1956), and *Report of the Joint Committee of the Senate and the House of Commons on Capital Punishment* (Ottawa: Department of Justice, 1956).

14 See Appendix in MacFarlane, "Instructions," 180.

15 Prior to Gallagher, and following the 1879-1913 reign of Augustus Power, various men held the position of chief remissions officer, but, arguably, none made as significant an impact on the daily operations of the branch and on the operation of the royal prerogative of mercy.

16 Ibid., 190-91.

17 See Government of Canada, National Parole Board, "History of Parole in Canada – Part 3: People behind the Reforms in the Years after the Second World War," http://www.npb-cnlc.gc.ca/about/part3_e.htm.

18 Quoted in Strange, "Comment," 193.

19 Quoted in ibid., 190-91.

20 The Lassandro case predates Gallagher's 1924 promotion to chief officer. W. Walsh, J.S.C., to the honourable secretary of state, 4 December 1922, 9, Florence Lassandro (1922), LAC, RG 13, vol. 1524, part 5.1, file CC146.

21 M.F. Gallagher, "The King vs Emilio Piccariello & Florence Lassandra [sic]," 12 April 1923, 2, Lassandro (1922), LAC, RG 13, vol. 1524, part 5.1, file CC146.

22 See J.V. Roberts et al., *Penal Populism and Public Opinion: Lessons from Five Countries* (Oxford: Oxford University Press, 2003), and Mariana Valverde, *Law's Dream of a Common Knowledge* (Princeton: Princeton University Press, 2003).

23 F.H. Allport (1937), quoted in Martin Roiser, "Commonsense, Science and Public Opinion," *Journal for the Theory of Social Behaviour* 17, 4 (1987): 416. For other contemporary studies on the media as representing public opinion and on ways in which judges continue to gauge public opinion or community standards in sentencing decisions, see Douglas Walton, *Appeal to Popular Opinion* (University Park: Pennsylvania State University Press, 1999); Roberts et al., *Penal Populism;* and Valverde, *Law's Dream,* 47-48.

24 For good examples of the theoretical and empirical use of approaches to text analysis and constructionism, see Robert Menzies, *Survival of the Sanest: Order and Disorder in a Pre-Trial Psychiatric Clinic* (Toronto: University of Toronto Press, 1989); Jeff Coulter, *The Social Construction of Mind: Studies in Ethnomethodology and Linguistic Philosophy* (Totowa, NJ: Macmillan, 1979); Ian Hacking, *The Social Construction of What?* (Cambridge, MA: Harvard University Press, 1999); Steve Woolgar, ed., *Knowledge and Reflexivity: New Frontiers in the Sociology of Knowledge* (London: Sage Publications, 1988); Gale Miller and Robert Digwall, eds., *Context and Method in Qualitative Research* (London: Sage Publications, 1997); James Holstein and Gale Miller, eds., *Challenges and Choices: Constructionist Perspectives on Social Problems* (Hawthorne, NY: Aldine de Gruyter, 2003); Gale Miller, "Toward Ethnographies of Institutional Discourse," *Journal of Contemporary Ethnography* 23, 3 (1994): 280-306; Robin Williams, "Sociology and the Vernacular Voice: Text, Context and the Sociological Imagination," *History of Human Sciences* 13, 4 (2000): 73-95; Mark Peyrot, "Psychological Testing and Forensic Decision Making: The Properties-in-Use of the MMPI," *Social Problems* 42, 4 (1995): 574-86; Derrol Palmer, "Identifying Delusional Discourse: Issues of Rationality, Reality and Power," *Sociology of Health and Illness* 22, 5 (2000): 661-78; Martyn Hammersley, "Conversation Analysis and Discourse Analysis: Methods or Paradigms?" *Discourse and Society* 14, 6 (2003): 751-81; Sarah Bailyn, "Who Makes the Rules? Using Wittgenstein in Social Theory," *Journal for the Theory of Social Behaviour* 32, 3 (2002): 311-29; Melvin Pollner, "Left of Ethnomethodology: The Rise and Decline of Radical Reflexivity," *American Sociological Review* 56 (1991): 370-80; Jaber Gubrium and James Holstein, "Narrative Practice and the Coherence of Personal Stories," *Sociological Quarterly* 39, 1 (1998): 163-87; and Umphrey, "Dialogics."

25 The semiotic approach to reading textual material was inspired by Ferdinand de Saussure's theory of structural linguistics, which Roland Barthes further developed. Barthes argued that the message, or meaning, of a text cannot be found in the words of the text itself but is embodied in the system of codes that structured the text. "Semiotics" is therefore the analytical process of uncovering those codes and employing them as a way to access the meaning of a given text. The fundamental components of text analysis used throughout this book were drawn especially from the works of Louis Althusser, Michel Foucault, and Jacques Derrida. For other examples, see David McNally, *Bodies of Meaning* (New York: State University of New York Press, 2001); Floyd Merrell, *Sign, Textuality, World* (Bloomington: University of Indiana Press, 1992); Andrew McKenna, *Violence and Difference: Girard, Derrida and Deconstruction* (Urbana: University of Illinois Press, 1992); Dorothy E. Smith, *The Conceptual Practices of Power: A Feminist Sociology of Knowledge* (Toronto: University of Toronto Press, 1990), and Smith, *Writing the Social: Critique, Theory and Investigation* (Toronto: University

of Toronto Press, 1999). For three excellent applied examples of text analysis, see Menzies, *Survival of the Sanest;* Ruth Harris, *Murders and Madness: Medicine, Law, and Society in the Fin de Siècle* (Oxford: Clarendon Press, 1989); and Alison Young, *Imagining Crime* (London: Sage Publications, 1986).

26 John Scott, *A Matter of Record: Documentary Sources in Social Research* (Cambridge: Polity Press, 1990), argues that we must consider the complex of social and interpersonal factors that intervene between the author, text, and audience to transform the messages found in the text. He suggests that to interpret the meaning of a text, we must recognize key moments in the "movement of the text from author to audience" (34). The internal meaning of a text cannot be known independent of its reception by an audience, and the moment we approach a text to interpret its meaning, we become part of that audience.

27 I refer here to the extended notion of "text" used by Pierre Bourdieu and others to include not only written records but also the structures and procedures that characterize a particular social/cultural/political/institutional site and that shaped the meaning and expression of the written texts. See Pierre Bourdieu, "The Force of Law: Toward a Sociology of the Juridical Field," *Hastings Law Journal* 38 (1987): 814-53.

Chapter 3: Criminological Thinking and Ways of "Knowing" the Criminal

1 See Dawn Moore and Mariana Valverde, "Maidens at Risk: 'Date Rape Drugs' and the Formation of Hybrid Risk Knowledges," *Economy and Society* 29, 4 (2000): 514-31. The authors argue that in assessing risk knowledges, it is "not always necessary or appropriate to divide knowledges using the binary opposition of expert vs. lay, scientific vs. common-sense." It is more often the case that many forms of knowledge – "hybrid knowledges" – are represented in discourses of risk (520). I think this best describes the dynamic of responsibility knowledge as well.

2 For secondary works on determinism, eugenics, public health, and the regulation of deviance in Canadian history, see Ian Dowbiggin, *Keeping America Sane: Psychiatry and Eugenics in the United States and Canada, 1880-1940* (Ithaca and London: Cornell University Press, 1997); Angus McLaren, "The Creation of a Haven for 'Human Thoroughbreds': The Sterilization of the Feeble-Minded and the Mentally Ill in British Columbia," *Canadian Historical Review* 67, 2 (1986): 127-50, and McLaren, *Our Own Master Race: Eugenics in Canada, 1855-1945* (Toronto: Oxford University Press, 1990); and Mariana Valverde, *The Age of Light, Soap and Water: Moral Reform in English Canada, 1885-1925* (Toronto: McClelland and Stewart, 1991). For good primary examples, see William L. Hutton, "A Brief for the Sterilization of the Feeble-Minded" (report prepared for Association of Ontario Mayors Annual Conference, Toronto, Ontario, June 1936); and generally the writings of Dr. Charles Kirk Clarke, including "A Clinic for Nervous and Mental Diseases," *Bulletin of the Ontario Hospitals for the Insane* 4 (January 1911): 73-77; Clarke, "Notes of a Clinical Case: The Case of W.M.B. – Moral Imbecility," *Bulletin of the Ontario Hospitals for the Insane* 7, 4 (July 1914): 207-31; Clarke, "The Defective Immigrant," *Public Health Journal* 7, 11 (November 1916): 462-65; Clarke, "Immigration," *Public Health Journal* 10, 10 (October 1919): 441-44; Clarke with C.B. Farrar, "One Thousand Psychiatric Cases from the Canadian Army," *Canadian Journal of Mental Hygiene* 1 (1919-20): 313-17; and Clarke, "The Mental Hygiene Movement" (paper presented at the Saskatchewan Educational Association, Saskatoon, 5 April 1920), Biographical Files, C.K. Clarke, Griffin-Greenland Collection, Archives of Canadian Psychiatry and Mental Health Services, Toronto, Ontario, file 2 a. 3.

3 See, particularly, works by the American physician Isaac Ray (1807-81), who was medical superintendent of the State Hospital for the Insane at Augusta, Georgia, and later, in 1845, at the Butler Hospital at Providence, Rhode Island. His most noteworthy book, *A Treatise on the Medical Jurisprudence of Insanity,* was published in 1838 and went through six editions. Dr. Ray reportedly published over 100 articles and books on mental illness in his career. His work is summarized in Arthur Fink, *Causes of Crime: Biological Theories in the United States 1800-1915* (New York: A.S. Barnes, 1938). Also see Charles Mercier, *Criminal Responsibility* (New York: Physicians and Surgeons Book Company, 1931); George W. Jacoby, *The Unsound Mind and the Law: A Presentation of Forensic Psychiatry* (New York and London: Funk

and Wagnalls, 1918); Ben Karpman, *Case Studies in the Psychopathology of Crime: A Reference Source for Research in Criminal Materials,* vol. 3 (Washington: Medical Science Press, 1948); and Dr. E. Mendel, *Text-Book of Psychiatry: A Psychological Study of Insanity for Practitioners and Students,* trans. William C. Krauss (Philadelphia: Physicians and Surgeons Book Company, 1907).

4 Mark Tebbit, *Philosophy of Law: An Introduction* (New York and London: Routledge, 2000), 140.

5 See H.B. Spaulding, "Insanity and Criminal Responsibility from the Legal Point of View," *Ontario Journal of Neuropsychiatry* (March 1933): 11-24; Charles A. Rymer, "The Insanity Plea in Crime: An Evaluation of the 1927 Law," *American Journal of Psychiatry* 105 (February 1949): 594-600; D.O. Lynch, "Some Observations on the Criminally Insane with Special Reference to Those Charged with Murder," *Ontario Journal of Neuropsychiatry* 12 (December 1937): 39-52; Joseph Moore, "Insanity as a Defense for Crime," *American Journal of Psychiatry* 85 (September 1929): 263-67; Carlos MacDonald, "Should the Plea of Insanity as a Defense to an Indictment for Crime Be Abolished?" *American Journal of Insanity* 76 (January 1920): 295-302; J.C. McRuer, "Insanity as a Legal Defence," *Canadian Medical Association Journal* 61 (November 1949): 489-95; and G.H. Stevenson, "Insanity as a Criminal Defence: The Psychiatric Viewpoint," *Canadian Medical Association Journal* 58 (February 1948): 174-78.

6 McLaren, *Our Own Master Race.*

7 Abraham Myerson, "Nature of Feeble-Mindedness," *American Journal of Psychiatry* 89 (May 1933): 1205-6. Also see Dr. Myerson's *Inheritance of Mental Diseases* (Baltimore: Williams, 1925).

8 Myerson, "Nature of Feeble-Mindedness," 1206-7.

9 Ibid., 1211.

10 The *Canadian Journal of Mental Hygiene* was a publication of the Canadian National Committee for Mental Hygiene.

11 Quoted in McLaren, *Our Own Master Race,* 60.

12 The following are two good examples of standard medical school texts: Aaron Rosanoff, ed., *Manual of Psychiatry,* 5th ed. (New York: Wiley, 1920), and Mendel, *Text-Book of Psychiatry.*

13 See, particularly, works by Dr. Charles Mercier, including *Criminal Responsibility.* Mercier was considered the leading North American authority on criminal insanity. Also see Fink, *Causes of Crime,* written for "students of criminology."

14 Sheila Jasanoff, *Science at the Bar: Law, Science and Technology in America* (Cambridge, MA: Harvard University Press, 1995), 47-48.

15 See, for instance, Angus McLaren, "Males, Migrants, and Murder in British Columbia, 1900-1923," in F. Iacovetta and W. Mitchinson, eds., *On the Case: Explorations in Social History* (Toronto: University of Toronto Press, 1998), 158-80; Robert Menzies, "The Making of Criminal Insanity in British Columbia: Granby Farrant and the Provincial Mental Home, Colquitz, 1919-1933," in Hamar Foster and John McLaren, eds., *Essays in the History of Canadian Law Volume 6* (Toronto: University of Toronto Press, 1995), 274-313; and Menzies, *Survival of the Sanest: Order and Disorder in a Pre-Trial Psychiatric Clinic* (Toronto: University of Toronto Press, 1989). For other good examples, see the following: Michael Clark and Catherine Crawford, eds., *Legal Medicine in History* (Cambridge: Cambridge University Press, 1994); J.E. Goldstein, *Console and Classify: The French Psychiatric Profession in the Nineteenth Century* (Cambridge: Cambridge University Press, 1987); G.N. Grob, *Mental Illness and American Society, 1875-1940* (Princeton: Princeton University Press, 1983); Andrew Scull, *Social Order/ Mental Disorder: Anglo-American Psychiatry in Historical Perspective* (London: Routledge, 1989); and Roger Smith, *Trial by Medicine: Insanity and Responsibility in Victorian Trial* (Edinburgh: Edinburgh University Press, 1981).

16 *R. v. M'Naghten* (1843), 10 Cl. and F. 200, 8 E.R. 718.

17 For texts on the early laws of evidence, see the following primary examples: John Davison Lawson, *The Law of Expert and Opinion Evidence Reduced to Rules* (Chicago: T.H. Flood, 1900); William Renwick Riddell, "The Medical Man as a Witness," *Canadian Journal of Medicine and Surgery* (December 1910): 1-26; Edmund Powell, *Principles and Practice of the Law of Evidence: Canadian Notes by Hon. Mr. Justice Russell* (London: Butterworth, 1911); Sidney

L. Phipson, *The Law of Evidence,* 8th ed. (Toronto: Carswell, 1930); Sir James Fitzjames Stephen, *A Digest of the Law of Evidence*, 12th ed. (London: Macmillan, 1936); John Henry Wigmore, *A Treatise on the Anglo-American System of Evidence in Trials at Common Law: Including the Statutes and Judicial Decisions of All Jurisdictions of the United States and Canada* (Boston: Little, Brown, 1923); John MacArthur Maguire, *Evidence: Common Sense and Common Law* (Chicago: Foundation Press, 1947); Kenneth G. Gray, *Law and the Practice of Medicine* (Toronto: Ryerson Press, 1947); and Henry Roscoe, *Roscoe's Criminal Evidence: The Law, Evidence and Practice in Criminal Cases* (Toronto: Carswell, 1952). For a secondary study on the history of evidence, see William Twining and Iain Hampsher-Monk, eds., *Evidence and Inference in History and Law: Interdisciplinary Dialogues* (Evanston, IL: Northwestern University Press, 2003). For contemporary references on evidence law and the expert witness, see Michael R. Grover, *Expert Witness: The Forensic Appraiser* (Winnipeg: Appraisal Institute of Canada, 1991); David J. Doust, *The Expert Witness* (Ayer's Cliff, QC: Pachelle, 1997); Law Society of Upper Canada, *The Law of Evidence* (Toronto: Irwin Law, 2004); and John Sopinka, *The Law of Evidence in Canada* (Markham, ON: Butterworths, 2004).

18 Gray, *Law and the Practice,* 15.

19 Ibid.

20 Sidney L. Phipson, quoted in ibid., 14.

21 Stephen, *A Digest of the Law,* 12th ed., 69 (emphasis added).

22 Jasanoff, *Science at the Bar,* 47-48.

23 Tony Ward, "Law, Common Sense and the Authority of Science: Expert Witnesses and Criminal Insanity in England, ca. 1840-1940," *Social and Legal Studies* 6, 3 (1997): 343-62. See also Chapter 2 of this book.

24 This idea is explored in a contemporary context in Mariana Valverde, "Social Facticity and the Law: A Social Expert's Account of Law," *Social and Legal Studies* 5, 2 (1996): 201-17.

25 Technically, the defences of provocation and self-defence would negate a defence of insanity: both assume intent, whereas insanity assumes a lack of intent.

26 Trial transcripts, 102, Frances Harrop (1940), Library and Archives Canada (LAC), Ottawa, Ontario, RG 13, vol. 1625, part 3, file CC514.

27 Ibid., 16-17.

28 Ibid.

29 Ibid., 17.

30 Ibid., 18.

31 See Chapter 2 for more on the perceived effects of poverty and other environmental conditions on mental health.

32 Ibid., 21.

33 Ibid., 114-20. One procedural difficulty that emerged repeatedly with expert testimony during this period was the fact that much of their evidence was based on hearsay. To get around this legal technicality, a witness was not permitted to report directly on what the accused or others said to him. He was, however, permitted to give his opinions, which were, of course, based primarily on the very interviews he could not report.

34 Ibid., 128-29.

35 Ibid.

36 In the case of Albert Le Beaux (1921), for example, the trial judge commented in his report to the minister of justice that the jury was "composed entirely of English speaking Protestants." Also, F. Murray Greenwood and Beverley Boissery show that before the 1950s the only provinces to theoretically qualify women for jury duty were British Columbia (in 1922) and Nova Scotia (in 1929), although women were not actually called to jury duty in Nova Scotia until 1951. Greenwood and Boissery, *Uncertain Justice* (Toronto: Dundurn Press, 2000), 126-32. There were no women jurors in the cases analyzed for this book.

37 Greenwood and Boissery, *Uncertain Justice,* 135.

38 "Judge's Charge," 136, Frances Harrop (1940), LAC, RG 13, vol. 1625, part 3, file CC514.

39 Ibid. This again was largely due to the limitations of legal language to directly incorporate psychiatric dogma into law. Frances Harrop's material conditions were readily entered as factual evidence; however, evidence pertaining to her past state of mind was somehow less discernible.

40 Carlos F. MacDonald, "The Ethical Aspects of Expert Testimony in Relation to the Plea of Insanity as a Defense to an Indictment for Crime," *American Journal of Insanity* 67 (1910-11): 241.
41 Ibid. For other examples of legal commentary on the role and value of the expert witness and psychiatry, see F. Dodd, "The Legal and Medical Theories of Mental Disease in Criminal Cases," *American Journal of Insanity* 39 (April 1883): 456-69; Riddell, "Medical Man"; Ainsworth Mitchell, *The Expert Witness* (Cambridge: W. Heffer and Sons, 1923); Roscoe Pound, "Science and Legal Procedure," *American Journal of Psychiatry* 85 (July 1928): 33-51; Kenneth Gray, "Psychiatry and the Criminal Code," *Ontario Journal of Neuropsychiatry* 10 (December 1935): 44-55; and Manfred Guttmacher and Henry Weihofen, *The Role of Psychiatry in the Law* (Springfield, IL: Thomas, 1968).
42 D. Plouffe, "The Attitude of the Psychiatrists as Experts in Criminal Courts," *Ontario Journal of Neuropsychiatry* 12 (December 1937): 28. For additional commentaries from the medical perspective on legal insanity and the role of expert evidence, see Daniel Clark, "Medical Evidence in Courts of Law," *American Journal of Insanity* 35 (January 1879): 375-99; William Francis Drewry, "The Scope of the Activities of the Alienist," *American Journal of Insanity* 67, 1 (July 1910): 1-16; Henry Stedman et al., "Report of the Committee on Medical Expert Testimony of the American Medico-Psychological Association," *American Journal of Insanity* 67 (1910-11): 177-86; William Nelson, "Psychiatry and Its Relationship to the Administration of the Criminal Law," *American Journal of Psychiatry* 89 (January 1933): 703-23; and J.D. Heaslip, "The Position of Medicine in the Treatment of Crime," *Ontario Journal of Neuropsychiatry* 12 (December 1937): 33-38.
43 Plouffe, "Attitude of the Psychiatrists," 28.
44 Spaulding, "Insanity and Criminal Responsibility," 22.
45 Ruth Harris, *Murders and Madness: Medicine, Law, and Society in the Fin de Siècle* (Oxford: Clarendon Press, 1989), 11, 130, 151, and 266. Harris argues that, in many French cases, the defendant's self-characterization hardly differed from that advanced by the psychiatrist. While delivering their professional diagnoses and opinions during courtroom questioning, experts often reiterated defendants' own statements regarding the cause(s) of their behaviour and mind-state. Harris further argues that, in most cases, both judges and doctors were "eager to ferret out physical and mental signs of disorder" (264). However, there were also exceptions. In fewer cases, Harris shows that when psychiatrists digressed from their normal use of lay language to assert their diagnostic authority by offering a strict scientific description of the defendant, they were faced with resistance. By providing detailed information about family histories and personal illnesses, Harris shows how defendants actively participated in the creation of their psychological and physiological difference – whether or not the expert agreed with their self-characterization.
46 Trial transcripts, 100-1, Mary Smith (1935), LAC, RG 13, vol. 1599, part 3, file CC439.
47 There is not much evidence to suggest that experts saw themselves competing in law with the common sensibilities of women, or other marginalized populations.
48 Charles Kirk Clarke, "Canadian Law in Regard to Responsibility," *Queen's Quarterly* (n.d.): 274-75, C.K. Clarke Archives (CKCA), Farrar Library, Clarke Institute of Psychiatry, Toronto, Ontario, vol. 2, file 13.
49 Ibid., 286.
50 Ibid.
51 Joel Peter Eigen, *Witnessing Insanity: Madness and Mad-Doctors in the English Court* (New Haven: Yale University Press, 1995), 94.
52 Douglas Walton, *Appeal to Popular Opinion* (University Park: Pennsylvania State University Press, 1999), 107.
53 Ward, "Law, Common Sense," 357. Alan Norrie, *Crime, Reason and History* (London: Butterworths, 1993), quoted in ibid., 357.
54 Michel Foucault, "About the Concept of the Dangerous Individual in Nineteenth Century Legal Psychiatry," *International Journal of Law and Psychiatry* 1 (1978): 6. This is a very simplistic interpretation of a complex paradigm developed throughout Foucault's work: see particularly his *The Birth of the Clinic: An Archaeology of Medical Perception*, trans. A.M. Sheridan Smith (New York: Vintage Books, 1973), which he later expands to consider more subtle

forms of self-regulation. However, most applications of Foucault's approach in medical-legal literature tend to reconstruct a unidirectional top-down model in which the powerful regulate the powerless.

55 For abstracts and excerpts from primary literature dating back to the sixteenth century, see R. Hunter and I. Macalpine, eds., *Three Hundred Years of Psychiatry: 1535-1860* (London: Oxford University Press, 1963).

56 Nigel Walker, *Crime and Insanity in England* (Edinburgh: Edinburgh University Press, 1968), 246.

Chapter 4: Negotiating Responsibility in Law's "Marketplace"

1 Michel Foucault described the trial as "an event that provided the intersection of discourses that differed in origin, form, organization, and function." Foucault, ed., *"I, Pierre Rivière, Having Slaughtered My Mother, My Sister, and My Brother" ... A Case of Parricide in the 19th Century* (Lincoln: University of Nebraska Press, 1975), x-xi.

2 Michael MacDonald, "Madness, Suicide and the Computer," in Roy Porter and Andrew Wear, eds., *Problems and Methods in the History of Medicine* (London: Croom, 1987), 211.

3 Because none of the capital case files I examined included an insanity defence that successfully quashed a conviction, they did not permit a comprehensive study of this defence in Canada. What is interesting, however, is that the question of a defendant's state of mind was usually on the table at some point in each case, even in the absence of an insanity defence. For instance, of the sixty-six capital cases analyzed for this study, only nineteen (29 percent) involved a formal plea of insanity. Yet, of the remaining forty-seven "non-insanity" cases, the defendant's mental capacity was raised as a primary issue in thirty-two (68 percent) examples. This indicates that the defendant's state of mind was at issue during some stage of the trial or commutation process in 77 percent of the cases. This finding alone points to the need for a more qualitative reading of capital case files.

4 In England, the verdict would read "guilty but insane"; in the US, it was "not guilty by reason of insanity." In Canada, we have since adopted the US wording.

5 H.B. Spaulding, "Insanity and Criminal Responsibility from the Legal Point of View," *Ontario Journal of Neuropsychiatry* (March 1933): 11-24.

6 This supports Gerry Johnston's findings regarding the role of psychiatry in early English criminal cases. According to him, "there is a widespread perception, which some psychiatrists have re-enforced, that psychiatry seeks to undermine notions of moral responsibility, that it seeks a relaxation of law and ethics. The courts no doubt recognized that the notion of moral responsibility is indispensable to the functioning of modern society, and have therefore been reluctant to recognize psychiatric doctrines *in the courtroom*. Once the criminal and the crime have been censured, however, the objection to psychiatry becomes less noticeable." Johnston, "From Experts on Responsibility to Advisors on Punishment: The Role of Psychiatrists in Penal Matters," in P. Rush, S. McVeigh, and A. Young, eds., *Criminal Legal Doctrine* (Brookfield, VT: Ashgate, 1997), 101.

7 In 29 percent of the cases used for this study, a formal plea of insanity was introduced at trial and ultimately failed. Yet a closer reading of trial and post-trial documentation shows that the subject of mental capacity was raised at some point in approximately 80 percent of cases.

8 According to s. 201 of the *Criminal Code of Canada* (1955), culpable homicide is murder

> (a) where the person who causes the death of a human being (i) means to cause his death, or (ii) means to cause him bodily harm that he knows is likely to cause his death, and is reckless whether death ensues or not;
>
> (b) where a person, meaning to cause death to a human being or meaning to cause his death, and being reckless whether death ensues or not, by accident or mistake causes death to another human being, notwithstanding that he does not mean to cause death or bodily harm to that human being; or
>
> (c) where a person, for an unlawful object, does anything that he knows or ought to know is likely to cause death, and thereby causes death to a human being, notwithstanding that he desires to effect his object without causing death or bodily harm to any human being.

Section 201 was formerly s. 259. It was s. 277 in the Code of 1892 and s. 147 of the *English Draft Code.*

9 *R. v. Tolson* (1889), 23 Q.B.D. 168, quoted in Martin Friedland, ed., *Cases and Materials on Criminal Law and Procedure,* 5th ed. (Toronto: University of Toronto Press, 1978), 404. *Cases and Materials* is a classic Canadian text on criminal law and procedure.

10 Benjamin Andoh, "The M'Naghten Rules – The Story so Far," *Medical-Legal Journal* 61, 2 (Spring 1993): 98.

11 Jonathan Glover, *Responsibility* (New York: Humanities Press, 1970), 3, 20.

12 In 1948-49, s. 19 became what is now s. 16 of the *Criminal Code.* For a good overview of the history of the M'Naghten rules, along with a breakdown of the main criticisms and reform proposals, see Andoh, "The M'Naghten Rules," 93-103.

13 Ibid., 96-97.

14 See, for example, Carlos MacDonald, "Should the Plea of Insanity as a Defense to an Indictment for Crime Be Abolished?" *American Journal of Psychiatry* 76 (January 1920): 295-302, and Joseph Moore, "Insanity as a Defense for Crime," *American Journal of Psychiatry* 85 (September 1928): 263-67.

15 For other primary discussions of the practice of the insanity defence and the use of the M'Naghten rules in Canada and the United States, see Charles A. Rymer, "The Insanity Plea in Crime: An Evaluation of the 1927 Law," *American Journal of Psychiatry* 105 (February 1949): 594-600; D.O. Lynch, "Some Observations on the Criminally Insane with Special Reference to Those Charged with Murder," *Ontario Journal of Neuropsychiatry* 12 (December 1937): 39-52; J.C. McRuer, "Insanity as a Legal Defence," *Canadian Medical Association Journal* 61 (November 1949): 489-95; G.H. Stevenson, "Insanity as a Criminal Defence: The Psychiatric Viewpoint," *Canadian Medical Association Journal* 58 (February 1949): 174-78; Charles North, "A Proposed Change in the Criminal Law," *American Journal of Insanity* 70 (January 1914): 683-94; John Charles Bucknill, "The Plea of Insanity in the Case of Charles Julius Guiteau," *American Journal of Insanity* 39 (October 1882): 181-212; P.H. Winfield, ed., *Mental Abnormality and Crime* (London: Macmillan, 1944); and Jerome Hall, "Responsibility and Law: Defense of the McNaghten Rules," *American Bar Association Journal* 12 (October 1956): 917-90.

16 The law regarding opinion evidence and the admittance of expert testimony is outlined in Kenneth G. Gray, *Law and the Practice of Medicine* (Toronto: Ryerson Press, 1947). According to this text, "the general rule is that a witness is not permitted to testify as to his opinion or beliefs ... One exception to this rule prevails in the case of a qualified expert witness, who may give an opinion upon the facts, even in a case with which he has had no association except as a witness. The opinions of skilled witnesses are admissible whenever the subject is one upon which competency to form an opinion can only be acquired by a course of special study or experience" (14).

17 Spaulding, "Insanity and Criminal Responsibility," 12-13. Spaulding's article was originally presented as a paper at the Toronto Psychiatric Hospital Seminar, Toronto, 28 January 1933.

18 Ibid., 17.

19 Charles Kirk Clarke, "Canadian Law in Regard to Responsibility," *Queen's Quarterly* (n.d.): 274-78, C.K. Clarke Archives (CKCA), Farrar Library, Clarke Institute of Psychiatry, Toronto, Ontario, vol. 2, file 13.

20 Forty-two percent of defendants who pleaded insanity received recommendations to mercy from the judge/jury, and 63 percent were commuted or ordered new trials. The odds of escaping execution through evidence of insanity were only slightly better than for the larger sample of convicted murderers who did not use this defence: these received recommendations to mercy in 42 percent of cases (where information was available); 55 percent of them escaped execution.

21 Although the interpretation of insanity law was quite flexible, the language that could be used and the theories that were recognized as valid articulations of insanity were doctrinally bound.

22 M.F. Gallagher, "Memorandum for the Right Honourable the Minister of Justice," 1-2, Marie Anne Houde (Gagnon) (1920), Library and Archives Canada (LAC), Ottawa, Ontario, RG 13, vol. 1507, part 1.2, file CC143.

23 "The Gagnon Case. To the Editor of the Gazette" (newspaper clipping stamped 28 September 1920), Houde (1920), LAC, RG 13, vol. 1507, file CC143.
24 Ibid.
25 See also Canadian Prisoners' Welfare Association (CPWA) to Right Hon. C.J. Doherty, minister of justice, 17 September 1920, Houde (1920), LAC, RG 13, vol. 1507, file CC143. The CPWA organized a substantial petition-signing campaign and claimed that the signatures represented "all classes of society and, though mostly from this province [Quebec], include some signatures from further afield. Clergymen, prominent commercial men, medical men, lawyers and industrial workers are among the signatories."
26 For a similar analysis of the competing and simultaneous characterizations of a condemned Canadian woman, see Karen Dubinsky and Franka Iacovetta, "Murder, Womanly Virtue, and Motherhood: The Case of Angelina Napolitano, 1911-1922," *Canadian Historical Review* 72, 4 (1991): 505.
27 Letter titled "Is a Woman to Hang?" from the CPWA, 7 August 1920, Houde (1920), LAC, RG 13, vol. 1507, file CC143.
28 "The Gagnon Case. To the Editor of the Gazette" (newspaper clipping stamped 28 September 1920), Houde (1920), LAC, RG 13, vol. 1507, file CC143.
29 Thomas Vieu to Hon. J.C. Doherty, minister of justice, 16 September 1920, Houde (1920), LAC, RG 13, vol. 1507, file CC143.
30 This is supported by the 1987 edition of *Criminal Pleading and Practice in Canada,* in which E.G. Ewaschuk comments that, although there is no formal defence of diminished responsibility in Canada, "an unarticulated form of diminished responsibility existed in Canada in the sense that evidence of mental disorder short of legal insanity is considered in determining specific intent together with other relevant factors." Quoted in Judith Ablett Kerr, "A Licence to Kill or an Overdue Reform? The Case of Diminished Responsibility," *Otago Law Review* 9, 1 (1997): 3.
31 "Charge to the Jury," in trial transcripts, 321, William Monchuk (1938), LAC, RG 13, vol. 1614, file CC483.
32 According to s. 261 of the *Criminal Code,* the defence of provocation could justify a reduction of a charge from murder to manslaughter but only if the victim had caused the provocation. The provocation defence was easily accepted by the appeal court and the public for the killing of Mr. John Seabright, Monchuk's rival neighbour. However, it was debated whether Monchuk was so provoked by his dispute with Seabright that it also justified a manslaughter charge for the killing of Seabright's wife and daughter.
33 McRuer's comments appeared in an article entitled "Conclude Hearing Death Appeal," stamped 15 June 1938, Monchuk (1938), LAC, RG 13, vol. 1614, file CC483. Note also the various spellings of Monchuk's name, including Manchuck and Munchuk. The most frequent version is Monchuk.
34 J.J. Bench, KC, to M.F. Gallagher, 14 May 1938, Monchuk (1938), LAC, RG 13, vol. 1614, file CC483.
35 E. Whitman, secretary of the Women's Auxiliary to U.M.M.A., Calgary, Alberta, to Hon. Hugh Guthrie, minister of justice, 16 October 1934, Dina Dranchuk (1934), LAC, RG 13, vol. 1592, part 1, file CC418.
36 Mrs. C.D. Adam, secretary Women's Section of the Canadian Labor Party, to Hugh Guthrie, minister of justice, 16 October 1934, Dranchuk (1934), LAC, RG 13, vol. 1592, part 1, file CC418.
37 E. Clare Darling, barrister, solicitor, notary, to minister of justice, 5 October 1994, Dranchuk (1934), LAC, RG 13, vol. 1592, part 1, file CC418.
38 Ibid.
39 This was not the trend of executive clemency decisions during the 1930s, which actually saw the highest execution rate in post-Confederation history.
40 Percy Farebrother to "Minister of Justice," 19 October 1940, Annie Rubletz (1940), LAC, RG 13, vol. 1627, part 1, file CC522. Her surname is also spelled "Rubelietz."
41 "British Justice in Canada," *Prairie Citizen* (date unknown), Rubletz (1940), LAC, RG 13, vol. 1627, part 1, file CC522.

42 Ibid. We can also see how the social conditions created by war, and the experiences of individuals in that social context, shaped the significance of particular responses to cases involving men who were identified as soldiers. For example, it was standard practice to include their military records as part of the documentary information passed on to the minister of justice. And a soldier's behaviour during service was typically entered as evidence of "character." In the case of William Hainen (1945), the point was raised that the accused was "in uniform" when he beat a woman to death with a piece of wood. Hainen's defence at trial was insanity and drunkenness, both brought on by his war experience. However, despite expert testimony and recommendations to mercy from the trial judge and jury, Hainen was executed.

43 Mrs. E. Eaton to "Hon Earnest Lapointe," minister of justice, 24 October 1940, Rubletz (1940), LAC, RG 13, vol. 1627, part 1, file CC522.

44 Another Mother, "Calls for Mercy," *Regina Leader-Post,* 18 October 1940, Rubletz (1940), LAC, RG 13, vol. 1627, part 1, file CC522.

45 Arthur Davies to Hon. Ernest Lapointe, 19 October 1940, Rubletz (1940), LAC, RG 13, vol. 1627, part 1, file CC522.

46 Miss Mary L. Kennedy to minister of justice, stamped 15 June 1940, 2 (underlining in original), Frances Harrop (1940), LAC, RG 13, vol. 1625, part 1, file CC514.

47 W.L. Lockhead, "Genetics: The Science of Breeding," *Canadian Bookman* 1 (July 1919): 66, quoted in Angus McLaren, *Our Own Master Race: Eugenics in Canada, 1855-1945* (Toronto: Oxford University Press, 1990), 13.

48 McLaren, *Our Own Master Race,* 99.

49 Terry L. Chapman, "The Early Eugenics Movement in Western Canada," *Alberta History* 25 (1977): 14.

50 *An Act Respecting Sexual Sterilization,* S.B.C. 1933, c. 59. See also McLaren, *Our Own Master Race,* 90-91.

51 See Mariana Valverde, *The Age of Light, Soap and Water: Moral Reform in English Canada, 1885-1925* (Toronto: McClelland and Stewart, 1991), and McLaren, *Our Own Master Race.*

52 See, generally, the file of Annie Rubletz (1940), LAC, for many opinions regarding the "uncivilized" and "un-Christian" practice of executing women.

53 "Welland Burglaries Are Heard," *St. Catharines Star,* Harry Rudka (1922), LAC, RG 13, vol. 1520, part 2, file 694A/CC118.

54 W.M. German to Sir Lomer Gouin, K.C.M.G., minister of justice, 13 January 1932, Harry Rudka (1922), LAC, RG 13, vol. 1520, part 2, file 694A/CC118.

55 Quoted in "Four Sentenced to Hang in Torture Murder of Woman," *Ottawa Journal,* 13 September 1944, William Schmidt (1944), LAC, RG 13, vol. 1645, part 2.1, file CC568.

56 C.R. Fitch to M.F. Gallagher, for the deputy minister of justice, 30 November 1944, 1, Schmidt (1944), LAC, RG 13, vol. 1645, part 2.1, file CC568.

57 John Haddad to minister of justice, 11 January 1942, Frank Patrick (1941), LAC, RG 13, vol. 1633, part 2.2, file CC539.

58 Muriel D. Beatty to minister of justice, 12 January 1942, Patrick (1941), LAC, RG 13, vol. 1633, part 2.2, file CC539.

59 Rev. Jules Pirot, parish priest, Esterhazy, Saskatchewan, to minister of justice, 26 December 1941, 1, Patrick (1941), LAC, RG 13, vol. 1633, part 2.2, file CC539.

60 Ibid.

61 Ibid., 2.

62 Ibid.

63 Ibid., 3.

64 James Fitzjames Stephen, *A Digest of the Law of Evidence,* 12th ed. (London: Macmillan, 1936), article 57 on "Evidence of Character in Criminal Cases by Witnesses Other than the Accused," 74 (emphasis added).

65 Ibid., article 59 on the "Meaning of Character," 77.

66 "Judge's charge" to jury, 10-11, James McGrath (1931), LAC, RG 13, vol. 1572, part 3, file CC360.

67 The *Criminal Code of Canada,* 1955, s. 16(2), previously s. 19(1), notes that "a person is insane when he is in a state of natural imbecility or has a disease of the mind to an extent that renders him incapable of appreciating the nature and quality of an act or omission or of knowing that the act was wrong."

68 Dr. Loggie's testimony, trial transcripts, 216-18, Sarah Jackson (1920), LAC, RG 13, vol. 1509, part 2.2, file 654A/CC147.

69 "Judge's charge" to the jury, McGrath (1931), LAC, RG 13, vol. 1572, part 3, file CC360.

70 In his analysis of British medical-legal history, Joel Eigen shows that when reason was "dethroned" and "the will no longer restrained by judgment," the sufferer was considered in a "common sense philosophy" to be "driven mad by his or her passions." Passion, Eigen explains, "clearly had autonomous power to produce madness." Eigen, *Witnessing Insanity: Madness and Mad-Doctors in the English Court* (New Haven: Yale University Press, 1995), 77. See also Michel Foucault, *Madness and Civilization: A History of Insanity in the Age of Reason* (New York: Vintage Books, 1965).

71 Loggie's testimony, Jackson (1920), LAC.

72 E.H. Cooke, medical superintendent of the Provincial Mental Hospital, Ponoka, Alberta, to "The Deputy Attorney General, Edmonton," 22 November 1930, George Dvernichuk (1930), LAC, RG 13, vol. 1564, file CC332.

73 See Valverde, *The Age of Light;* Carolyn Strange, *Toronto's Girl Problem: The Perils and Pleasures of the City, 1880-1930* (Toronto: University of Toronto Press, 1995); Strange, ed., *Qualities of Mercy* (Vancouver: UBC Press, 1997); McLaren, *Our Own Master Race;* Mona Gleason, *Normalizing the Ideal: Psychology, Schooling, and the Family in Postwar Canada* (Toronto: University of Toronto Press, 1999); Robert Menzies, "The Making of Criminal Insanity in British Columbia: Granby Farrant and the Provincial Mental Home, Colquitz 1919-1933," in Hamar Foster and John McLaren, eds., *Essays in the History of Canadian Law Volume 6* (Toronto: University of Toronto Press, 1995), 274-313; Kimberley White-Mair, "Experts and Ordinary Men: Locating *R. v. Lavallée,* Battered Woman Syndrome, and the 'New' Psychiatric Expertise on Women within Canadian Legal History," *Canadian Journal of Women and the Law* 12, 2 (2000): 406-38, and White, "Making Sense and Doing Justice: Exploring Criminal Justice Interpretations of Psychiatric Expert Evidence in Early-20th Century Canada," in Claire Dolan, ed., *Entre justice et justiciables: Les auxiliaires de la justice du Moyen Age au XXe siècle* (Laval: Presses de l'Université Laval, 2005), 789-804.

74 Eigen, *Witnessing Insanity,* 6.

75 The question of who had the right to decide matters of mind-state and criminal responsibility would later become a central issue in the 1953 Royal Commission on the Law of Insanity and again in Gilbert Sharpe, *Mental Disorder Project – Criminal Law Review: Final Report* (Ottawa: Department of Justice, 1985).

Chapter 5: The Racialization of Criminal Responsibility

1 For historical studies, see James Walker, *"Race," Rights and the Law in the Supreme Court of Canada* (Waterloo, ON: Wilfrid Laurier University Press, 1997), and Constance Backhouse, *Colour-Coded: A Legal History of Racism in Canada, 1900-1950* (Toronto: University of Toronto Press, 1999).

2 For instance, Avio shows that being Native Canadian increased the odds of execution by a factor of 6.1 over the rate found for Anglo-Canadians. See Avio, "Capital Punishment in Canada: Statistical Evidence and Constitutional Issues," *Canadian Journal of Criminology* 30, 3 (October 1988): Table 1, "Execution Risk Disparities," 340.

3 Walker, *"Race," Rights and the Law,* 19-21; Backhouse, *Colour-Coded,* 6-12.

4 William L. Hutton, "A Brief for the Sterilization of the Feeble-Minded" (report prepared for Association of Ontario Mayors Annual Conference, Toronto, Ontario, June 1936), 4.

5 Walker, *"Race," Rights and the Law,* 30. The following statement about the order of things was expressed in 1900 by Gilbert Murray, a prominent English scholar: "There is in the world a hierarchy of races ... [Some] will direct and rule the others, and the lower work of the world will tend in the long run to be done by the lower breeds of men. This much we of the ruling colour will no doubt accept as obvious." Quoted in ibid., 12.

6 For a thorough examination of the construction of "Indian" identity in early Canadian society, see, generally, works by Tina Loo, particularly her "Dan Cranmer's Potlatch: Law as Coercion, Symbol, and Rhetoric in British Columbia, 1884-1951," *Canadian Historical Review* 73, 2 (1992): 125-65; "The Road from Bute Inlet: Crime and Colonial Identity in British Columbia," in Jim Phillips, Tina Loo, and Susan Lewthwaite, eds., *Essays in the History of Canadian Law,* vol. 5, *Crime and Criminal Justice* (Toronto: Osgoode Society, 1994), 112-42; "Native Culture and the Modification of Capital Punishment in Nineteenth-Century British Columbia," in Carolyn Strange, ed., *Qualities of Mercy* (Vancouver: UBC Press, 1997), 104-29. See also works by Sarah Carter, in particular her *Aboriginal People and Colonizers of Western Canada to 1900* (Toronto: University of Toronto Press, 1999).

7 Trial transcripts, 12, Albert Le Beaux (1921), Library and Archives Canada (LAC), Ottawa, Ontario, RG 13, vol. 1513, file CC166.

8 Ibid., 15.

9 Ibid., 15, 43.

10 Lucien Dubuc (trial judge), to the secretary of state, Re: The King vs Le Beaux, 30 June 1921, 5, Le Beaux (1921), LAC, RG 13, vol. 1513, file CC166.

11 Bishop G. Breynat is quoted in the summary report titled "Memorandum for the Right Honourable the Minister of Justice," 9, Le Beaux (1921), LAC, RG 13, vol. 1513, file 670A/CC166.

12 Ibid., 10.

13 Ibid., 6.

14 Ibid., 9.

15 M.F. Gallagher, "Memorandum for the Honourable the Acting Minister of Justice," 2, 12, Sarah Jackson (1920), LAC, RG 13, vol. 1509, part 2.1, file CC147.

16 H.C. Reynolds to C.J. Doherty, minister of justice, Jackson (1920), LAC, RG 13, vol. 1509, part 2.1, file CC147.

17 "In the Wilderness," *True Romance,* March 1962, 36.

18 Ibid., 84.

19 Ibid., 86.

20 Nellie L. McClung to C.J. Doherty, minister of justice, 3 November 1920, Jackson (1920), LAC, RG 13, vol. 1509, part 2.1, file CC147. For more information on McClung, see her *The Stream Runs Fast: My Own Story* (Toronto: Thomas Allen, 1945).

21 T.R.L. MacInnes to Michael Gallagher, 27 October 1944, Paul Abraham (1944), LAC, RG 13, vol. 1646, part 1, file CC570.

22 Ibid.

23 S.T. Wood to minister of justice, 19 October 1944, Abraham (1944), LAC, RG 13, vol. 1646, part 1, file CC570.

24 Dr. McLean's testimony, trial transcripts, 143, Abraham (1944), LAC, RG 13, vol. 1646, part 1, file CC570.

25 Ibid., 42.

26 Memorandum for the Minister: re: Paul Abraham – Capital Case – regarding Choice of Psychiatrist to Examine and Report, 2 December 1944, Abraham (1944), LAC, RG 13, vol. 1646, part 1, file CC570.

27 Harvey Clare, Memorandum for the Minister: re: Paul Abraham, 12 December 1944, Abraham (1944), LAC, RG 13, vol. 1646, part 1, file CC570. Harvey Clare provided post-trial reports for several cases in this study, including Debartoli (1925), Pasquale (1926), Carrier (1929), Johnston (1942), and Kisielewski (1943). In every instance, he reported that the offender was legally sane.

28 T.R.L. MacInnes to Michael Gallagher, 27 October 1944, 1-2, Abraham (1944), LAC, RG 13, vol. 1646, part 1, file CC570.

29 The full newsclip reads, "Indian Hanged: Edmonton, Dec. 20. Paul Abraham, 28-year old. White Court, Alta, Indian, was hanged at Fort Saskatchewan Jail at 11:37 am today. He was convicted of the murder of his wife at Cherhill last July 18" (source unknown).

30 Neither the shift in common-sense thinking about race, as described by Walker in *"Race," Rights and the Law,* nor corroboration of his argument that by the 1940s it became "unfashionable to be overtly racist" is reflected in the case files of those convicted for murder.

31 "Rex v. Mary C. Smith. Special Report of Chief Justice Brown for the Minister of Justice," 7 November 1935, 1 (emphasis added), Mary Smith (1935), LAC, RG 13, vol. 1599, part 1, file CC439.

32 "Condensed Summary," 1, Joseph Proulx (1945), LAC, RG 13, vol. 1650, part 2, file CC585.

33 See M.F. Gallagher, "Memorandum for the Honourable the Minister of Justice," 1; Harvey Clare, "The Homewood Sanitarium of Guelph," to M.F. Gallagher, 11 June 1926, 1; Mr. H.H. Stevens to the minister of justice, 14 May 1926; and "Crime Report. Vancouver (Spring 1926) Assizes," Benito Pasquale (1926), LAC, RG 13, vol. 1538, part 1, file CC147.

34 M.F. Gallagher, "Memorandum for the Honourable the Minister of Justice," 1, Pasquale (1926), LAC, RG 13, vol. 1538, part 1, file CC147.

35 Harvey Clare to M.F. Gallagher, 1-2, Pasquale (1926), LAC, RG 13, vol. 1538, part 1, file CC147.

36 "In re Louis Jones," Mr. John Mahoney writing from the law office of A.W. Jones, KC, and John F. Mahoney, MPP, Barristers and Solicitors, to Michael Gallagher, chief of the remissions branch, 25 November 1927, 3-4, Louis Jones (1927), LAC, RG 13, vol. 1545, part 1, file CC267.

37 Ibid.

38 W.M. Bevis, "Psychological Traits of the Southern Negro with Observations as to Some of His Psychosis," *American Journal of Psychiatry* 1 (July 1921): 69.

39 Ibid.

40 Ibid., 70-72.

41 Trial transcripts, 25 October 1927, 102, Jones (1927), LAC, RG 13, vol. 1545, part 3, file CC267.

42 Ibid.

43 Mahoney to Gallagher, 3, Jones (1927), LAC, RG 13, vol. 1545, part 1, file CC267.

44 Ibid., 4.

45 Ibid., 3.

46 Ibid.

47 Charles Kirk Clarke, "The Defective Immigrant," *Public Health Journal* 7, 11 (November 1916): 462.

48 Ibid., 465.

49 Cited in Angus McLaren, "The Creation of a Haven for 'Human Thoroughbreds': The Sterilization of the Feeble-Minded and Mentally Ill in British Columbia," *Canadian Historical Review* 67, 2 (1986): 127.

50 According to Angus McLaren, the desirability of a particular immigrant group depended on its perceived closeness to the white Anglo-Saxon ideal and its ability to be "Canadianized." He recounts that "British and Americans were viewed as the most desirable, next northern and western Europeans (including the Jews), and last of all the Asians and blacks." Quoting Arthur Doughty, Adam Shortt, and James S. Woodsworth, McLaren describes the predominant characterization of Galicians as "mentally slow," "addicted to drunken sprees and animalized." The Italians, he continues, were perceived as naturally "devoid of shame; the Turks, Armenians, and Syrians as undesirable; the Greeks, Macedonians, and Bulgarians as liars; the Chinese as addicted to opium and gambling; and the arrival of Jews and Negroes as entirely unsolicited." McLaren, *Our Own Master Race,* 47.

51 Ian Dowbiggin, "Keeping This Young Country Sane: C.K. Clarke, Immigration Restriction, and Canadian Psychiatry, 1890-1925," *Canadian Historical Review* 76, 4 (1995): 661.

52 Ibid.

53 R.C. Rathbone, "Alberta Provincial Police," Edmonton, 23 December 1930, 1, George Dvernichuk (1930), LAC, RG 13, vol. 1564, part 1, file CC332.

54 For example, it was reported "on good authority" that Dvernichuk "thought nothing of throwing a live cat into a burning furnace." Ibid., 1-2.

55 E.H. Cooke, Provincial Mental Hospital, to deputy attorney general, Edmonton, 22 November 1930, Dvernichuk (1930), LAC, RG 13, vol. 1564, part 1, file CC332. See also Dr. D.L. McCullough (acting medical superintendent), "Provincial Mental Hospital, Ponoka,

Alberta, 23rd January, 1931. Re Katie Eremko" (Dvernichuk's sister), Dvernichuk (1930), LAC, RG 13, vol. 1564, part 1, file CC332.

56 Frank Ford, justice of the Supreme Court of Alberta, "Report of the Honourable Mr. Justice Ford upon the Proceedings in Connection with the Trial of George Dvernichuk," 6-7, Dvernichuk (1930), LAC, RG 13, vol. 1564, part 1, file CC332.

57 Ibid., 2.

58 Deputy attorney general, "re Dvernichuk," 3 February 1931, Dvernichuk (1930), LAC, RG 13, vol. 1564, part 1, file CC332.

59 "Report of the Honourable Mr. Justice Ford," 5, Dvernichuk (1930), LAC, RG 13, vol. 1564, part 1, file CC332.

60 M.F. Gallagher, "Memorandum for the Honourable the Minister of Justice," 3, Catherine Tratch (1924), LAC, RG 13, vol. 1528, part 2, file CC216. Tratch was also identified in various documents as Ruthenian.

61 J.H. Currie, the Currie Company Limited, to minister of justice, 2, Tratch (1924), LAC, RG 13, vol. 1528, part 1, file CC216.

62 J. Harvey Hearne to Wallace Stewart, MP, 25 April 1924, 1-2, Tratch (1924), LAC, RG 13, vol. 1528, part 1, file CC216.

63 J.F.L. Embury to honourable secretary of state for Canada, 18 February 1924, 2, Tratch (1924), LAC, RG 13, vol. 1528, part 1, file CC216.

64 Ibid.

65 C.W. Stewart to M.F. Gallagher, 12 May 1924, Tratch (1924), LAC, RG 13, vol. 1528, part 1, file CC216.

66 Ibid.

67 C.W. Stewart to Hon. E. Lapointe, minister of justice, 12 May 1924, Tratch (1924), LAC, RG 13, vol. 1528, part 1, file CC216.

68 M.F. Gallagher, "Memorandum for the Honourable the Minister of Justice," 1-2, Tratch (1924), LAC, RG 13, vol. 1528, part 2, file CC216.

69 See the English "Translation of Judge's Charge to the Jury," 11, Tommasina Teolis (1934), LAC, RG 13, vol. 1592, part 1, file CC422.

70 Ibid., 15-17.

71 Backhouse, *Colour-Coded,* 13.

Chapter 6: Murder between "Wives" and "Husbands"

1 "Charge to the Jury," 3, James McGrath (1931), Library and Archives Canada (LAC), Ottawa, Ontario, RG 13, vol. 1572, part 3, file CC360.

2 Mona Gleason examines the role of the social sciences and expert knowledge in shaping the experiences of "ordinary Canadians." Her project traces the promotion and construction of what "normal family life" came to mean in post-war society and how psychological discourses endorsed and naturalized the "dominance of Anglo/Celtic (as opposed to 'ethnic'), middle-class, heterosexual, and patriarchal values." Gleason argues that this "normalized ideal," defined through expert evaluations of "normalcy," was intended to "collapse and consolidate the diversity of family life." Therefore, those who fell outside the domestic ideal, including working-class, non-Anglo, and decidedly non-Christian families, were, according to Gleason, excluded, classified, and pathologized as "abnormal" and "poorly adjusted." Although Gleason does not make clear distinctions between psychology and psychiatry, which emerged from quite different starting points, her analysis illustrates the influence of a widespread social science movement on representations of conjugality in mid-twentieth-century Canada. Gleason, *Normalizing the Ideal: Psychology, Schooling, and the Family in Postwar Canada* (Toronto: University of Toronto Press, 1999), 4-5.

3 For further explorations in moral, gender, and/or sexual regulation in early Canadian society, see Mariana Valverde, *The Age of Light, Soap and Water: Moral Reform in English Canada, 1885-1925* (Toronto: McClelland and Stewart, 1991); Carolyn Strange, *Toronto's Girl Problem: The Perils and Pleasures of the City, 1880-1930* (Toronto: University of Toronto Press, 1995); Cecilia Morgan, *Public Men and Virtuous Women: The Gendered Languages of Religion and Politics in Upper Canada, 1791-1850* (Toronto: University of Toronto Press, 1996); and

Angus McLaren, *The Trials of Masculinity: Policing Sexual Boundaries, 1870-1930* (Chicago: University of Chicago Press, 1997).

4 See Dorothy E. Chunn, "Rehabilitating Deviant Families through Family Courts: The Birth of 'Socialized' Justice in Ontario, 1920-1940," *International Journal of the Sociology of Law* 16 (1988): 137.

5 See, for example, Annalee E. Gölz, "If a Man's Wife Does Not Obey Him, What Can He Do? Marital Breakdown and Wife Abuse in Late Nineteenth-Century and Early Twentieth-Century Ontario," in Louis A. Knafla and Susan W.S. Binnie, eds., *Law, Society, and the State: Essays in Modern Legal History* (Toronto: University of Toronto Press, 1995), 323-50; and Ruth Harris, *Murders and Madness: Medicine, Law, and Society in the Fin de Siècle* (Oxford: Clarendon Press, 1989).

6 For studies showing the propensity toward leniency in cases of intimate heterosexual violence and murder, see Terry L. Chapman, "'Til Death Do Us Part': Wife Beating in Alberta, 1905-1920," *Alberta History* 36, 4 (Autumn 1988): 13-22; Gölz, "If a Man's Wife"; Karen Dubinsky, *Improper Advances: Rape and Heterosexual Conflict in Ontario, 1880-1929* (Chicago: University of Chicago Press, 1993); Harris, "Melodrama, Hysteria," 30, and Harris, *Murders and Madness*. For further studies in the history of domestic and family violence, see Linda Gordon, *Heroes of Their Own Lives: The Politics and History of Family Violence* (New York: Viking Press, 1988); Elizabeth Pleck, *Domestic Tyranny: The Making of Social Policy against Family Violence from Colonial Times to the Present* (New York: Oxford University Press, 1987); Katherine Harvey, "To Love, Honour and Obey: Wife-Battering in Working-Class Montreal, 1869-1879," *Urban History Review* 19, 2 (October 1990): 128-40; James S. Snell, *In the Shadow of the Law: Divorce in Canada, 1900-1939* (Toronto: University of Toronto Press, 1991); and Chunn, "Rehabilitating Deviant Families."

7 Recommendations to mercy were more numerous for this group than for men who had committed non-spousal murder; of these, 28 percent (nine of thirty-two) received such recommendations.

8 Boyko's original death sentence was commuted; however, he later killed a man in prison, and after being tried and sentenced to death again by the same judge, he was hanged. See also cases of Jacob Wied (1948), LAC, RG 13, vol. 1676, file CC663; and James Fosbraey (1950), LAC, RG 13, vols. 1690 and 1691, file CC708.

9 See Joan Sangster, "'Pardon Tales' from Magistrate's Court: Women, Crime and the Court in Peterborough County, 1920-1950," *Canadian Historical Review* 74, 2 (1993): 161-97.

10 See cases of Louis Jones (1920), LAC, RG 13, vol. 1545, file CC267; Frank Dolan (1937), LAC, RG 13, vol. 1612, file CC477; and R.A. Wright (1939), LAC, RG 13, vol. 1621, file CC498.

11 In two cases, Marie (Viau) Beaulne (1929), LAC, RG 13, vol. 1555, file CC304, and Tommasina Teolis (1934), LAC, RG 13, vols. 1592 and 1593, file CC422, the male conspirators were also hanged.

12 "Judges' Chambers, the Supreme Court of Alberta, Edmonton, September 29th, 1934," 1, 4-5, Dina Dranchuk (1934), LAC, RG 13, vol. 1592, part 1, file CC418.

13 See English "Translation of Judge's Charge to the Jury," 30, Teolis (1934), LAC, RG 13, vol. 1592, part 1, file CC422.

14 Ibid., 31-32.

15 "Two Must Hang for Poisoning at Montpellier," *Ottawa Citizen,* 13 June 1929, 1, 19, Beaulne (1929), LAC, RG 13, vol. 1555, file CC304.

16 Angus McLaren, "Males, Migrants, and Murder in British Columbia, 1900-1923," in F. Iacovetta and W. Mitchinson, eds., *On the Case: Explorations in Social History* (Toronto: University of Toronto Press, 1998), 168.

17 "Two Must Hang," *Ottawa Citizen,* 19.

18 Ibid.

19 Ibid.

20 "The Penalty of Murder," *Ottawa Journal,* 14 June 1929.

21 "Are Opposed to Hanging in Hull: Prominent Citizens against Double Execution and Readily Sign Petitions," *Ottawa Evening Citizen,* 13 August 1929, Beaulne (1929), LAC, RG 13, vol. 1555, file CC304.

22 "17 Reasons Are Advanced with Clemency Plea: Petition in Behalf of Condemned Couple from Montpellier Being Presented This Week," *Ottawa Evening Citizen,* 31 July 1929, 29, Beaulne (1929), LAC, RG 13, vol. 1555, file CC304.

23 See Chunn, "Rehabilitating Deviant Families"; Harris, *Murders and Madness;* McLaren, *Trials of Masculinity;* Karen Dubinsky and Franka Iacovetta, "Murder, Womanly Virtue, and Motherhood: The Case of Angelina Napolitano, 1911-1922," *Canadian Historical Review* 72, 4 (1991): 505-31.

24 See, generally, the case files of Dranchuk (1934), LAC, RG 13, vol. 1592, file CC418, and Frances Harrop (1940), LAC, RG 13, vol. 1625, part 3, file CC514.

25 "Judges' Chambers, the Supreme Court of Alberta, Edmonton, September 29th, 1934," 1, Dranchuk (1934), LAC, RG 13, vol. 1592, part 1, file CC418.

26 Ibid., 4. Dr. Taylor's remarks are referred to in the main text of the judge's report.

27 Ibid., 5, 1.

28 For example, Joel Eigen examined the trends in lay testimony with regard to madness in eighteenth- to nineteenth-century England and found that witnesses blamed madness on everything from "bad falls to bad husbands." "Family distress" was the second-most frequent emotional cause of insanity cited by lay witnesses. Eigen, *Witnessing Insanity: Madness and Mad-Doctors in the English Court* (New Haven: Yale University Press, 1995), 100-1.

29 See Harris, *Murders and Madness;* Gölz, "If a Man's Wife"; Kimberley White-Mair, "Experts and Ordinary Men: Locating *R. v. Lavallée,* Battered Woman Syndrome, and the 'New' Psychiatric Expertise on Women within Canadian Legal History," *Canadian Journal of Women and the Law* 12, 2 (2000): 406-38, and White-Mair, "Negotiating Responsibility: Representations of Criminality and Mind-State in Canadian Law, Medicine and Society, 1920-1950" (PhD thesis, University of Toronto, 2001). Prior to 1948, s. 54 of the *Criminal Code of Canada* read, "everyone who has without justification assaulted another, or has provoked an assault from that other, may nevertheless justify force subsequent to such assault, if he uses such force under reasonable apprehension of death or grievous bodily harm from the violence of the person first assaulted or provoked, and in the belief, on reasonable grounds, that it is necessary for his own preservation from death or grievous bodily harm, if he did not commence the assault with intent to kill or do grievous bodily harm, and did not endeavour, at any time before the necessity for preserving himself arose, to kill or do grievous and bodily harm, and if before such necessity arose, he declined further conflict, and quitted or retreated from it as far as was practicable. (2) Provocation, within the meaning of this section may be given by blows, words or gestures."

30 Recall the judge's words to the jury in the Teolis case (1934): "Gentlemen, one can understand that a man can kill for love, jealousy, anger, but to kill in cold blood." The same argument was made in response to Beaulne's case (1929): "There might have been some excuse for a crime of passion committed in the heat of a fury, but not for such a sinister, calculated, deliberate, traitorous killing." "The Penalty of Murder," *Ottawa Journal,* 14 June 1920, LAC, RG 13, vol. 1555, file CC304.

31 For example, Mary Smith, charged with murdering her husband, related that he had threatened her with violence for telling a neighbour how cheaply she could run her household. Owing money to several people in their small town of Duck Lake, Saskatchewan, he shook his finger at her when she asked if he meant to beat her up again, answering, "Yes, and when I do you will not have so much to say." "Statement Made by Accused," 1, Mary Smith (1935), LAC, RG 13, vol. 1599, part 1, file CC439.

32 John Mahoney to M.F. Gallagher, 25 November 1927, 4, Jones (1927), LAC, RG 13, vol. 1545, part 1, file CC267. See also the judge's report in the case of R.A. Wright (1939), an "American Negro" who killed his common-law wife because he feared she would leave him. In both cases, the "status" of the couple's relationship and the presumed "loose character" of the victims were discussed. "The Supreme Court of British Columbia, Vancouver, B.C., April 3, 1939," to "The Honourable the Secretary of State," 1, LAC, RG 13, vol. 1621, part 3.1, file CC498.

33 Trial transcripts, 48-50 (emphasis added), Paul Abraham (1944), LAC, RG 13, vol. 1646, part 3, file CC570.

34 See T.R.L. MacInnis, secretary, Indian Affairs Branch of the Department of Mines and Resources, to Gallagher, 27 October 1944. MacInnis' letter was later quoted in Gallagher's "Condensed Summary" to the minister of justice, 3, Abraham (1944), LAC, RG 13, vol. 1646, part 1, file CC570.
35 "Charge to the Jury," 3, McGrath (1931), LAC, RG 13, vol. 1572, part 3, file CC360.
36 Ibid., 4.
37 Police report, 4, McGrath (1931), LAC, RG 13, vol. 1572, part 3, file CC360.
38 Trial transcripts, 200-5, McGrath (1931), LAC, RG 13, vol. 1572, part 3, file CC360.
39 Ibid.
40 See judge's report, "Rex v. Mary C. Smith Special Report of Chief Justice Brown for the Minister of Justice," 3, Smith (1935), LAC, RG 13, vol. 1599, part 1, file CC439.
41 Ibid., 3.
42 Ibid., 5-6.
43 Ibid., 4.
44 Dr. MacNiel's testimony, trial transcripts, 95, Smith (1935), LAC, RG 13, vol. 1599, part 3, file CC439. At the time of Smith's trial, MacNiel had been the superintendent in charge of the mental hospital at Battleford for twenty-three years and was by legal standards qualified to give expert evidence on the issue of mental defectiveness.
45 Ibid., 96-98.
46 Smith received a recommendation to mercy from the jury and judge; she was ordered a new trial on appeal, and her sentence was reduced.
47 Judge's report, 4-5, Smith (1935), LAC.
48 Trial transcripts, 102, Smith (1935), LAC, RG 13, vol. 1599, part 3, file CC439.
49 Matt O'Reilly, "Anxious to Have Sentence Commuted," *Calgary Herald,* n.d., Dranchuk (1934), LAC, RG 13, vol. 1592, part 1, file CC418.
50 A MERE MAN, "Letters to the Editor: Women and the Law," *Calgary Albertan,* 25 October 1935, Dranchuk (1934), LAC, RG 13, vol. 1592, part 1, file CC418.
51 Mrs. Mary Healey, secretary, Florence Nightingale Rebekah Lodge 21, to "The Remissions Branch, Department of the Secretary of State," 23 May 1940, Harrop (1940), LAC, RG 13, vol. 1625, part 1, file CC514. Also see Miss Mary L. Kennedy to "the Hon. the Minister of Justice," (n.d.) in the same volume and file.
52 "Home Welfare Association" to minister of justice, Harrop (1940), LAC, RG 13, vol. 1625, part 1, file CC514.

Chapter 7: Concluding Thoughts

1 Kimberley White-Mair, "Experts and Ordinary Men: Locating *R. v. Lavallée,* Battered Woman Syndrome, and the 'New' Psychiatric Expertise on Women within Canadian Legal History," *Canadian Journal of Women and the Law* 12, 2 (2000): 406-38.
2 *Lavallée v. R.* (1990), 1 S.C.R. 852, 55 C.C.C. (3rd) 97.
3 *R. v. Gladue* (1999), 1 S.C.R. 688.
4 Elizabeth Sheehy, "Review of the Self-Defence Review," *Canadian Journal of Women and the Law* 12, 1 (2000): 197-234. For scholarly reflections on the rise and use of "battered women's syndrome" in criminal law, see Donna Martinson, Marilyn MacCrimmon, Isabel Grant, and Christine Boyle, "A Forum on Lavallée v. R.: Women and Self-Defence," *U.B.C. Law Review* 31 (1991): 23-68; Wendy Chan, "A Feminist Critique of Self-Defence and Provocation in Battered Women's Cases," *Women and Criminal Justice* 6, 1 (1994): 39-65; Christine Bell and Marie Fox, "Telling Stories of Women Who Kill," *Social and Legal Studies* 5, 4 (1996): 471-94; Martha Shafer, "The Battered Woman Syndrome Revisited: Some Compelling Thoughts Five Years after *R. v. Lavallée*?" *University of Toronto Law Journal* 47 (1997): 1-33; and Sheehy, "Review of the Self-Defence Review."
5 For comments and analysis of the *Gladue* decisions, see Kent Roach and Jonathan Rudin, "Gladue: The Judicial and Political Reception of a Promising Decision," *Canadian Journal of Criminology* 42 (2000): 355-88; Roach and Rudin, "Broken Promises: A Response to Stenning and Roberts' 'Empty Promises,'" *Saskatchewan Law Review* 65 (2002): 3-34; Leonard Rotman, "Development in Aboriginal Law: The 1998-99 Term [of the Supreme Court of Canada],"

Supreme Court Law Review 11 (2000): 1-36; and Philip Stenning and Julian Roberts, "Empty Promises: Parliament, the Supreme Court, and the Sentencing of Aboriginal Offenders," *Saskatchewan Law Review* 64 (2001): 137-68.

Bibliography

Archival Collections

Archives of Canadian Psychiatry and Mental Health Services (ACP), Queen Street Mental Health Centre, Toronto, Ontario.

C.K. Clarke Archives (CKCA), Farrar Library, Clarke Institute of Psychiatry, Toronto, Ontario.

Griffin-Greenland Archives on the History of Canadian Psychiatry (GGA), Queen Street Mental Health Centre, Toronto, Ontario.

Library and Archives Canada (LAC), Records of the Department of Justice (RG 13) and Records of Federal Royal Commissions (RG 33), Ottawa, Ontario.

Public Archives of Ontario (PAO), Criminal Justice Records, Toronto, Ontario.

University of Toronto Archives (UTA), American medical periodicals, 1797-1900.

Professional Journals

American Journal of Insanity (1844-1921)

American Journal of Psychiatry

British Journal of Medical Psychology (1923-53)

Bulletin of the Ontario Hospitals for the Insane (1907-16)

Canadian Journal of Criminology

Canadian Journal of Mental Hygiene (1919-21)

Canadian Journal of Psychology

Canadian Medical Association Journal

International Journal of Psychoanalysis (1920-29)

Journal of Mental Science/British Journal of Psychiatry (1858-1962)

Journal of Psychiatric Social Work (1948-55)

Mental Health Journal (Canadian)

Mental Hygiene (1917-72)

Psychiatric Quarterly (1927-74)

Psychological Bulletin (1904-11)

Journal Articles and Book Chapters

Alexander, L. "*Mens Rea* and Inchoate Crimes." *Journal of Criminal Law and Criminology* 87 (Summer 1997): 1138-93.

Andoh, Benjamin. "The M'Naghten Rules – The Story So Far." *Medico-Legal Journal* 61 (1993): 93-103.

Ashley, Scott. "The Poetics of Race in 1890s Ireland: An Ethnography of the Aran Islands." *Patterns of Prejudice* 35, 2 (April 2001): 5-18.

Avio, Kenneth L. "Capital Punishment in Canada: Statistical Evidence and Constitutional Issues." *Canadian Journal of Criminology* 30, 3 (October 1988): 331-49.

–. "The Quality of Mercy: Exercise of the Royal Prerogative in Canada." *Canadian Public Policy* 12 (1987): 366-79.

Bailyn, Sarah. "Who Makes the Rules? Using Wittgenstein in Social Theory." *Journal for the Theory of Social Behaviour* 32, 3 (2002): 311-29.
Bartlett, Peter. "Legal Madness in the Nineteenth Century." *Social History of Medicine* 14, 1 (2001): 107-31.
Bayles, M. "Character, Purpose and Criminal Responsibility." *Law and Philosophy* 1 (1982): 5-20.
Beard, G.M. "Correspondence: Dr. G.M. Beard on Insanity." *American Journal of Insanity* 37 (October 1880): 229-37.
Bearnard, Alan. "Anthropology, Race, and Englishness: Changing Notions of Complexion and Character." *Eighteenth-Century Life* 25, 3 (2001): 94-102.
Bell, Christine, and Marie Fox. "Telling Stories of Women Who Kill." *Social and Legal Studies* 5, 4 (1996): 471-94.
Bevis, W.M. "Psychological Traits of the Southern Negro with Observations as to Some of His Psychosis." *American Journal of Psychiatry* 78, 1 (July 1921): 69-78.
Boldt, Richard C. "The Construction of Responsibility in Criminal Law." *University of Pennsylvania Law Review* 140, 6 (1992): 245-332.
Bourdieu, Pierre. "The Force of Law: Toward a Sociology of the Juridical Field." *Hastings Law Journal* 38 (1987): 814-53.
Briggs, L. Vernon. "Problems with the Insane." *American Journal of Insanity* 70 (October 1913): 467-75.
Brush, Edward. "Our Work as Psychiatrists and Its Opportunities." *American Journal of Insanity* 73, 1 (July 1916): 1-17.
Bucke, Richard Maurice. "Surgery among the Insane in Canada." *American Journal of Insanity* 55 (July 1898): 1-19.
Bucknill, John Charles. "The Plea of Insanity in the Case of Charles Julius Guiteau." *American Journal of Insanity* 39 (October 1882): 181-98.
Busch, R., N. Robertson, and H. Lapsley. "Gap: Battered Women's Experience of the Justice System in New Zealand." *Canadian Journal of Women and the Law* 8 (1995): 190-223.
Caplan, Leonard. "The Expert Witness." *Medico-Legal Journal* 47 (1979): 124-37.
Carey, Ruth. "'USELESS' (UOSLAS) v. the Bar: The Struggle of the Ottawa Student Clinic to Represent Battered Women." *Journal of Law and Social Policy* 8 (1992): 54-81.
Chan, Wendy. "A Feminist Critique of Self-Defence and Provocation in Battered Women's Cases." *Women and Criminal Justice* 6, 1 (1994): 39-65.
Chapman, Terry L. "The Early Eugenics Movement in Western Canada." *Alberta History* 25 (1977): 9-16.
–. "'Til Death Do Us Part': Wife Beating in Alberta, 1905-1920." *Alberta History* 36, 4 (Autumn 1988): 13-22.
Chunn, Dorothy E. "Rehabilitating Deviant Families through Family Courts: The Birth of 'Socialized' Justice in Ontario, 1920-1940." *International Journal of the Sociology of Law* 16 (1988): 137-58.
–, and Robert Menzies. "Gender, Madness and Crime: The Reproduction of Patriarchal and Class Relations in a Psychiatric Court Clinic." *Journal of Human Justice* 1, 2 (Spring 1990): 33-54.
Clark, Daniel. "Medical Evidence in Courts of Law." *American Journal of Insanity* 35 (January 1879): 375-99.
–. "A Psycho-Medical History of Louis Riel." *American Journal of Insanity* 44 (1887-88): 33-55.
Clarke, Charles Kirk. "The Care and Treatment of the Criminal." *Canadian Journal of Medicine and Surgery* 15, 1 (January 1904): 1-14.
–. "A Clinic for Nervous and Mental Diseases." *Bulletin of the Ontario Hospitals for the Insane* 4 (January 1911): 73-77.
–. "The Defective Immigrant." *Public Health Journal* 7, 11 (November 1916): 462-65.
–. "Immigration." *Public Health Journal* 10, 10 (October 1919): 441-44.
–. "Notes of a Clinical Case: The Case of W.M.B. – Moral Imbecility." *Bulletin of the Ontario Hospitals for the Insane* 7, 4 (July 1914): 207-31.
–, with C.B. Farrar. "One Thousand Psychiatric Cases from the Canadian Army." *Canadian Journal of Mental Hygiene* 1 (1919-20): 313-17.

Coles, E. "A Psychological Perspective on the Legal Concepts of 'Volition' and 'Intent.'" *Journal of Law and Medicine* 4 (August 1996): 60-71.

Compton, J. "Expert Witness Testimony and the Diminished Capacity Defense." *American Journal of Trial Advocacy* 20 (Winter 1996-97): 381-408.

Crawford, C. "Legalizing Medicine: Early Modern Legal Systems and the Growth of Medico-Legal Knowledge." In Michael Clark and Catherine Crawford, eds., *Legal Medicine in History,* 89-116. Cambridge: Cambridge University Press, 1994.

–. "The Rejection of Psychological Approaches to Mental Disorder in Late Nineteenth-Century British Psychiatry." In Andrew Scull, ed., *Madhouses, Mad-Doctors, and Madmen: The Social History of Psychiatry in the Victorian Era,* 271-312. Philadelphia: University of Pennsylvania Press, 1981.

D'Agostino, Peter. "Craniums, Criminals, and the 'Cursed Race': Italian Anthropology in American Racial Thought, 1861-1924." *Comparative Studies in Society and History* 44, 2 (2002): 319-43.

Dodd, F. "The Legal and Medical Theories of Mental Disease in Criminal Cases." *American Journal of Insanity* 39 (April 1883): 456-69.

Dowbiggin, I. "Degeneration and Hereditarianism in French Mental Medicine, 1840-90." In W.F. Bynum, R. Porter, and M. Shepherd, eds., *The Anatomy of Madness: Essays in the History of Psychiatry,* vol. 3: 188-232. London: Tavistock Publishers, 1985.

Drewry, William Francis. "The Scope of the Activities of the Alienist." *American Journal of Insanity* 67, 1 (July 1910): 1-16.

Dubinsky, Karen, and Franka Iacovetta. "Murder, Womanly Virtue, and Motherhood: The Case of Angelina Napolitano, 1911-1922." *Canadian Historical Review* 72, 4 (1991): 505-31.

Eigen, Joel Peter. "I Answer as a Physician." In Michael Clark and Catherine Crawford, eds., *Legal Medicine in History,* 167-99. Cambridge, UK: Cambridge University Press, 1994.

–, and Gregory Andoll. "From Mad-Doctor to Forensic Witness: The Evolution of Early English Court Psychiatry." *International Journal of Law and Psychiatry* 9 (1986): 159-69.

Ewick, Patricia, and Susan Silbey. "Common Knowledge and Ideological Critique: The Significance of Knowing that the 'Haves' Come out Ahead." *Law and Society Review* 33, 4 (1999): 1025-44.

Farley, J., and G.L. Geison. "Science, Politics and Spontaneous Generation in Nineteenth Century France: The Pasteur-Pouchet Debate." *Bulletin of the History of Medicine* 48 (1974): 161-98.

Farrar, Clarence. "The Neuropsychiatric Service of the Department of Soldiers' Civil Re-Establishment, Canada." *American Journal of Psychiatry* 79 (April 1923): 163-83.

Ferguson, Robert. "The Commonalities of Common Sense." *William and Mary Quarterly,* 3rd ser., 57, 3 (2000): 465-504.

Flint, Austin. "Methods of Dealing with the Criminal Insane – Defects in Present Methods and Suggested Remedies." *American Journal of Insanity* 67 (October 1910): 227-40.

Forbes, Thomas R. "Early Forensic Medicine in England: The Angus Murder Trial." *Journal of the History of Medicine* 36 (1981): 296-309.

Foucault, Michel. "About the Concept of the Dangerous Individual in Nineteenth Century Legal Psychiatry." *International Journal of Law and Psychiatry* 1 (1978): 1-18.

France, Simon. "Gains and Lost Opportunities in Canadian Constitutional Mens Rea." *Queen's Law Journal* 20 (Spring 1995): 533-56.

Girard, Philip. "From Subversion to Liberation: Homosexuals and the Immigration Act 1952-1977." *Canadian Journal of Law and Society* 2 (1987): 1-28.

Godler, Zlata. "Doctors and the New Immigrants." *Canadian Ethnic Studies* 9 (1977): 6-17.

Goldstein, Anne. "History, Homosexuality, and Political Values: Searching for the Hidden Determinants of *Bowers v. Hardwick.*" *Yale Law Journal* 97, 6 (1988): 1073-1104.

Goldstein, J.E. "'Moral Contagion': A Professional Ideology of Medicine and Psychiatry in Eighteenth and Nineteenth Century France." In G.L. Geison, ed., *Professions and the French State, 1700-1900,* 181-222. Philadelphia: University of Pennsylvania Press, 1984.

Goldstein, Jan. "Professional Knowledge and Professional Self-Interest: The Rise and Fall of Monomania in 19th-Century France." *International Journal of Law and Psychiatry* 21, 4 (1998): 385-96.

Gölz, Annalee E. "If a Man's Wife Does Not Obey Him, What Can He Do? Marital Breakdown and Wife Abuse in Late Nineteenth-Century and Early Twentieth-Century Ontario." In Louis A. Knafla and Susan W.S. Binnie, eds., *Law, Society, and the State: Essays in Modern Legal History*, 323-50. Toronto: University of Toronto Press, 1995.

Gray, Kenneth. "Psychiatry and the *Criminal Code*." *Ontario Journal of Neuropsychiatry* 10 (December 1935): 44-55.

Gubrium, Jaber, and James Holstein. "Narrative Practice and the Coherence of Personal Stories." *Sociological Quarterly* 39, 1 (1998): 163-87.

Hall, Jerome. "Responsibility and Law: Defense of the McNaghten Rules." *American Bar Association Journal* 12 (October 1956): 917-90.

Haller, John. "Concepts of Race Inferiority in Nineteenth-Century Anthropology." *Journal of the History of Medicine and Allied Sciences* 25, 1 (1970): 247-61.

Hamlin, Christopher. "Intoxication in the Codification of Canadian Criminal Law." *Canadian Bar Review* 73 (1994): 515-52.

–. "Scientific Method and Expert Witnessing: Victorian Perspectives on a Modern Problem." *Social Studies of Science* 16 (1986): 485-513.

Hammersley, Martyn. "Conversation Analysis and Discourse Analysis: Methods or Paradigms?" *Discourse and Society* 14, 6 (2003): 751-81.

–. "Understanding the Terrorist: Anarchism, Medicine and Politics in Fin-de-Siècle France." In Michael Clark and Catherine Crawford, eds., *Legal Medicine in History*, 200-22. Cambridge: Cambridge University Press, 1994.

Harvey, Katherine. "To Love, Honour and Obey: Wife-Battering in Working-Class Montreal, 1868-1979." *Urban History Review* 19, 2 (October 1990): 128-40.

Heaslip, J.D. "The Position of Medicine in the Treatment of Crime." *Ontario Journal of Neuropsychiatry* 12 (December 1937): 33-38.

Herbert, Christopher. "Epilogue: Ethnography and Evolution." *Victorian Studies* 41, 3 (1998): 485-94.

Johnson, David. "Two Faces of Justice: A Milestone in Quantitative Cross-Cultural Research." *Law and Society Inquiry* 19 (Summer 1994): 667-86.

Johnston, Gerry. "From Experts in Responsibility to Advisers on Punishment: The Role of Psychiatrists in Penal Matters." In P. Rush, S. McVeigh, and A. Young, eds., *Criminal Legal Doctrine*, 84-103. Brookfield, VT: Ashgate, 1997.

Kazan, Patricia. "Reasonableness, Gender Difference, and Self-Defense Law." *Manitoba Law Journal* 24 (1997): 549-76.

Kelman, M. "Interpretive Construction in the Substantive Criminal Law." *Stanford Law Review* 33 (1981): 591-674.

Kerr, Judith Ablett. "A Licence to Kill or an Overdue Reform? The Case of Diminished Responsibility." *Otago Law Review* 9, 1 (1997): 1-13.

Larimer, Douglas. "Theoretical Racism in Late-Victorian Anthropology, 1870-1900." *Victorian Studies* 31, 3 (1988): 405-30.

Leavitt, Frederic. "Psychiatry and the Criminal." *American Journal of Psychiatry* 89, 3 (November 1932): 541-54.

Lee, Evan. "Cancelling Crime." *Connecticut Law Review* 30 (Fall 1997): 117-56.

Lloyd, James Hendrie. "The Trial of the Insane for Crime: A Historical Retrospect." *American Journal of Psychiatry* 64, 1 (July 1907): 35-51.

Lockhead, W.L. "Genetics: The Science of Breeding." *Canadian Bookman* 1 (July 1919): 65-66.

Loo, Tina. "Dan Cranmer's Potlatch: Law as Coercion, Symbol, and Rhetoric in British Columbia, 1884-1951." *Canadian Historical Review* 73, 2 (1992): 125-65.

–. "Native Culture and the Modification of Capital Punishment in Nineteenth-Century British Columbia." In Carolyn Strange, ed., *Qualities of Mercy*, 104-29. Vancouver: UBC Press, 1997.

–. "The Road from Bute Inlet: Crime and Colonial Identity in British Columbia." In Jim Phillips, Tina Loo, and Susan Lewthwaite, eds., *Essays in the History of Canadian Law*. Vol. 5, *Crime and Criminal Justice*, 112-42. Toronto: Osgoode Society, 1994.

Loseke, Donileen, and Spencer Cahill. "The Social Construction of Deviance: Experts on Battered Women." *Social Problems* 31, 3 (February 1984): 296-310.

Lynch, D.O. "Some Observations on the Criminally Insane with Special Reference to Those Charged with Murder." *Ontario Journal of Neuropsychiatry* 12 (December 1937): 39-52.

MacDonald, Carlos F. "The Ethical Aspects of Expert Testimony in Relation to the Plea of Insanity as a Defense to an Indictment for Crime." *American Journal of Insanity* 67 (1910): 227-40.

–. "Should the Plea of Insanity as a Defense to an Indictment for Crime Be Abolished?" *American Journal of Psychiatry* 76 (January 1920): 295-302.

MacDonald, Michael. "Madness, Suicide and the Computer." In Roy Porter and Andrew Wear, eds., *Problems and Methods in the History of Medicine,* 207-29. London: Croom, 1987.

MacFarlane, Bruce. "Instructions to the Executioner." *Criminal Law Quarterly* 14 (1998): 178-83.

Martinson, Donna, Marilyn MacCrimmon, Isabel Grant, and Christine Boyle. "A Forum on Lavallée v. R.: Women and Self-Defence." *U.B.C. Law Review* 31 (1991): 23-68.

May, James. "Statistical Studies of the Insane." *American Journal of Insanity* 70 (October 1913): 427-39.

Maynard, Stephen. "Through a Hole in the Lavatory Wall: Homosexual Subcultures, Police Surveillance, and the Dialectics of Discovery, Toronto, 1890-1930." *Journal of the History of Sexuality* 5, 2 (1994): 207-42.

McCord, Clinton P. "Social Psychiatry – Its Significance as a Specialty." *American Journal of Psychiatry* 82 (October 1925): 233-40.

McLaren, Angus. "The Creation of a Haven for 'Human Thoroughbreds': The Sterilization of the Feeble-Minded and Mentally Ill in British Columbia." *Canadian Historical Review* 67, 2 (1986): 127-50.

–. "Males, Migrants, and Murder in British Columbia, 1900-1923." In F. Iacovetta and W. Mitchinson, eds., *On the Case: Explorations in Social History,* 158-80. Toronto: University of Toronto Press, 1998.

McRuer, J.C. "Insanity as a Legal Defence." *Canadian Medical Association Journal* 61 (November 1949): 489-95.

Menninger, William. "The Role of Psychiatry in the World Today." *American Journal of Psychiatry* 104 (September 1947): 155-63.

Menzies, Robert. "'I Do Not Care for a Lunatic's Role': Modes of Regulation and Resistance inside the Colquitz Mental Home for the 'Criminally Insane,' 1919-1933." *Canadian Bulletin of Medical History* 16, 2 (1999): 181-213.

–. "The Making of Criminal Insanity in British Columbia: Granby Farrant and the Provincial Mental Home, Colquitz, 1919-1933." In Hamar Foster and John McLaren, eds., *Essays in the History of Canadian Law Volume 6,* 274-313. Toronto: University of Toronto Press, 1995.

–. "Race, Reason and Regulation: British Columbia's Mass Exile of Chinese 'Lunatics' aboard the CPSS Express of Russia, 9 February 1935." In J. Mclaren, R. Menzies, and D.E. Chunn, eds., *Regulating Lives: Social Control, Law and the State in British Columbia History,* 196-230. Vancouver: UBC Press, 2002.

Miller, Gale. "Toward Ethnographies of Institutional Discourse." *Journal of Contemporary Ethnography* 23, 3 (1994): 280-306.

Mooij, Antoine. "Kant on Criminal Law and Psychiatry." *International Journal of Law and Psychiatry* 21, 4 (1998): 335-41.

Moore, Dawn, and Mariana Valverde. "Maidens at Risk: 'Date Rape Drugs' and the Formation of Hybrid Risk Knowledges." *Economy and Society* 29, 4 (2000): 514-31.

Moore, Joseph. "Insanity as a Defense for Crime." *American Journal of Psychiatry* 85 (September 1928): 263-67.

Moore, Michael. "The Relevance of Philosophy to Law and Psychiatry." *International Journal of Law and Psychiatry* 6, 2 (1983): 177-92.

Moran, Richard. "The Origin of Insanity as a Special Verdict: The Trial for Treason of James Hadfield." *Law and Society Review* 19, 3 (1985): 487-519.

Myerson, Abraham. "Nature of Feeble-Mindedness." *American Journal of Psychiatry* 89 (May 1933): 1205-26.

Nelson, William. "Psychiatry and Its Relationship to the Administration of the Criminal Law." *American Journal of Psychiatry* 89 (January 1933): 703-23.

North, Charles. "A Proposed Change in the Criminal Law." *American Journal of Insanity* 70 (January 1914): 683-94.

Nye, R. "Heredity or Milieu: The Foundations of Modern European Criminological Theory." *Isis* 67 (1976): 334-55.

Oberndorf, C.P. "Psychiatry and Psychoanalysis." *American Journal of Psychiatry* 82 (April 1926): 605-14.

Palmer, Derrol. "Identifying Delusional Discourse: Issues of Rationality, Reality and Power." *Sociology of Health and Illness* 22, 5 (2000): 661-78.

Penfold, P. Susan. "Drugged, Exploited, Labelled and Blamed: How Psychiatry Oppresses Women." In Susan Boyd, Dorothy Chunn, and Robert Menzies, eds., *(Ab)Using Power: The Canadian Experience,* 174-84. Halifax: Fernwood Publishing, 2001.

Peyrot, Mark. "Psychological Testing and Forensic Decision Making: The Properties-in-Use of the MMPI." *Social Problems* 42, 4 (1995): 574-86.

Phillips, Jim. "The Operation of the Royal Pardon in Nova Scotia, 1749-1815." *University of Toronto Law Journal* 42 (1992): 401-49.

Plouffe, D. "The Attitude of the Psychiatrists as Experts in Criminal Courts." *Ontario Journal of Neuropsychiatry* 12 (December 1937): 27-32.

Pollner, Melvin. "Left of Ethnomethodology: The Rise and Decline of Radical Reflexivity." *American Sociological Review* 56 (1991): 370-80.

Pollock, Horatio. "Mental Disease in the United States in Relation to Environment, Sex and Age, 1922." *American Journal of Psychiatry* 82 (October 1925): 219-32.

Porter, Roy. "Lay Medical Knowledge in the Eighteenth Century: The Evidence of *The Gentleman's Magazine*." *Medical History* 29 (1985): 138-69.

Pound, Roscoe. "Science and Legal Procedure." *American Journal of Psychiatry* 85 (July 1928): 33-51.

Reed, Alan. "Duress and Provocation as Excuses to Murder: Salutary Lessons for Recent Anglo-American Jurisprudence." *Journal of Transnational Law and Policy* 6 (Fall 1996): 51-92.

Riddell, William Renwick. "The Medical Man as a Witness." *Canadian Journal of Medicine and Surgery* (December 1910): 1-26.

Roach, Kent, and Jonathan Rudin. "Broken Promises: A Response to Stenning and Roberts' 'Empty Promises.'" *Saskatchewan Law Review* 65 (2002): 3-34.

–. "Gladue: The Judicial and Political Reception of a Promising Decision." *Canadian Journal of Criminology* 42 (2000): 355-88.

Roiser, Martin. "Commonsense, Science and Public Opinion." *Journal for the Theory of Social Behaviour* 17, 4 (1987): 411-32.

Rosanoff, A.J. "Intellectual Efficiency in Relation to Insanity." *American Journal of Insanity* 73 (July 1916): 43-77.

Rotman, Leonard. "Development in Aboriginal Law: The 1998-99 Term [of the Supreme Court of Canada]." *Supreme Court Law Review* 11 (2000): 1-36.

Rymer, Charles A. "The Insanity Plea in Crime: An Evaluation of the 1927 Law." *American Journal of Psychiatry* 105 (February 1949): 594-600.

–, and Marion Reinhardt Rymer. "Psychological Medicine as Practiced by the Quack." *American Journal of Psychiatry* 92 (November 1935): 695-707.

Salter, Michael. "Common Sense and the Resistance to Legal Theory." *Ratio Juris* 5, 2 (1992): 212-29.

Sanders, Joseph. "Is There a 'Common Law' of Responsibility? The Effect of Demographic Variables on Judgments of Wrongdoing." *Law and Human Behaviour* 11 (December 1987): 277-98.

Sangster, Joan. "'Pardon Tales' from Magistrate's Court: Women, Crime and the Court in Peterborough County, 1920-1950." *Canadian Historical Review* 74, 2 (1993): 161-97.

Scull, Andrew. "From Madness to Mental Illness: Medical Men as Moral Entrepreneurs." *Archives européennes de sociologie* 16 (1975): 218-61.

Shafer, Martha. "The Battered Woman Syndrome Revisited: Some Compelling Thoughts Five Years after *R. v. Lavallée*?" *University of Toronto Law Journal* 47 (1997): 1-33.

Sheehy, Elizabeth. "Review of the Self-Defence Review." *Canadian Journal of Women and the Law* 12, 1 (2000): 197-234.

Smart, Carol. "Criminological Theory: Its Ideology and Implications Concerning Women." *British Journal of Sociology* 28, 1 (1977): 89-100.

Smith, Roger. "The Boundary between Insanity and Criminal Responsibility in Nineteenth-Century England." In Andrew Scull, ed., *Madhouses, Mad-Doctors, and Madmen: The Social History of Psychiatry in the Victorian Era,* 339-63. Philadelphia: University of Pennsylvania Press, 1981.

–. "Expertise and Causal Attribution in Deciding between Crime and Mental Disorder." *Social Studies in Science* 15 (1985): 67-98.

Sousa, Elizabeth S. "Lay versus Scientific Knowledge: The Value of a Dichotomy." *European Bulletin of Cognitive Psychology* 11, 3 (1991): 307-22.

Spaulding, H.B. "Insanity and Criminal Responsibility from the Legal Point of View." *Ontario Journal of Neuropsychiatry* (March 1933): 11-24.

Staum, Martin. "Paris Ethnology and the Perfectibility of 'Races.'" *Canadian Journal of History* 35, 3 (2000): 453-73.

Stedman, Henry, Carlos MacDonald, Charles Mills, Charles Baincroft, and H.A. Tomlinson. "Report of the Committee on Medical Expert Testimony of the American Medico-Psychological Association." *American Journal of Insanity* 67 (1910-11): 177-86.

Stenning, Philip, and Julian Roberts. "Empty Promises: Parliament, the Supreme Court, and the Sentencing of Aboriginal Offenders." *Saskatchewan Law Review* 64 (2001): 137-68.

Stevenson, G.H. "Insanity as a Criminal Defence: The Psychiatric Viewpoint." *Canadian Medical Association Journal* 58 (February 1948): 174-78.

Strachan, C., and D. Dutton. "The Role of Power and Gender in Anger Responses to Sexual Jealousy." *Journal of Applied Social Psychology* 22, 22 (1992): 1721-40.

Strange, Carolyn. "Comment: Capital Case Procedure Manual." *Criminal Law Quarterly* 14 (1998): 184-97.

–. "The Lottery of Death: Capital Punishment in Canada, 1867-1976." *Manitoba Law Journal* 23, 2 (1995): 594-619.

–. "Masculinities, Intimate Femicide and the Death Penalty in Australia, 1890-1920." *British Journal of Criminology* 43, 2 (2003): 310-39.

–. "Mercy for Murderers? A Historical Perspective on the Royal Prerogative of Mercy." *Saskatchewan Law Review* 64, 2 (2001): 559-72.

–. "Wounded Womanhood and Dead Men: Chivalry and the Trials of Clara Ford and Carrie Davies." In F. Iacovetta and M. Valverde, eds., *Gender Conflicts: New Essays in Women's History,* 149-88. Toronto: University of Toronto Press, 1992.

Stubbs, Julie, and Julia Tolmie. "Race, Gender, and the Battered Woman Syndrome: An Australia Case Study." *Canadian Journal of Women and the Law* 8 (1995): 122-58.

Sullivan, Edmond V. "Commonsense and Valuing." *Religious Education* 78, 1 (1983): 5-12.

Swainger, Jonathan. "A Distant Edge of Authority: Capital Punishment and the Prerogative of Mercy in British Columbia, 1872-1880." In Hamar Foster and John McLaren, eds., *Essays in the History of Canadian Law Volume IV,* 204-41. Toronto: University of Toronto Press, 1995.

Tighe, Janet. "The New York Medico-Legal Society: Legitimating the Union of Law and Psychiatry, 1867-1918." *International Journal of Law and Psychiatry* 9 (1986): 231-43.

Umphrey, Martha Merril. "The Dialogics of Legal Meaning: Spectacular Trials, the Unwritten Law, and Narratives of Criminal Responsibility." *Law and Society Review* 33, 2 (1999): 393-423.

Valverde, Mariana. "Social Facticity and the Law: A Social Expert's Account of Law." *Social and Legal Studies* 5, 2 (1996): 201-17.

–. "When the Mother of the Race Is Free: Race, Reproduction, and Sexuality in First-Wave Feminism." In F. Iacovetta and M. Valverde, eds., *Gender Conflicts: New Essays in Women's History,* 3-26. Toronto: University of Toronto Press, 1992.

Ward, Tony. "Law, Common Sense and the Authority of Science: Expert Witnesses and Criminal Insanity in England, ca. 1840-1940." *Social and Legal Studies* 6, 3 (1997): 343-62.

White, Brenda. "Training Medical Policemen: Forensic Medicine and Public Health in Nineteenth-Century Scotland." In Michael Clark and Catherine Crawford, eds., *Legal Medicine in History,* 145-66. Cambridge, UK: Cambridge University Press, 1994.

White, Kimberley. "Making Sense and Doing Justice: Exploring Criminal Justice Interpretations of Psychiatric Expert Evidence in Early-20th Century Canada." In Claire Dolan, ed., *Entre justice et justiciables: Les auxiliaires de la justice du Moyen Age au XXe siècle,* 789-804. Laval: Presses de l'Université Laval, 2005.

White-Mair, Kimberley. "Experts and Ordinary Men: Locating *R. v. Lavallée,* Battered Woman Syndrome, and the 'New' Psychiatric Expertise on Women within Canadian Legal History." *Canadian Journal of Women and the Law* 12, 2 (2000): 406-38.

Williams, Robin. "Sociology and the Vernacular Voice: Text, Context and the Sociological Imagination." *History of Human Sciences* 13, 4 (2000): 73-95.

Workman, Joseph. "Moral Insanity – What Is It?" *American Journal of Insanity* 39 (January 1883): 334-48.

Young, Alison. "Femininity as Marginalia: Conjugal Homicide and the Conjugation of Sexual Difference." In P. Rush, S. McVeigh, and A. Young, eds., *Criminal Legal Doctrine,* 127-55. Portland: Book News, 1997.

Books

Abrahamsen, David. *Crime and the Human Mind.* New York: Columbia University Press, 1944.

Ackerknecht, Erwin H. *A Short History of Medicine.* Baltimore and London: Johns Hopkins University Press, 1982.

Angus, Ian. *A Border Within: National Identity, Cultural Plurality, and Wilderness.* Montreal and Kingston: McGill-Queen's University Press, 1997.

Arrigo, Bruce. *The Contours of Psychiatric Justice: A Postmodern Critique of Mental Illness, Criminal Insanity and the Law.* New York and London: Garland Publishing, 1996.

Aylward, C. *Canadian Critical Race Theory: Racism and the Law.* Halifax: Fernwood Publishing, 1999.

Backhouse, Constance. *Colour-Coded: A Legal History of Racism in Canada, 1900-1950.* Toronto: Osgoode Society for Canadian Legal History, University of Toronto Press, 1999.

–. *Petticoats and Prejudice: Women and Law in Nineteenth-Century Canada.* Toronto: Osgoode Society, Women's Press, 1991.

Baird, R., and S. Rosenbaum, eds. *Punishment and the Death Penalty.* New York: Prometheus Books, 1995.

Barrett, Frank. *Disease and Geography: The History of an Idea.* Toronto: Atkinson College, Department of Geography, 2000.

Baruch, G., and A. Treacher. *Psychiatry Observed.* London: Routledge and Kegan Paul, 1978.

Beattie, John M. *Crime and the Courts in England, 1600-1800.* Princeton, NJ: Princeton University Press, 1986.

Bockover, Mary I., ed. *Rules, Rituals, and Responsibility.* La Salle, IL: Open Court, 1991.

Boritch, Helen. *Fallen Women: Female Crime and Criminal Justice in Canada.* Scarborough: Nelson Canada, 1997.

Bromberg, Walter. *Psychiatry between the Wars, 1918-1945: A Recollection.* Westport: Greenwood Press, 1982.

Bullock, A., and S. Trombley, eds. *The New Fontana Dictionary of Modern Thought.* London: HarperCollins, 1999.

Bynum, W.F., R. Porter, and M. Shepherd, eds. *The Anatomy of Madness: Essays in the History of Psychiatry.* 3 vols. London: Routledge, 1985-88.

Carter, Sarah. *Aboriginal People and Colonizers of Western Canada to 1900.* Toronto: University of Toronto Press, 1999.

Chafetz, Morris E. *The Tyranny of Experts: Blowing the Whistle on the Cult of Expertise.* New York: Madison Books, 1996.

Chandler, David. *Capital Punishment in Canada.* Toronto: McClelland and Stewart, 1976.

Clark, Michael, and Catherine Crawford, eds. *Legal Medicine in History.* Cambridge: Cambridge University Press, 1994.

Conrad, P., and J.W. Schnieder. *Deviance and Medicalization.* Columbus: Temple University Press, 1985.

Cooper, D. *The Language of Madness.* New York, NY: Viking Press, 1978.

Coulter, Jeff. *The Social Construction of Mind: Studies in Ethnomethodology and Linguistic Philosophy.* Totowa, NJ: Macmillan, 1979.

Dell, Susanne. *Murder into Manslaughter: The Diminished Responsibility Defence in Practice.* Oxford, UK: Oxford University Press, 1984.

Digby, Anne. *Madness, Morality and Medicine: A Study of the York Retreat, 1796-1914.* Cambridge, UK: Cambridge University Press, 1985.

Doust, David J. *The Expert Witness.* Ayer's Cliff, QC: Pachelle, 1997.

Dowbiggin, Ian. *Keeping America Sane: Psychiatry and Eugenics in the United States and Canada, 1880-1940.* Ithaca and London: Cornell University Press, 1997.

Dubinsky, Karen. *Improper Advances: Rape and Heterosexual Conflict in Ontario, 1880-1929.* Chicago: University of Chicago Press, 1993.

Duff, R.A. *Trials and Punishments.* Cambridge, UK: Cambridge University Press, 1986.

Eigen, Joel Peter. *Witnessing Insanity: Madness and Mad-Doctors in the English Court.* New Haven: Yale University Press, 1995.

Elliot, C. *The Rules of Insanity: Moral Responsibility and the Mentally Ill Offender.* New York: State University of New York Press, 1996.

Esquirol, E. *Mental Maladies: A Treatise on Insanity.* Trans. E.K. Hunt. Philadelphia: Hafner, 1945.

Fink, Arthur. *Causes of Crime: Biological Theories in the United States, 1800-1915.* New York: A.S. Barnes, 1938.

Foot, P. *Virtue and Vices and Other Essays in Moral Philosophy.* Oxford, UK: Oxford University Press, 1978.

Foucault, Michel. *The Birth of the Clinic: An Archaeology of Medical Perception.* Trans. A.M. Sheridan Smith. New York: Vintage Books, 1973.

–. *The History of Sexuality.* Trans. Robert Hurley. Vol. 1, *An Introduction.* New York: Pantheon Books, 1978.

–, ed. *"I Pierre Rivière, Having Slaughtered My Mother, My Sister, and My Brother" ... A Case of Parricide in the 19th Century.* Lincoln: University of Nebraska Press, 1975.

–. *Madness and Civilization: A History of Insanity in the Age of Reason.* Trans. Richard Howard. New York: Vintage Books, 1965.

–. *The Order of Things: An Archaeology of the Human Sciences.* Trans. A.M. Sheridan Smith. New York: Tavistock Publications, 1994.

Friedland, M.L. *The Case of Valentine Shortis: A True Story of Crime and Politics in Canada.* Toronto: University of Toronto Press, 1986.

–, ed. *Cases and Materials on Criminal Law and Procedure.* 5th ed. Toronto: Emond Montgomery Publications, 1997.

Friedrich, Carl. *Responsibility.* New York: Liberal Arts Press, 1960.

Gleason, Mona. *Normalizing the Ideal: Psychology, Schooling, and the Family in Postwar Canada.* Toronto: University of Toronto Press, 1999.

Glover, Jonathan. *Responsibility.* New York: Humanities Press, 1970.

Goldstein, J.E. *Console and Classify: The French Psychiatric Profession in the Nineteenth Century.* Cambridge, UK: Cambridge University Press, 1987.

Gordon, Linda. *Heroes of Their Own Lives: The Politics and History of Family Violence.* New York: Viking Press, 1988.

Gray, Kenneth G. *Law and the Practice of Medicine.* Toronto: Ryerson Press, 1947.

Greenwood, F. Murray, and Beverley Boissery. *Uncertain Justice: Canadian Women and Capital Punishment 1754-1953.* Toronto: Dundurn Press, 2000.

Grob, G.N. *Mental Illness and American Society, 1875-1940.* Princeton: Princeton University Press, 1983.

Grover, Michael R. *Expert Witness: The Forensic Appraiser.* Winnipeg: Appraisal Institute of Canada, 1991.

Guttmacher, Manfred, and Henry Weihofen. *The Role of Psychiatry in the Law.* Springfield, IL: Thomas, 1968.

Hacking, Ian. *The Social Construction of What?* Cambridge, MA: Harvard University Press, 1999.

Hall, Stuart. *The Hard Road to Renewal: Thatcherism and the Crisis of the Left.* New York: Verso, 1988.

Hamilton, R., and M. Barrett, eds. *The Politics of Diversity: Feminism, Marxism and Nationalism.* Montreal: Book Centre, 1986.

Harris, Ruth. *Murders and Madness: Medicine, Law, and Society in the Fin de Siècle.* Oxford: Clarendon Press, 1989.

Hart, H.L.A. *Punishment and Responsibility: Essays in the Philosophy of Law.* Oxford: Clarendon Press, 1968.

Hay, D., P. Linebaugh, J.G. Rule, E.P. Thompson, and C. Winslow. *Albion's Fatal Tree: Crime and Society in Eighteenth-Century England.* New York, NY: Pantheon Books, 1975.

Hoehne, Dieter. *Legal Aid in Canada.* Lewiston, NY: E. Mellen Press, 1989.

Holstein, James, and Gale Miller, eds. *Challenges and Choices: Constructionist Perspectives on Social Problems.* Hawthorne, NY: Aldine de Gruyter, 2003.

Hook, Sidney, ed. *Law and Philosophy: A Symposium.* New York, NY: New York University Press, 1964.

Hunter, R., and I. Macalpine, eds. *Three Hundred Years of Psychiatry: 1535-1860.* London: Oxford University Press, 1963.

Iacovetta, F., and Wendy Mitchinson, eds. *On the Case: Explorations in Social History.* Toronto: University of Toronto Press, 1998.

Iacovetta, F., and M. Valverde. *Gender Conflicts: New Essays in Women's History.* Toronto: University of Toronto Press, 1992.

Jack, D. *Rogues, Rebels and Geniuses: The Story of Canadian Medicine.* Toronto: Doubleday Canada, 1981.

Jacoby, George W. *The Unsound Mind and the Law: A Presentation of Forensic Psychiatry.* New York and London: Funk and Wagnalls, 1918.

Jasanoff, Sheila. *Science at the Bar: Law, Science and Technology in America.* Cambridge, MA: Harvard University Press, 1995.

Jaywardene, C.H.S. *The Penalty of Death: The Canadian Experiment.* Lexington, MA: Lexington Books, 1977.

Jones, Carol. *Expert Witnesses: Science, Medicine and the Practice of Law.* Oxford: Clarendon Press, 1993.

Karolus, H., ed. *International Symposium on Society, Medicine and the Law.* Amsterdam: Elsevier, Scientific Publishing, 1973.

Karpman, Ben. *Case Studies in the Psychopathology of Crime: A Reference Source for Research in Criminal Materials.* Vol. 3. Washington: Medical Science Press, 1948.

Kramar, Kirsten. *Unwilling Mothers, Unwanted Babies: Infanticide in Canada.* Vancouver: UBC Press, 2005.

Lacey, Nicola. *State Punishment: Political Principles and Community Values.* New York: Routledge, 1988.

Law Society of Upper Canada. *The Law of Evidence.* Toronto: Irwin Law, 2004.

Lawson, John Davison. *The Law of Expert and Opinion Evidence Reduced to Rules.* Chicago: T.H. Flood, 1900.

Lucas, J.R. *Responsibility.* Oxford: Clarendon Press, 1993.

Lunbeck, Elizabeth. *The Psychiatric Persuasion: Knowledge, Gender and Power in Modern America.* Princeton, NJ: Princeton University Press, 1994.

Lundberg, F., and M. Farnham. *Modern Woman: The Lost Sex.* New York: Harper and Brothers, 1947.

Machover, S. *Cultural and Racial Variations in Pattern of Intellect: Performance of Negro and White Criminals on the Bellevue Adult Intelligence Scale.* New York: AMS Press, 1943.

MacNiven, Don. *Creative Morality.* New York: Routledge, 1993.

Maguire, John MacArthur. *Evidence: Common Sense and Common Law.* Chicago: Foundation Press, 1947.

Martin, James. *Gramsci's Political Analysis: A Critical Introduction.* New York: Macmillan, 1998.

McAuley, Finbarr. *Insanity, Psychiatry and Criminal Responsibility.* Dublin: Round Hall Press, 1993.

McClung, Nellie. *The Stream Runs Fast: My Own Story.* Toronto: Thomas Allen, 1945.

McConnell, Ray Madding. *Criminal Responsibility and Social Constraint.* New York: Charles Scribner's Sons, 1913.

McKenna, Andrew. *Violence and Difference: Girard, Derrida and Deconstruction.* Urbana: University of Illinois Press, 1992.

McLaren, Angus. *Our Own Master Race: Eugenics in Canada, 1855-1945.* Toronto: Oxford University Press, 1990.

–. *The Trials of Masculinity: Policing Sexual Boundaries 1870-1930.* Chicago: University of Chicago Press, 1997.

McNally, David. *Bodies of Meaning.* New York: State University of New York Press, 2001.

McRuer, James. *The Evolution of the Judicial Process.* Toronto: Clark, Irwin, 1957.

Mendel, E. *Text-Book of Psychiatry: A Psychological Study of Insanity for Practitioners and Students.* Trans. William C. Krauss. Philadelphia: Physicians and Surgeons Book Company, 1907.

Menzies, R. *Survival of the Sanest: Order and Disorder in a Pre-Trial Psychiatric Clinic.* Toronto: University of Toronto Press, 1989.

Mercier, Charles. *Criminal Responsibility.* New York: Physicians and Surgeons Book Company, 1931.

Merrell, Floyd. *Sign, Textuality, World.* Bloomington, IN: University of Indiana Press, 1992.

Miller, Gale, and Robert Digwall, eds. *Context and Method in Qualitative Research.* London: Sage Publications, 1997.

Mitchell, Ainsworth. *The Expert Witness.* Cambridge: W. Heffer and Sons, 1923.

Moran, Richard. *Knowing Right from Wrong: The Insanity Defense of Daniel McNaughtan.* London: Collier Macmillan, 1981.

Morgan, Cecilia. *Public Men and Virtuous Women: The Gendered Languages of Religion and Politics in Upper Canada, 1791-1850.* Toronto: University of Toronto Press, 1996.

Mort, Frank. *Dangerous Sexualities: Medico-Moral Politics in England since 1830.* London: Routledge and Kegan Paul, 1987.

Myerson, Abraham. *Inheritance of Mental Diseases.* Baltimore: Williams, 1925.

Nye, R. *Crime, Madness and Politics in Modern France: The Medical Concept of National Decline.* Princeton, NJ: Princeton University Press, 1984.

Paul, E., F. Miller, and J. Paul, eds. *Crime, Culpability, and Remedy.* Oxford: Blackwell, 1990.

Peterson, Ingrid. *Four Theories of Responsibility.* Lund, Sweden: Lund University Press, 1990.

Phipson, Sidney L. *The Law of Evidence.* 8th ed. Toronto: Carswell, 1930.

Pitch, Tamar. *Limited Responsibilities: Social Movements and Criminal Justice.* New York: Routledge, 1995.

Pleck, Elizabeth. *Domestic Tyranny: The Making of Social Policy against Family Violence from Colonial Times to the Present.* New York: Oxford University Press, 1987.

Porter, Roy. *A Social History of Madness: Stories of the Insane.* London: Weidenfeld and Nicolson, 1987.

Powell, Edmund. *Principles and Practice of the Law of Evidence: Canadian Notes by Hon. Mr. Justice Russell.* London: Butterworth, 1911.

Radden, Jennifer. *Madness and Reason.* London: G. Allen and Unwin, 1985.

Razack, S. *Looking White People in the Eye: Gender, Race, and Culture in Courtrooms and Classrooms.* Toronto: University of Toronto Press, 1998.

Reid, R., and R. Holland. *Advocacy: Views from the Bench.* Aurora, ON: Canada Law Book, 1984.

Reznek, Lawrie. *Evil or Ill? Justifying the Insanity Defense.* New York: Routledge, 1997.

Roberts, J.V., L.J. Stalans, D. Indemaur, and M. Hough. *Penal Populism and Public Opinion: Lessons from Five Countries.* New York, NY: Oxford University Press, 2003.

Robinson, Daniel N. *Wild Beasts and Idle Humours: The Insanity Defense from Antiquity to the Present.* Cambridge, MA: Harvard University Press, 1996.

Rosanoff, Aaron, ed. *Manual of Psychiatry.* 5th ed. New York: Wiley, 1920.

Roscoe, Henry. *Roscoe's Criminal Evidence: The Law, Evidence and Practice in Criminal Cases.* Toronto: Carswell, 1952.
Rush, P., S. McVeigh, and A. Young, eds. *Criminal Legal Doctrine.* Brookfield, VT: Ashgate, 1997.
Sanders, Byrne Hope. *Emily Murphy: Crusader.* Toronto: Macmillan Company of Canada, 1945.
Santos, Bonaventura de Sousa, trans. *Toward a New Common Sense: Law, Science and Politics in the Paradigmatic Transition.* New York: Routledge, 1995.
Scott, John. *A Matter of Record: Documentary Sources in Social Research.* Cambridge, UK: Polity Press, 1990.
Scull, Andrew, ed. *Madhouses, Mad-Doctors, and Madmen: The Social History of Psychiatry in the Victorian Era.* Philadelphia: University of Pennsylvania Press, 1981.
–. *Social Order/Mental Disorder: Anglo-American Psychiatry in Historical Perspective.* London: Routledge, 1989.
Short, S.E.D., ed. *Medicine in Canadian Society: Historical Perspectives.* Montreal and Kingston: McGill-Queen's University Press, 1981.
Shorter, Edward. *A History of Psychiatry: From the Era of the Asylum to the Age of Prozac.* Toronto: John Wiley and Sons, 1997.
Showstack Sassoon, Anne. *Gramsci and Contemporary Politics: Beyond Pessimism of the Intellect.* New York: Routledge, 2000.
–. *Gramsci's Politics.* 2nd ed. Minneapolis: University of Minnesota Press, 1987.
Smart, Carol. *Women, Crime and Criminology: A Feminist Critique.* London: Routledge and Kegan Paul, 1976.
Smith, Dorothy E. *The Conceptual Practices of Power: A Feminist Sociology of Knowledge.* Toronto: University of Toronto Press, 1990.
–. *Writing the Social. Critique, Theory and Investigation.* Toronto: University of Toronto Press, 1999.
Smith, Roger. *Trial by Medicine: Insanity and Responsibility in Victorian Trial.* Edinburgh: Edinburgh University Press, 1981.
Snell, James. *In the Shadow of the Law: Divorce in Canada, 1900-1939.* Toronto: University of Toronto Press, 1991.
Sopinka, John. *The Law of Evidence in Canada.* Markham, ON: Butterworths, 1998.
Stephen, James Fitzjames. *A Digest of the Law of Evidence.* 12th ed. London: Macmillan, 1936.
Stern, E., and S. Hamilton. *Mental Illness.* New York: Harper and Row, 1942.
Stoler, Ann. *Race and the Education of Desire.* Durham and London: Duke University Press, 1995.
Strange, Carolyn, ed. *Qualities of Mercy.* Vancouver: UBC Press, 1997.
–. *Toronto's Girl Problem: The Perils and Pleasures of the City, 1880-1930.* Toronto: University of Toronto Press, 1995.
Strecker, Edward. *Fundamentals of Psychiatry.* Philadelphia: Lippincott, 1941.
Szasz, Thomas. *Ideology and Insanity: Essays on the Psychiatric Dehumanization of Man.* Garden City, NY: Anchor Books, 1970.
Tebbit, Mark. *Philosophy of Law: An Introduction.* New York and London: Routledge, 2000.
Thomas, Alexander, and Samuel Sillen. *Racism and Psychiatry.* New York: Brunner/Mazel, 1973.
Twining, William, and Iain Hampsher-Monk, eds. *Evidence and Inference in History and Law: Interdisciplinary Dialogues.* Evanston, IL: Northwestern University Press, 2003.
Valverde, Mariana. *The Age of Light, Soap and Water: Moral Reform in English Canada, 1885-1925.* Toronto: McClelland and Stewart, 1991.
–. *Diseases of the Will: Alcohol and the Dilemmas of Freedom.* Cambridge, UK: Cambridge University Press, 1998.
–. *Law's Dream of a Common Knowledge.* Princeton: Princeton University Press, 2003.
Walker, James. *"Race," Rights and the Law in the Supreme Court of Canada.* Waterloo, ON: Wilfrid Laurier University Press, 1997.
Walker, Nigel. *Crime and Insanity in England.* Edinburgh: Edinburgh University Press, 1968.

Walton, Douglas. *Appeal to Popular Opinion.* University Park: Pennsylvania State University Press, 1999.

Weeks, Jeffrey. *Invented Moralities: Sexual Values in an Age of Uncertainty.* Cambridge, UK: Polity Press, 1995.

–, ed. *The Lesser Evil and the Greater Good: The Theory and Politics of Social Diversity.* London: Rivers Oram Press, 1994.

Weiner, Bernard. *Judgments of Responsibility: A Foundation for a Theory of Social Conduct.* New York: Guilford Press, 1995.

Weisberg, Kelly, ed. *Women and the Law: A Social Historical Perspective,* Vol. 1: *Women and the Criminal Law.* Cambridge, MA: Schenkman, 1982.

Weisstub, D.N., ed. *Law and Psychiatry in the Canadian Context.* New York: Pergamon Press, 1980.

Wigmore, John Henry. *A Treatise on the Anglo-American System of Evidence in Trials at Common Law: Including the Statutes and Judicial Decisions of All Jurisdictions of the United States and Canada.* Boston: Little, Brown, 1923.

Williamson, W.H. *Annals of Crime: Some Extraordinary Women.* London: G. Routledge, 1930.

Winfield, P.H., ed. *Mental Abnormality and Crime.* London: Macmillan, 1944.

Woolgar, Steve, ed. *Knowledge and Reflexivity: New Frontiers in the Sociology of Knowledge.* London: Sage Publications, 1988.

Wright, P., and A. Treacher. *The Problem of Medical Knowledge: Examining the Social Construction of Medicine.* Edinburgh: Edinburgh University Press, 1982.

Young, Alison. *Imagining Crime.* London: Sage Publications, 1996.

Reports, Records, and Government Documents

Canada. Department of Justice. *Report of a Committee Appointed to Inquire into the Principles and Procedures Followed in the Remission Service of the Department of Justice of Canada.* Ottawa: Department of Justice, 1956.

–. *Report of the Joint Committee of the Senate and the House of Commons on Capital Punishment.* Ottawa: Department of Justice, 1956.

–. *Royal Commission on the Law of Insanity as a Defense in Criminal Cases, 1952-1956* (Final Report). Ottawa and Hull: E. Cloutier, Queen's Printer, 1956.

Canadian Criminal Code (1955).

Dominion Borough of Canada. *Statistics of Criminal and Other Offences.* Ottawa: Statistics Canada, Justice Statistics Division, 1926-50.

Gadoury, L., and A. Lechasseur. "Persons Sentenced to Death in Canada, 1867-1976: An Inventory of Capital Case Files in the Records of the Department of Justice (RG 13)." Government Archives Division, Library and Archives Canada, 1992.

Hutton, William L. "A Brief for the Sterilization of the Feeble-Minded." Report prepared for the Association of Ontario Mayors Annual Conference, Toronto, Ontario, June 1936.

Minister of Trade and Commerce. *Criminal Statistics.* Ottawa: Government of Canada, 1912-25.

Sharpe, Gilbert. *Mental Disorder Project – Criminal Law Review: Final Project.* Ottawa: Department of Justice, 1985.

Unpublished Manuscripts

Alexander, M. "The Administration of Madness and Attitudes towards the Insane in Nineteenth-Century Paris." PhD thesis, Johns Hopkins University, 1976.

Clark, M.J. "The Data of Alienism: Evolutionary Neurology, Physiological Psychology, and the Reconstruction of British Psychiatric Theory, c. 1850-1900." D. Phil. thesis, Oxford University, 1982.

Clarke, C.K. "The Mental Hygiene Movement." Paper presented at the Saskatchewan Educational Association, Saskatoon, 5 April 1920.

Crawford, C. "The Emergence of English Forensic Medicine: Medical Evidence in Common-Law Courts, 1730-1830." PhD thesis, Oxford University, 1987.

Goldstein, J.E. "French Psychiatry in Social and Political Context: The Formation of a New Profession, 1820-1860." PhD thesis, Columbia University, 1978.

Greenland, Cyril. "C.K. Clarke's Portrait; '... the Uses of Adversity.'" McMaster University, School of Social Work (April 1980), ACP, Griffin-Greenland Collection, Biographical Files, C.K. Clarke.

White-Mair, Kimberley. "Negotiating Responsibility: Representations of Criminality and Mind-State in Canadian Law, Medicine and Society, 1920-1950." PhD thesis, University of Toronto, 2001.

Index

Note: "(t)" after a page number indicates a table

LAW AND SOCIETY

Lori G. Beaman
Defining Harm: Religious Freedom and the Limits of the Law (2007)

Stephen Tierney (ed.)
Multiculturalism and the Canadian Constitution (2007)

Julie Macfarlane
The New Lawyer: How Settlement Is Transforming the Practice of Law (2007)

Dawn Moore
Criminal Artefacts: Governing Drugs and Users (2007)

Hamar Foster, Heather Raven, and Jeremy Webber (eds.)
Let Right Be Done: Aboriginal Title, the Calder Case, and the Future of Indigenous Rights (2007)

Dorothy E. Chunn, Susan B. Boyd, and Hester Lessard (eds.)
Reaction and Resistance: Feminism, Law, and Social Change (2007)

Margot Young, Susan B. Boyd, Gwen Brodsky, and Shelagh Day (eds.)
Poverty: Rights, Social Citizenship, and Legal Activism (2007)

Rosanna L. Langer
Defining Rights and Wrongs: Bureaucracy, Human Rights, and Public Accountability (2007)

C.L. Ostberg and Matthew E. Wetstein
Attitudinal Decision Making in the Supreme Court of Canada (2007)

Chris Clarkson
Domestic Reforms: Political Visions and Family Regulation in British Columbia, 1862-1940 (2007)

Jean McKenzie Leiper
Bar Codes: Women in the Legal Profession (2006)

Gerald Baier
Courts and Federalism: Judicial Doctrine in the United States, Australia, and Canada (2006)

Avigail Eisenberg (ed.)
Diversity and Equality: The Changing Framework of Freedom in Canada (2006)

Randy K. Lippert
Sanctuary, Sovereignty, Sacrifice: Canadian Sanctuary Incidents, Power, and Law (2005)

James B. Kelly
Governing with the Charter: Legislative and Judicial Activism and Framers' Intent (2005)

Dianne Pothier and Richard Devlin (eds.)
Critical Disability Theory: Essays in Philosophy, Politics, Policy, and Law (2005)

Susan G. Drummond
Mapping Marriage Law in Spanish Gitano Communities (2005)

Louis A. Knafla and Jonathan Swainger (eds.)
Laws and Societies in the Canadian Prairie West, 1670-1940 (2005)

Ikechi Mgbeoji
Global Biopiracy: Patents, Plants, and Indigenous Knowledge (2005)

Florian Sauvageau, David Schneiderman, and David Taras, with Ruth Klinkhammer and Pierre Trudel
The Last Word: Media Coverage of the Supreme Court of Canada (2005)

Gerald Kernerman
Multicultural Nationalism: Civilizing Difference, Constituting Community (2005)

Pamela A. Jordan
Defending Rights in Russia: Lawyers, the State, and Legal Reform in the Post-Soviet Era (2005)

Anna Pratt
Securing Borders: Detention and Deportation in Canada (2005)

Kirsten Johnson Kramar
Unwilling Mothers, Unwanted Babies: Infanticide in Canada (2005)

W.A. Bogart
Good Government? Good Citizens? Courts, Politics, and Markets in a Changing Canada (2005)

Catherine Dauvergne
Humanitarianism, Identity, and Nation: Migration Laws in Canada and Australia (2005)

Michael Lee Ross
First Nations Sacred Sites in Canada's Courts (2005)

Andrew Woolford
Between Justice and Certainty: Treaty Making in British Columbia (2005)

John McLaren, Andrew Buck, and Nancy Wright (eds.)
Despotic Dominion: Property Rights in British Settler Societies (2004)

Georges Campeau
From UI to EI: Waging War on the Welfare State (2004)

Alvin J. Esau
The Courts and the Colonies: The Litigation of Hutterite Church Disputes (2004)

Christopher N. Kendall
Gay Male Pornography: An Issue of Sex Discrimination (2004)

Roy B. Flemming
Tournament of Appeals: Granting Judicial Review in Canada (2004)

Constance Backhouse and Nancy L. Backhouse
The Heiress vs the Establishment: Mrs. Campbell's Campaign for Legal Justice (2004)

Christopher P. Manfredi
Feminist Activism in the Supreme Court: Legal Mobilization and the Women's Legal Education and Action Fund (2004)

Annalise Acorn
Compulsory Compassion: A Critique of Restorative Justice (2004)

Jonathan Swainger and Constance Backhouse (eds.)
People and Place: Historical Influences on Legal Culture (2003)

Jim Phillips and Rosemary Gartner
Murdering Holiness: The Trials of Franz Creffield and George Mitchell (2003)

David R. Boyd
Unnatural Law: Rethinking Canadian Environmental Law and Policy (2003)

Ikechi Mgbeoji
Collective Insecurity: The Liberian Crisis, Unilateralism, and Global Order (2003)

Rebecca Johnson
Taxing Choices: The Intersection of Class, Gender, Parenthood, and the Law (2002)

John McLaren, Robert Menzies, and Dorothy E. Chunn (eds.)
Regulating Lives: Historical Essays on the State, Society, the Individual, and the Law (2002)

Joan Brockman
Gender in the Legal Profession: Fitting or Breaking the Mould (2001)